REIGNS OF TERROR

Reigns of Terror

Patricia Marchak

McGill-Queen's University Press
Montreal & Kingston · London · Ithaca

© McGill-Queen's University Press 2003

ISBN 0-7735-2641-2 (cloth)
ISBN 0-7735-2642-0 (paper)

Legal deposit fourth quarter 2003
Bibliothèque nationale du Québec

Printed in Canada on acid-free paper that is 100% ancient forest free
(100% post-consumer recycled), processed chlorine free.

This book has been published with the help of a grant from the Humanities
and Social Sciences Federation of Canada, using funds provided by the
Social Sciences and Humanities Research Council of Canada.

McGill-Queen's University Press acknowledges the financial support of the
Government of Canada through the Book Publishing Industry
Development Program (BPIDP) for its activities. It also acknowledges the
support of the Canada Council for the Arts for its publishing program.

National Library of Canada Cataloguing in Publication

Marchak, M. Patricia, 1936–
    Reigns of terror / Patricia Marchak.

Includes bibliographical references and index.
ISBN 0-7735-2641-2 (bnd)
ISBN 0-7735-2642-0 (pkb)

1. Crimes against humanity. 2. Genocide – Sociological aspects.
3. Genocide – History – 20th century. 4. Political atrocities – History –
20th century. I. Title.

JC571.M335 2003   304.6'63   C2003-903363-5

This book was typeset by Dynagram Inc. in 10/13 Sabon.

Contents

Preface

Reigns of Terror was well under way before the infamous terrorist attacks on the Pentagon in Washington and the World Trade Center in New York on September 11, 2001. The term "terrorist" has been so frequently invoked to describe the hijackers who perpetrated the attacks that we are in danger of overlooking a much more lethal and widespread form of terror: terror that is sponsored by states. Both today and historically, the vast majority of crimes against humanity, and by far the largest number of deaths and disappearances, have been caused not by small groups of revolutionaries, but by organized states against their own citizens and the citizens of other countries. This book is an inquiry into the conditions that lead to states committing gross human rights crimes against their own citizens.

A new governing elite in the Ottoman Empire ordered the deportation and certain death of up to 800,000 Armenians in 1915–16. Stalin instigated a deliberate policy of mass starvation against peasants in the Eastern Ukraine when they resisted collectivization: from 5 to 8 million people starved to death in an eighteen-month period beginning in 1932. The Nazi Holocaust claimed about 6 million victims. Guatemala's army staged a thirty-six-year war against the country's Mayan population that took the lives of between 200,000 and 300,000. In Rwanda up to one million were killed in a few months in 1994. The Khmer Rouge in Cambodia killed or forced into starvation up to 2 million people in a forty-four-month period of the late-1970s. Augusto Pinochet's army and his secret intelligence service killed or caused the disappearances of an estimated 3,000 Chileans in the 1970s, while the military junta in neighbouring Argentina tortured and "disappeared" up to 30,000. Thousands of Bosnian Muslims were killed by Serb forces during the final stages of the breakup of the former Yugoslavia. And on it goes, one country after another, different cultures, different histories, different ways the crimes against civilians occurred, but always the same themes, the same arguments that blame the victims and excuse the perpetrators. The question we ask in this book is why do states turn on their own citizens? Why do states inflict genocide and other crimes against humanity on their own people?

Current theories about state crimes against their own citizens revolve in large part around the concept of racism. This concept has variations ranging from xenophobia to tribalism, but the basic theme is that people, defining themselves and others by their ethnic roots, turn on minorities when they feel threatened in one way or another. The UN Genocide Convention (1951) defines genocide as an attempt to eradicate a people identified in terms of race or religion. But many state crimes are aimed at populations that are no different in ethnic terms from the majority. The victims are chosen on the basis of their territorial locations, their occupations, their lifestyles, their class situation, their political beliefs, or even their age. For such crimes the word "politicide" has been coined, and it is helpful in expanding understanding, but terminology does not in itself provide an explanation.

Most genocidal episodes are attempts to eradicate a people altogether. Some politicides are identical; they, too, are designed to completely obliterate people defined in terms other than race and religion. Other politicides are designed to remove power from a class of people or prevent them from acting in certain ways, and some politicides are aimed at killing ideas by killing the ideological leaders and as many followers as can be found, and destroying books linked to social movements. There are differences between politicides and genocide as defined in the United Nations Convention, but, in all instances where states turn on their own people, similar destructive actions are paramount and the victims are invariably described, often in heavy propaganda, in extreme terms as evil-doers who threaten the security and well-being of other citizens.

I will argue, contrary to much of the current literature on genocide, that these crimes against citizens are always instrumental, the ultimate objectives being the retention or creation of unequal citizens and the appropriation of territory, other property, or services belonging to the victims. The ethnic dimension provides the excuse and the ideological rationale for the action; it is important, especially where there has been a long history of ethnic conflict or discrimination, but it is not the explanation for the events. The attempt to eliminate ideas is, likewise, aimed at preventing social change that involves upsets in the rankings of citizens. This argument runs contrary to a substantial literature linking genocide directly to anti-Semitism in Europe and to ethnic cleansing there and elsewhere. I will argue that the definition of genocide, emerging in the aftermath of the Second World War, has become an obstacle to our understanding of state crimes unless we recognize genocide as a subset of crimes against humanity. Genocide, together with politicide in all its dimensions, needs to be located within its political contexts, rather than in simple terms of the ethnic origins of either victims or perpetrators.

Reigns of Terror has two parts and an epilogue. The first part consists of arguments about the causes and nature of state crimes. The second part is a series of concise histories of nine societies where, over the past century, agents of the state have abducted, raped, tortured, starved, deported, and killed citizens. Readers are provided with information on the preceding events and context, a brief description of the crimes, and identification of the perpetrators and the victims. Where available, witness and participant statements are quoted. Debates and disagreements in the literature are noted, and references are copiously provided for readers who wish to delve more deeply into these events. Sources of information for Armenia, the Eastern Ukraine, Nazi Germany, Cambodia, Burundi and Rwanda, and the former Yugoslavia are historians, diplomats, social scientists, and journalists who have specialized in studies of these areas or who were witnesses at the time. A column in a recent edition of the *Turkish Daily News* is quoted at length with the writer's permission: it was published while I was in Turkey. Sources for Chile and Argentina include the same range of informants as for other studies, together with the author's research fieldnotes and excerpts from recent interviews I conducted with William Marchak in those countries.

The historical studies are placed in Part Two, rather than preceding the analysis and argument, because readers will have different levels of familiarity with the instances of these state crimes. Readers who are unfamiliar with these histories may prefer to read this part first, before reading the more analytical material in Part One. Other readers may want to refresh their memories about particular instances and selectively read the histories of countries with which they are least familiar. The analytical chapters refer to the studies, so readers who need more information about a particular case can turn to that country's history to brief themselves.

The choice of case studies was made not on the basis of a prior theory but with reference to their diversity in historical, cultural, and geo-political terms, and to the availability of solid scholarship about the events. In examining both the differences and the similarities, I hoped we could discern what they have in common to lead us to an explanation of the events. The theory expounded in Part One grew out of an examination of these and other instances that occurred during the past few centuries.

In Part One I put forward an argument about the nature of modern states and their links to the inequality of citizens. Chapter 1 presents an overview of the argument, defines several key terms, and provides a discussion of international conventions pertinent to the subject. Chapter 2 considers theories that deal with racism, tribalism, and identity, and concludes that they are manifestations of the drive to sustain inequalities between populations, but not in themselves sufficient explanations for state crimes. Chapter 3 moves further towards considering class, territory, and regional inequalities as the bases for state crimes. Chapter 4 examines the cultural contexts for and the ideologies that are created as justifications for state crimes. Chapter 5 is concerned with issues of rationality, obedience, conformity, and bureaucracy in modern states. And chapter 6 summarizes the arguments and deliberates on the utility of diverse forms of intervention in states most susceptible to commission of these crimes. An epilogue considers some of the conflicts raging in 2003 in relation to the themes of the book.

This study is about the causes or, more accurately, the conditions that lead to state crimes; it is not an examination of the consequences, although, of course, the impact on citizens is discussed. The full extent of the consequences of state actions might include the impact on generations unborn at the time of the incidents. Such horrible experiences are not forgotten by victims; nor are terrible actions, taken in the heat of a political battle and under the influence of a bloodthirsty ideology, forgotten by the perpetrators. The more immediate consequences are both explicit and implicit in the descriptive chapters. But a focus on consequences is the task of another book, not this one. Here we are concentrating on the causes and conditions that underlie crimes against humanity conducted under the aegis of states. I trust that readers, already sensitive to the consequences, are also intent on considering why such events occur.

Methods of criminal actions vary a great deal. Gas chambers and all the technology of killing people under Nazi control have put an indelible imprint on our minds, but just as effective methods of killing citizens are forced starvation, mass deportations under conditions leading inevitably to death from exhaustion, forced labour without adequate food or sanitation, and many methods of torture and assassination. We cannot determine the causes from the methods, nor can we infer them from the numbers who were killed or maimed. Some state decisions of the past century have inflicted millions of deaths on selected populations. Others have targeted a few thousand individuals for torture and assassination. The numbers and the methods differ, but the point is that, beneath these differences, there are similar conditions. I will argue that the same kind of conditions led the Young Turks, Hitler, Stalin, Pol Pot, Hutu extremists, Serbian armies, and anti-communist juntas to kill perceived opponents, but I will also argue that there the similarities end: the consequences of their actions had variable outcomes depending on the size and composition of their populations, their previous history, their geo-political position in the world at that time, and the participation of external states in their affairs.

I have an agenda, one argued, I hope, with appropriate scholarly concern for objectivity and the fair reporting of others' positions. It is to support attempts by humanitarians to engage the world's states in helping one another to avoid these episodes, rather than ignoring them, merely lamenting them, or actively contributing to the conditions that cause them.

Acknowledgments

I am indebted to the Social Sciences and Humanities Research Council of Canada for continued funding for my research. It would be impossible to write books that require more than a passing familiarity with countries and cultures beyond Canada without such funding, and I am grateful that, even though I am now retired from teaching, the council has provided me with sufficient funds to continue with research and publication.

I am also indebted to the Centre of International Relations, headed by Brian Job, in the Liu Institute for the Study of Global Issues at University of British Columbia, for providing me with a much-appreciated office and also with colleagues who are deeply interested in what happens in this world and why it happens. I remain grateful to the Peter Wall Institute for Advanced Study for a most stimulating year as a Distinguished Scholar in Residence while Ken MacCrimmon was the director.

Thanks as always to Wasyl (Bill) Marchak, whose companionship, encouragement, and sense of humour sustain me. Friends are always cherished, but are especially appreciated while writing a book on a topic that can sometimes be depressing. Let me express my appreciation to friends at home and abroad, including, posthumously, Robert Earl (Bob) Johannes, whose gentle yet critical voice accompanied me for nearly half a century.

PART ONE

An Argument about Conditions
Leading to Crimes against Humanity

1

States, Armed Force, and Unequal Citizens

Much printers' ink has been devoted to the study of the Holocaust. Other terrible crimes against humanity perpetrated by the leaders and bureaucracies of states have filled a smaller but important niche in the historical literature. The vast majority of these studies have attributed the episodes to racism and authoritarian cultures. Earlier studies called the perpetrators monsters and psychopaths, but that identification is no longer assumed. Scholarly studies and legal interrogations have demonstrated that the perpetrators are more often ordinary people who are merely doing their job as they understand it. That finding is more terrifying than the previous belief in evil.

Reigns of Terror argues that racism and authoritarian cultures, while important components of any interpretation of terror, are insufficient as explanations for the events. Instead, we need to understand the structural constraints of states when changes are imposed on them either by internal developments or external pressures. The changes may be social, political, demographic, economic, or environmental. In all cases, states are incapable of proceeding with governance in the traditional mode and equally incapable of moving forward to another level without violence.

I argue this case in the first six chapters, which together make something of an extended essay on genocide (the eradication of people on the basis of ethnicity and religion) and politicide (the eradication of people for other reasons) as subsets of crimes against humanity committed by states. These interpretive chapters are followed by nine brief case studies, to which I will often refer during the argument. I do not attempt to cover all possible aspects of the subject; rather, I have selected some of the more salient aspects to enable us to understand the causes and the processes that lead to human rights abuses of such gross dimensions. The emphasis here is on causes or pre-conditions that combined in each instance to make the abduction, torture, rape, murder, or other brutal acts against some segment of the civilian population appear to be rational and even essential to the holders of state power. While the causes are similar, the methods of extermination and the consequences may be entirely dissimilar, encased as they are in the contexts of time and place.

NINE STATE CRIMES

The crimes against humanity examined here, all from the twentieth century, have these characteristics in common:

- Those who control the organs of the state intend to destroy subjects, citizens, or neighbours; these crimes are intentional, planned, and organized.*
- The instrument for eliminating people is an army or a specially trained militia, and often both. Frequently, those who control the organs of the state are the generals of an army. Sometimes the army has taken over the state by coup; other times, it has become the government by default when no political party is capable of maintaining the state. Militias are sometimes used by both civilian and military governments to collect information, target victims, and perform the actual crimes. In some cases, these special armed forces flank professional armies and are neither controlled nor approved by them.
- Few institutional sectors, or none at all, are independent of the state. In particular, those sectors that might otherwise express opposition, prevent rash actions, or at least spread the risk of various actions are either absent or immobilized. These sectors include unions, business associations, mass media, universities and schools, religious organizations, political parties, and voluntary associations.
- There is always social change on a substantial scale. A political crisis erupts before the planning of the onslaught, sometimes, but not invariably, connected to an economic crisis. Often the political situation brings on an economic crisis where there was not one previously.
- Between the planning stage and the action, a full-scale exclusionist ideology develops that justifies the elimination of a particular seg-

---

* See the section on intention and motivation later in this chapter.

ment of the population. This ideology generally builds on prejudices already rampant in the society, but it can also be of recent vintage, minted for current purposes. Ideology is the bridge between the actual inequalities and the commission of crimes either to defend or to dismantle existing inequalities.

- The victims are defined in terms that denote inequality of status or even of species. This inequality is understood to be eradicable only through violence, and it is so great, so offensive to the perpetrators, that they cannot bear to tolerate the victims any longer.
- All the crimes against humanity reported here can be explained in terms of the economic and political interests of the perpetrators. They are caused neither by sentiments or ideologies nor by ethnic animosities of long-standing or political beliefs of recent vintage. In all cases, however, such sentiments and ideologies flourished and influenced the selection of victims.

These characteristics imply the need for a theory that begins with recognition of the nature of states in the twentieth century and considers how such states deal with a range of inequalities, of which ethnic status is but one dimension. Other points include massive and often sudden social change that threatens to alter the relative status of diverse segments of the population; political paralysis in the wake of massive social change; the role of military forces, both professional and specially created; the development of ideology; and, above all, fundamental economic and political interests.

CHARACTERISTICS OF STATES

The state is the territorial and political unit of our analysis. States have governments, and governments at any moment are the actors on behalf of the state. We will talk about governments in specific contexts but refer to states in more general arguments. States also have numerous bureaucratic organizations and agencies that may continue through the tenures of several governments. They include armed forces, the judiciary, and all institutions and offices that deal with state business. The population subject to the jurisdiction of a state consists of citizens.

Political theorists of our age still call on the pre-eminent theorist of an earlier time, Max Weber (1864–1920), for a definition of the modern or capitalist state, and it continues to be a useful beginning: "A human community that (successfully) claims the *monopoly of the legitimate use of physical force within a given territory.* ... the right to use physical force is ascribed to other institutions or to individuals only to the extent that the state permits it. The state is considered the sole source of the 'right' to use violence" (Gerth and Mills, 1962: 78, emphasis added). Again, in another essay, he argues that the state "is ... a compulsory association with a territorial basis ... the use of force is regarded as legitimate only so far as it is either permitted by the state or prescribed by it. The claim of the modern state to monopolize the use of force is as essential to it as its character of compulsory jurisdiction and of continuous organization" (Parsons, 1966: 156).

The emphasis in both statements and throughout Weber's work is on the capacity to use force legitimately – indeed, to monopolize the legitimate use of force. This focus is central to our understanding, since we are examining state crimes against citizens when the state breaks down. Weber argues that the state is, in effect, "organized domination which calls for continuous administration," and "requires that human conduct be conditioned to obedience towards those masters who claim to be the bearers of legitimate power" (Gerth and Mills, 1958: 80).

The second essential feature of Weber's definition is that the state has a territorial basis. This aspect is critical because it is not only political turmoil that creates the conditions for state crimes but also conflict over land and resources. And nowhere is this basis more true than in those cases where different ethnic/religious or national groups occupy different regions of the same state.

Weber was focusing on the modern state, not on the city-states of ancient Greek and Roman periods, or the villages and small towns that were loosely governed by monarchs and landed gentry in Europe and their equivalents elsewhere following the fall of the Roman Empire. After the Thirty Years' War ended with the Peace of Westphalia in 1648, modern states began to form in Europe. But the conclusion of intra-European wars for that period merely allowed developing European states to spread their armies elsewhere. By the early twentieth century these states had subjugated other territories and peoples throughout the world to their imperial rule. Once the disastrous European war of 1914–18 was over, some of the lingering pre-modern empires were forcibly dissolved, and, after the next European war of 1939–45, most of the imperial empires were abandoned. The advantages of imperialism had declined. Transportation and manufacturing technologies had reduced the benefits of empires that required huge investments by way of armies, administrators, settlers, and other personnel from the home country. The focus here is on modern capitalist states or, in the case of Turkey and the Soviet Union, on emerging states within the context of a world embedded largely in capitalist market economies.

Citizens and Citizenship

Implied in Weber's definition of the state is the presence of citizens. In ancient Greece and Rome, citizenship was confined to free adult males. It carried with it specific obligations as well as privileges. With the development of states over the past four centuries, citizenship has taken on the meaning of all permanent residents in a territorially circumscribed state. But with the development of states has also arisen the expulsion of groups that other citizens deem unacceptable for citizenship. The notion of a "nation-state" is a state containing only the dominant ethnic group (now treated as a nationality), though that term has now lost its exclusive meaning in most of the world. "Ethnic cleansing" is the contemporary reformulation of that earlier objective. The expulsion of minorities is not a new phenomenon, and forced migrations of people have occurred throughout history. Even when the victim group has long resided in territories taken over by other groups under empires or imperialist regimes, it may not enjoy the status of full citizens with equal citizenship rights and duties. Such was the case with the Armenian population in the Ottoman Empire territories: they were identified as citizens, but their civil rights and opportunities were limited because of their ethnic status. The other genocidal incidents discussed in this book involve victims who were, at least formally, citizens before they were expelled or killed.

Legitimacy

Legitimacy is an implied and occasionally explicit agreement on the part of the governed and outsiders that a state has the right to determine the domestic rules for citizens, to act on their behalf, and to control the armed forces of the country. Yet the term is extremely flexible: what is regarded as legitimate in one context may be entirely unacceptable in another, even by the same population. Once a government finds it necessary to rule by force on more than an occasional basis, it is admitting to a loss of legitimacy. Governments may not be accepted as legitimate by the governments of other states if they have gained power in ways the other states oppose, whether for altruistic reasons or because they fear the example might be contagious. Legitimacy is a particular problem for democratic governments, since they are obliged to be accountable to electorates on a wide range of issues; the use of force is merely one facet of their operations. Democratic states have rules regarding succession, tenure, and limitations on governments by way of legitimizing their operations. Such rules are much less in evidence in non-democratic states, precisely because they do not ultimately rest on legitimacy; rather, they rest on force, or at least the potential use of force where ideology fails to achieve passive acceptance. But even in non-democratic capitalist states, legitimate control of armed force resides exclusively with governments; any other use of armed force is regarded as illegitimate and will be countered by state forces.

Military Forces

Armies are critical to the maintenance of legitimacy for governments, since only by controlling the armies can states govern peacefully yet retain the potential to use force. But armies consist of people who are trained to defend national interests as their leaders define them; if a government ceases to represent such interests, armies are capable of withdrawing their consent to the sustenance of civilian rule. They may stage a coup and take over state power. When they do so – a not infrequent occurrence where they are strong enough to control a population – they, too, have to establish credibility with the people. They require legitimation as state actors, just as the previous governments did. If they have to continue to employ force as the means of controlling citizens, they have no legitimacy. Under these circumstances the state is in a perpetual condition of paralysis, essentially unable to govern – a typical precondition for the onset of crimes against the citizenry.

Crimes against humanity require a large armed force relative to the population. A country such as Canada or Australia probably could not stage a genocidal episode today (even if either were so inclined), because neither has armed capacity to control its sprawling yet sparsely populated territories. European countries are rapidly following in the same direction, decreasing their military expenditures while increasing their social infrastructure. Indeed, of the large industrial countries, only the United States continues to invest heavily in military equipment and forces. And, considering only the logistics of crimes against humanity, the United States is alone in its capacity to stage a major armed offensive against its own people or its neighbours. However, among the less industrialized countries, there are still many whose spending priorities lean towards armaments and armed forces, rather than social infrastructure, and who face growing inequalities, together with the expanding capacity of their armed forces to impose their will on civilian populations.

The Burundi and Rwanda genocidal episodes are examples of states that never achieved internal legitimacy. After the departure of colonial powers, they tried to sustain hierarchical social relationships that were not regarded as legitimate by large parts of the population, institutional arrangements that excluded too many people, and population numbers that exceeded the carrying capacity of the land. The system was neither sustainable nor reproducible, and the hapless states in both countries relied entirely on armed force to maintain the power of narrow elites. Eventually the dominant elites in these states were the armies themselves, lacking in legitimacy and leaning on coercion, and eventually on murder, to establish their rule.

Nazi Germany and Pinochet's Chile are examples of states run by military forces, but where a large part of the execution of genocide and politicide was performed by auxiliary forces that were not directly accountable to the hierarchy of the professional armed forces. Both Hitler and Pinochet created these forces to carry out tasks that the professionals might be expected to refuse, even when they were in general agreement with the overall objectives of the operations. Such forces reduced the liability of professional armed forces for crimes and also provided the appearance of a separation between the government and the criminal organization.

The state is an organization with a monopoly of the legitimate use of armed force in a given territory. When either civilian governments or armies choose to conduct themselves as agents of crimes against humanity, they must have sufficient capacity – in terms of numbers and internal organization – to fully control the society with or without continued coercion. Armed force is an essential, though insufficient, condition for the conduct of these crimes. Moreover, a government has control of armed force only as long as the institutions of the armed forces consider that government legitimate.

A Hierarchy of Power

In feudal monarchies the right of sovereigns to use their power to maintain and increase the wealth of the court and the nobility was taken for granted. That was what kings did, and there was no point in expecting them to be concerned with the plight of the poor. Moreover, kings and nobles kept armies and spies to ensure that the population was under control at all times. The state, as represented in the monarchy, was always involved in sustaining and reproducing the system in place, with its hierarchy of power and wealth.

Democracies are not identical to monarchies, and the poor expect democratic governments to be concerned with their plight. But the basic function of the state has not changed as dramatically as we might believe. The state, as conducted by a government at any one time, continues to serve those with wealth and power even if it simultaneously strives to reduce the gap between the rich and the poor, or the powerful and the powerless. This is a normal condition, and no conspiracy theorist is required to discover it. Governments must be regarded as legitimate by the most powerful individuals and groups in their realm or they will be undermined, subjected to coups, or otherwise overthrown. For many democratic governments there is no quandary; their members assume that those with wealth create the jobs for those without. In this "trickle-down" theory of government, more should be given to those who have. For those governments that prefer a greater level of equality, there are distinct limits to reform. The precise limits vary by society, sources of wealth, size and strength of the army, and external interests in the affairs of the state.

Guatemala and Chile reached the limits when governments attempted to institute land reforms and other measures that favoured unions, workers, and the poor. In these and many kindred cases, those with wealth and the power it gave them were able to force governments out of office when they attempted such reforms. The army ceased to serve the government of the day, launched a coup, and served its opponents; indeed, it became the opponent and the replacement government, arguing that it had the duty to look after the long-term interests of the state. The judgments of the leaders of armies might well be influenced by their own level of wealth and influence and by what they imagine will best suit their institutional interests in the future, but their credibility will rest on whether they can persuade the population, and outsiders, that they are acting in the national interests. In both those cases, the army of the state was supported in its disobedience and coup by the military forces and government of the United States. States that are dependent on the economic and/or military strength of larger and more powerful states have limited capacities to make independent choices that are inimical to the interests of those dominant states.

Besides the potential defection of armies, governments should think long and hard about whether they can cope with a hostile upper class: to curtail power or reduce access to resources and ownership of wealth is to run a strong risk of capital flight or other forms of retaliation by those whose wealth and influence in the external world are generally required for the maintenance of the society. The same may be true of a dominant ethnic or religious group. In short, unless a government is prepared to lead a revolution or has come into power on the wave of a revolution it is unlikely to attack the hand that feeds it; and only then, when it is sure that another feeding source will be available.

This general understanding led both Karl Marx and Max Weber to argue that the capitalist state is an organization designed to enable the reproduction of the basic hierarchy of power and wealth in a society.* Neither was arguing that the state looks after a particular group of people; rather, that the state is engaged in ensuring that the system as a whole is maintained. All large-scale social systems have groups in both dominant positions and subordinate positions. These groups, together with those who occupy intermediate positions in relatively healthy societies, form a system, in the sense that while some commit capital or entrepreneurial skill to the ongoing sustenance of a total society, others contribute different kinds of skills, or their labour and time, in return for income or other forms of protection. In a system, the individual components don't operate in separate spheres: they are related to one another in their economic, political, and social dealings.

As an example of how a modern state might deal with its more powerful populations, we could consider the state that strives to gain investment in its industries by offering incentives to investment companies. At the same time, however, it may also impose the full force of a law against insider trading on the stock market against members of the same class of investors. The system in both cases is being nurtured and sustained; the overall hierarchy is being reproduced, even though the particular membership changes.

---

* In theoretical terms, the hierarchy is often phrased as "relations of domination and subordination."

The most basic internal manifestation of the inexorable hierarchy is the difference in power and wealth between a dominant class and subordinate classes, but, as we will see, that gap only begins to describe the range of inequalities within and between societies. The relationship between diverse ethnic and religious groups, often overlapping with class organization, involves differentials of power. The relationship between men and women is generally another dimension.

The relationships between countries, between both the states of countries and the economic hierarchies of countries, determine the range of independent power held by governments. They are another system where some are dominant and others are subordinate, and the two ends of the continuum are related to each other by economic or political dealings of many kinds. Those at the dominant end of the relationship naturally want to maintain their privileges; those at the subordinate end, just as naturally, want to move up the ladder or even cause the whole construction to fall apart. This pattern occurs whether the system is an empire, an imperialist organization, or a contemporary state: the tug of war is inevitable and persistent.

But these tugs of war are rarely overt, obvious, or simple. The poor are both exploited by the rich and enabled to survive by their wealth. Workers are subordinate, but they are employed; minorities may be despised but they may simultaneously be essential mediums for the transformations of wealth that ultimately sustain the whole edifice. And middle classes, so vital to the sustenance of any system over more than a single generation, are typically in thrall to the more powerful class above them, dependent for their fortunate employment and enjoying the advantages of the system for themselves and their progeny.

A revolutionary state has a task similar to that of a long-standing state, but it has to create as well as reproduce a hierarchy in which some are more powerful than others. Further, it must do so at high speed, since any delay encourages the reformation of previous elites and their supporters. To offset this potential, force is generally applied: revolutions are rarely pacific affairs. The task is to rid the state of potential saboteurs and establish a new hierarchy to displace the old one. Once established, the new state operates on essentially the same principle as before: it must sustain the system and retain the privileges of those whom it has empowered.

If a state is obliged to reproduce a hierarchy of human relationships, it may become paralyzed when that becomes impossible, in the sense that no government or other party is capable of sustaining the edifice peacefully. Alternatively, it may collapse altogether, in which case numerous armed groups may compete for control of the state; it may succumb to a revolution, often a coup by the armed forces; or it may identify internal or external enemies by way of reducing perceived threats or casting blame and postponing collapse. Any of these alternatives involves armed force against civilians, sooner or later. They are not mutually exclusive, and they may occur sequentially or in combination.

States have a mandate to sustain and reproduce systems of inequality among citizens; when they cannot reproduce the system, they have a high probability of committing crimes against humanity.

We now have the basic argument. States must reproduce a given system with its hierarchy, and it is when they cannot do so that they respond violently against citizens. By the time this outburst occurs, armies may have become the government of the state. Our next task is to consider the conditions under which states cannot reproduce a given hierarchy.

States and Fundamental Social Change

No form of social organization lasts forever. At a full millennium, the Byzantine Empire may have the prize for longevity. Even long-lasting empires have undergone substantial change over time. The sources of change are numerous, including internal cleavages and revolutions, environmental disasters, population expansion beyond the capacities of the resource base, changes in trade routes or markets, wars, conquests, and transformations in neighbouring states. A state's task, then, is to find ways of adjusting to change so that the system is not destroyed in the process. Again, this realization emphasizes that reproduction of the system does not imply creating a cloned version of the original but maintaining the general contours of power.

Barbara Harff (1986) does not take this general approach on the obligatory functions of the state, but she suggests a political explanation for genocide committed by states. She argues that "national upheaval sets the pre-conditions for the pursuit of genocidal policies against national minorities and powerless majorities." National upheaval is an "abrupt change in the political community" which might be caused by lost wars or other violent conflict. These structural changes are accompanied by "the existence of sharp internal cleavages prior to the upheaval."

National upheaval is often linked to external events, such as wars that spill over onto the national territory or the failure of external constraints on genocide. Harff does not show how these preconditions lead to crimes against humanity, but merely that they tend to occur together.

The argument can be furthered by viewing the state's function as the maintenance of the existing system with its hierarchy of power. Major and fundamental disturbances challenge existing relationships within the society. Those in positions of power are threatened with loss, and all the way down the line groups are confronted with major disruptions in their relationship to others. For some, changes are potentially beneficial; for others, profoundly distressing. Societies undergoing major disturbances in power relationships are extremely unstable, and it is this instability, brought on by whatever external or internal forces, that eventually causes the paralysis of states. This precondition leads to crimes against humanity.

The shock to the system may be abrupt and traumatic, but it may also be gradual and insidious. What we often call "modernization" is generally a gradual process of social change. Modernization, especially when enforced by revolutionary groups in a hurry, is typically a wrenching experience for an entire society. Heads topple, and other heads move into the vacuum. What was a viable occupation abruptly turns sour, useless; people's skills are rendered obsolete while unfamiliar skills become important to new industries. Whole institutional sectors – religious organizations, fraternal societies, craft guilds, schools, universities, communications sectors – can be pushed aside as irrelevant in a matter of a few years or less. There is no overnight possibility of turning blacksmiths into engineers or carriage drivers into auto mechanics; inevitably the changes are so unsettling that no peaceful accommodation is possible between those who are losing privileges, position, and wealth and upstarts who stand to gain new privileges and wealth. The disintegration of empires is akin to a pyramid eroding at the base. Everything tumbles down, and groups caught in the fall clutch at bricks and stones in their frantic attempts to save themselves. Simultaneously the groups that are using the same bricks to build new temples seek to destroy the old order when it interferes with their prospects for a better life in the new one. Not infrequently, bystanders are caught in the struggle as they attempt to ensure their own positions in the shifting sands. Recreating the society on a different basis typically involves economic penalties and great uncertainty. Leaders may have a grand vision (indeed, that is a prerequisite of leadership in these circumstances), but they are caught in economic squeezes while the *ancien régime* disintegrates and the fledgling replacement sputters into action. Uncertainty, ambiguity, fear: these are widespread emotional reactions to the transformation.

The changes incurred by the computer technologies of the late twentieth century are similar to earlier changes that we called "modernization." Now the engineers who succeeded the blacksmiths give way to robots; the auto mechanics are superseded by computer technicians. Universities that worried about over-size undergraduate classes are suddenly in competition with distance educational services. Companies that invested heavily in fixed plant are undermined by Internet companies with little fixed property selling the same wares. Countries are invaded by globally financed corporations that push aside domestic businesses or, equally likely, provide domestic businesses with new sales opportunities together with less independence. Globalization is a complex process, with consequences varying according to the geopolitical location of a country, its general economic stability, the willingness of its political units to facilitate global corporations, and the strength of its unions or the proportion of its poor – where either of these conditions might slow down corporate (in contrast to country) development (Marchak, 1991). Governments contending with the growth of computer technologies and their attendant changes on the manufacturing sectors, the telecommunications industry, all service sectors and all industries employing manual workers or clerical and management staffs – in short, the entire social infrastructure – are forced to implement changes in conditions that inevitably alter the relations among citizens. To these changes are added the consequences of vast social transformations throughout the world, such as huge excess populations relative to the employment available in any one region, or in excess to the availability of land for farming or of fish for fishing, and mass migrations and refugee populations demanding space in any country that might be able and willing to accommodate them. The consequences of these extreme conditions are immediately experienced by geographically immobile state organizations.

Under such circumstances, a purge of any group that appears as a potential threat to the well-being of the previously dominant elite may be the weapon for resisting change; or a purge by a newly dominant elite or its army and bureaucracy may be the only means of consolidating change. In the second situation, the former elite, if it is not transformed into a component of the new elite, exits stage right, and those of its members who fight back put their survival at stake. But threats do not come only from displaced elites; they also come from subordinate groups who see in the transformation an opportunity to gain independence or who seek a larger role in the new world. Either group constitutes a threat if its collective demands are out of step with the intentions of the new governors, and the more so if it is perceived as a potential collaborator with external interests against the new elites. The situation is often explosive, and the revolutionary leaders have to maintain the momentum of their revolution. They may reason that they have no choice but to eliminate real or potential sources of opposition. This is the kind of reasoning that was promulgated by the Young Turks for their forced evacuation of Armenians nearly a century ago and is still defensively argued by contemporary Turkish media.

If there were no state, no bureaucratic organization together with its army assigned to the task of maintaining the social system for a large population in its previous form, we would be describing an anarchic situation. Very small societies might survive with little more than a few elders and a hereditary chief. But societies with larger populations and a division of labour associated with essential functions for group survival require central political and regulatory organizations, and these institutions are massively challenged by fundamental social change. When the conditions are gradual – economic decline, say, rather than war or revolution – the state may attempt various strategies for dealing with them. In Chile and Argentina we see states undergoing frequent remodelling in governments as each strives to identify and cope with the changes that are actually beyond its capacity to contain. In Cambodia we see changes in government supported by external power, but also a general blindness to the nature of the changes the society is experiencing. Blindness makes it all the more difficult for governments to anticipate, let alone cope with, dangerous changes. When the system begins to collapse, the state experiences political paralysis. It cannot act. It is at this point that it may be taken over by the army or by a revolutionary party prepared to impose its will by force and cope with social change.

Fundamental social change that results in, or has the potential to result in, substantial alteration in the systemic inequalities of power constitutes a potential condition for the commission of state crimes against civilians.

We have to use the temporizing term "potential" because of the high variability among societies in their capacities for dealing with fundamental social change. Historically, yet still within the twentieth century, there have been empire-states, imperialist states, core states in contemporary capitalism, and the dependencies and colonies of all these forms, each differing in its generic capacities to cope with social change. There are also military and civilian dictatorships, oligarchies, and democracies. The democracies come in a multitude of forms, some involving the panoply of civil rights, rule of law, and widespread participation in various levels of government and voluntary associations. Some, however, are deemed democracies on the basis of little more than an occasional election. While democracies as a group are less prone to inflicting large-scale wounds on themselves than are autocratic and dictatorial states (as shown in extensive studies by R.J. Rummel, 1992, 1994), that in itself does not provide us with a strong indicator of which countries teeter on the brink of a breakdown. Not all dictatorships kill their citizens; not all democracies abstain. We will consider some of the differences between empires (or imperial powers) and subject realms (or colonies) further on.

Democracies are less likely to spawn reigns of terror on their own citizens than dictatorships or other autocratic systems.

Authoritarianism and the History of Civil Rights

The influence of culture, independent of an ideology generated for the purpose of justifying genocide or politicide, is extremely variable. These massive assaults on people who are already defined as vermin or enemies occur in a startling range of diverse cultures. All they seem to have in common is that they are located towards the more authoritarian end of a spectrum, for which the other end would be either liberal or permissive. Authoritarian cultures might be identified as those where the major social institutions emphasize the organic cohesion of the society; the importance of the state and other major institutions, such as the church, mosque, synagogue, or temple; the relative insignificance of individuals and tradition; and the right of the major institutions to establish rigid rules for the everyday behaviour of citizens together with harsh laws against disobedience. Authoritarian societies often have a long history of disregard for human rights, where violence has been a widespread feature of daily existence or where repression has been heavy on the shoulders of citizens. Such societies move more readily towards imposition of solutions by armed force than those where civil rights are embedded into law and daily life.

States in societies with an authoritarian culture, societies where civil rights are not established, and societies where repression is widespread and of long duration may be especially prone to use force against their own citizens for the solving of societal problems.

But we could easily be misled if we take authoritarianism to be a strong criterion for identifying societies at risk: not all authoritarian societies become genocidal; not all genocidal societies are rigidly authoritarian; and most societies are much too complex, culturally, to measure them on a single scale of authoritarianism. One problem with reliance on authoritarianism or long histories of repression as explanations is that societies undergo cultural changes under conditions of stress. A society that has a history of civil rights sometimes moves steadily away from its own traditions and law when its leaders define it as being under threat. In fact, we are seeing this phenomenon during the administration of George W. Bush in the United States following the bombing of the twin towers of the World Trade Center. In a country long distinguished by its outstanding dedication to civil liberties and the rule of law, a rapid change has taken place in its official dealings with immigrants, or even with citizens who appear to be of Middle Eastern descent or whose names or clothing indicate they might be Muslims. These people now are subjected to humiliating searches and detentions for no other reason than their appearance and name. After the war on Afghanistan, the United States administration incarcerated prisoners in Guantanamo Bay, Cuba, and other locations, without any of the protections required under international law for prisoners of war or any protections normally required under American law for detainees. They have not been charged with crimes or submitted to legal processes, their terms of imprisonment are not specific, and they have been subjected to persistent interrogations. Though many American citizens have protested, and civil liberties associations have mounted objections, public opinion polls indicate that popular support for these measures is strong throughout the United States. Dissenters experienced increasing hostility and even violent repercussions during the American and British attack on Iraq. These events suggest that a disturbing change is occurring in the world's most powerful state. (I will examine this change further in the epilogue to this book.)

Institutional Flexibility

Though cultures are malleable under stress, the basic institutions of a society tend to be firmer, if only because each of them has tasks to perform, long-term tenured employees with stakes in the system, and interlocking relations that are not quickly dismantled. Of particular importance are the institutions that are independent of the state and provide alternative visions for the society, or that freely comment on, and occasionally oppose, governments. These institutions might include the judiciary and universities, even if both are ultimately publicly funded institutional sectors, provided these organizations retain a large measure of independence. They would normally also include the mass media, business associations, unions, diverse religious organizations, voluntary associations, and political parties. The society that has a wide range of independent institutions between those of the state and the level of the family has cushions against the commission of state crimes. In relatively healthy societies there are numerous non-state activities of some importance that can voice critical opinions and actively oppose state behaviours that threaten citizens. The risk associated with state impotence may be dissipated by the presence of these alternative leadership groups that are able to pick up the slack and keep the operation rolling until governments sort out their difficulties.

These institutional sectors are sometimes referred to as "civil society," though the phrase has been overused and has developed too many different connotations. In Soviet-dominated subordinate societies of Eastern Europe, for example, it meant any organization opposed to the state. A World Bank officer once described the term as the important figures inside the society, as contrasted with outside "experts."* Government publications in several societies, together with United Nations publications, occasionally use the term in reference to non-governmental organizations (NGOs), where the term excludes such groups as the media, businesses, educational, medical, and religious institutions. And commentators who are strongly identified with minimal government political positions use the term in reference to everything, including,

---

* At the University of British Columbia at a meeting of World Bank personnel with UBC researchers, April 21, 1998.

especially, private corporations, but excluding the state, in arguments about the need for privatization and the removal of welfare and other protections of populations provided by states.

In societies with few and overlapping institutions (where a state church that invariably supports the government, or where armies control so much of the society's activities that voluntary organizations and mass media fail to emerge as separate entities), the weakness of the state becomes a widespread malaise throughout the society. Where states have intervened in higher education to the extent that they place state officials in classrooms or in the offices of deans and presidents, or where they have so intimidated the mass media that no independent journalism exists, the failure of the state can be catastrophic, because no alternatives are generated in a vacuum. We see these examples in concrete form in Argentina, before the military coup in 1976, where the military state and the Catholic Church so dominated the institutional life of the society that only through revolutionary violence could alternative visions of society or institutional capacities be created.

Societies with numerous institutional sectors separate from government have a greater capacity to withstand political paralysis than societies where the state is in control of major institutions, or where major institutions are closely allied with the state.

Each of these variables may be a necessary condition in a state before the onset of state crimes against citizens, though, on its own, it is insufficient. In combination, however, they are extremely volatile preconditions, leading the state in that direction.

Ideology

Ideology is often put forward as an explanation of state crimes, and, indeed, it is one more of the essential conditions. It acts as the medium between the intention and the act, between the motivation and the carrying out of genocidal attacks. It is the means by which the rest of the population, and sometimes external powers, are persuaded that the action is necessary. The general format of ideology is to persuade people that if the proposed victims are permitted to live, they will do great harm to the society at large. The harm may be in the form of transmitting impurities, preventing the extension of economic benefits from territorial resources, usurping power and threatening to turn good people into slaves, collaborating with enemies, undermining cultural values, or being committed to subversive behaviour. The effect of ideology, though it is rarely a conscious motivation, is to maintain or create inequality among members of the same population. Those who sponsor state crimes take the position that some citizens are more worthy of life and social benefits than others, and ideology is the means of justifying the inequalities.

Ideology is the bridge between the perception of a group as potential enemies and the determination to eradicate them.

Motivation

Humans are complex animals with many, sometimes conflicting, motivations in any situation. But an overriding theme in human affairs is greed, which may be entirely personal or, displaced, on behalf of a collectivity. Nationalism, when it covers for land-grabs, is a form of greed. While one cannot be privy to the private motivations of other people, it is a reasonable guess that in Armenia, Nazi Germany, Burundi, Rwanda, and Yugoslavia this greed was lurking not far beneath the ideological patinas of ethnic nationalism. In the case of the USSR, the scarcely hidden motivation was to obtain grain from reluctant peasants. In Chile and Argentina the motivation was, if anything, cruder: a raw defence of privilege against those who wanted to dilute it. The Cambodian case is the joker in the pack: it was the struggle against an overweening bureaucracy's greed.

Motivation is rarely declared, but intention, defined as actions with the foreseeable consequence of harm done to others, is more easily detectable. Indeed, the definition of intent used in the Genocide Convention carefully avoids the pitfalls of deliberating on the hidden motivations of actors. If those acting on behalf of the state do so with the knowledge that such actions will eradicate or massively harm a group or groups of citizens, they commit a crime against humanity irrespective of their motivation. But since we are trying to understand why they do so, we are concerned with motivation. I argue that the motivation, irrespective of the nature of the victims or the bespoken intent, generally includes a substantial degree of greed or envy of the victims. Their land, their other properties, their success at business or accumulation of wealth are subtly interlaced with perceptions of them as vermin, sick, poor, evil, subversive, or, as the Nazi state phrased it, "unworthy of life."

Political paralysis brought on by confrontation with fundamental social change that results in destabilization of the unequal powers of citizens, when combined with armed force capable of sustaining crimes against humanity and a paucity of institutions independent of the state, is the precondition for state crimes against citizens. The reasons may be expressed in many ideological frameworks that act as the bridge between motivation and action; the ultimate objectives may be instrumental and material. Autocratic forms of governance, an authoritarian culture, or cultures that have not hitherto included protection of civil rights may add to the probability of the commission of state crimes.

EXTERNAL INFLUENCES

The search for explanation is complicated by the fact that states as currently organized on the global stage vary considerably in their independence. The United States is the hegemonic power of our time, an imperial power during the nineteenth and twentieth centuries and capable now, through both its military and its economic power, of controlling many (possibly most) other societies. It is, at the beginning of the third millennium by our conventional calendar, a veritable empire in a world where there are no other empires and no other states capable of modifying its influence by ordinary economic or military means. Thus, when we try to understand the forces that led the governments of Central America, for example, to commit heinous crimes against their own citizens in the period following the Second World War right through to the 1990s and even today, we cannot make sense of events by reference solely to those governments. American companies such as United Fruit, ITT, Anaconda, and Kennecott, powerful agencies during the periods of turmoil in Central America and Chile, together with American intelligence services and military power, were important backdrops, if not primary actors, in many dramas. Similarly, we cannot explain the sequence of events in Iran, Iraq, Isreal, or Pakistan over the period from, say, the 1940s to the late 1980s or in Chad, Vietnam, Korea, and Cambodia without reference to both US and Soviet policies and the enmity between the Cold War powers. In other countries defined as satellites, components, or affiliates of the USSR, including Poland, East Germany, Romania, Hungary, and the Baltic States, Soviet policies during the Cold War were determining factors that have to be given priority in explanations of repression suffered in those regions. In some cases both of the dominant world powers during the Cold War were involved in local situations. To explain the rise and decade-long power of the Taliban in Afghanistan, for example, we have to deal with an earlier decade of Soviet-dominated government combined with American-dominated opposition that led to a political vacuum, anarchy, and internal war for several years before the Taliban gained ascendancy.

A kindred difficulty arises in consideration of empires and imperial governments, or very strong states living next to very weak states with which they are in conflict. The relative strengths of groups under all these circumstances is pertinent: the imperial state can kill and maim or enslave thousands of people in its colonies, and it has often done so with impunity under the guise of its own state sovereignty within its territories, even if on another continent. The core state of an empire, likewise, can commit a one-sided war against the population of a peripheral substate within its regions and can often get away with murder because, again, it claims control over the whole of its territories. The same is true, even though the claim is less believable, when a very strong state bullies a weaker neighbour. These caveats oblige the theorist to specify carefully the larger context of state actions while trying to explain the actions themselves

INTERVENTION

If the approach presented here is valid, it follows that crimes against humanity committed by states – and there are many – cannot be pre-empted or stopped by soothing words, pleas, or interventions by other states unless those other states are prepared to ensure that at least one of the following conditions is imposed: the inequality in question is preserved and those who object to it are stymied in their attempts to overturn the hierarchy (never a long-term solution); the perpetrators and the intended victims are physically separated for a lengthy period by peacekeeping troops (never a satisfactory solution); or the army and/or state elite that is attempting to maintain or create it is itself eradicated (which involves another form of politicide). The longer-term solution would have to include the development of diverse institutional sectors, but external powers are rarely in a position to oblige societies to create them.

On a more optimistic note, these episodes might be predictable and therefore preventable by actions that reduce the severity of the conditions that bring on state paralysis and that introduce alternative options. Much of the contemporary agony in Third World countries, for example, is caused by internal weaknesses combined with the extreme demands for dismantling of the public sector by the International Monetary Fund (IMF) (see Stiglitz, 2002a, 2002b; Soros, 2002a). A more sophisticated understanding of the internal inequalities and institutional capabilities might reduce the pressures on weak states and devise options for creative governance that does not rest on violence against citizens. Further, international legal sanctions, including an International Criminal Court, would have a function parallel to the development of national law in societies. Law imposes on governments and individuals demands for accountability, transparency, and responsibility. International law and sanctions against state crimes would have a restraining power on governments, armies, and bureaucracies that might otherwise repeat the crimes that were, until recently, committed the world over with impunity and under the cloak of national sovereignty. Since greed for land and other property often lies at the base of these crimes, the global community needs to address that greed through negotiation, if possible, or by united counter-force, if negotiation is impossible. We will pick up on this theme in chapter 6.

ESSENTIAL CONCEPTS

Some international conventions deal with the ideas basic to this study. There are also a few terms that are frequently employed in discussions of crimes against humanity. Before continuing with the analysis, readers might find it useful to remind themselves of the definition of these terms.

Crimes against Humanity

The concept of crimes against humanity was initially defined in the Charter for the Nuremberg Tribunal to try Nazi leaders after the Second World War. Such crimes have since been codified and implemented in international agreements including the Universal Declaration of Human Rights (1948), the U.N. Convention on the Prevention and Punishment of the Crime of Genocide (1948, in force as of 1951), the Geneva Conventions on War Crimes (1949 and later addenda), the Convention against Torture and Other Cruel, Inhuman or Degrading Treatment or Punishment (1984), and a range of other conventions and agreements of varying character and strength. These crimes refer to those committed by governments, including murder, extermination, enslavement, deportation, imprisonment, torture, sexual violence, persecution, or any other inhumane act that is committed against any civilian population or any identifiable group as part of a systematic and widespread attack. Incidental, accidental, or singular crimes are not included: the systemic nature of the events is essential to the definition of any set of crimes as being against humanity.

These crimes may be identified and prosecuted under national criminal or customary law, if such exists in a country, but they are more likely to be prosecuted where there is an international agreement ratified by the country or by other countries where perpetrators of such crimes might seek safety. Some countries, operating under the Napoleonic civil law tradition or accepting as national law whatever international laws they have ratified, automatically incorporate international law into their national law. Others have to create national laws specifically stating their adherence to international agreements. Britain, for example, did so, and it was under that implementing legislation that British police, in 1998, had the authority to detain General Augusto Pinochet, former president and chief of the armed forces in Chile, in response to a request for extradition by a Spanish judge.

Genocide

The first attempt to legally codify genocide was made by Rafael Lemkin, a Jewish refugee from Poland, in his book *Axis Rule in Occupied Europe* (1944). He took it to be the planned annihilation of a national, religious, or racial group through multiple acts of persecution and destruction. He included attacks on political and social institutions, culture, language, religion, national sentiments, and economic underpinnings of the victimized group. He created a typology of genocidal cases. The first is the total extermination of a group or a nation; the second, the destruction of a culture; the third, a combination of the first two whereby some groups are slated for extermination, others for forced assimilation.

The codification of genocide underwent debate and change in the post–Second World War period. The United Nations Convention on the Prevention and Punishment of Genocide (UNGC) of 1951 emphasizes the intent to destroy ethnic, racial, or religious groups. (In legal terminology, "intent" refers to a situation where there are foreseeable ends or consequences of actions, in contrast to motive, which refers to the reasons for the actions) (Fein, 1990: 15–20). Article 11 of the

convention reads: "Genocide means any of the following acts committed with intent to destroy, in whole or in part, a national, ethnical,
racial or religious group as such: (a) Killing members of the group;
(b) Causing serious bodily or mental harm to members of the group;
(c) Deliberately inflicting on the group conditions of life calculated to
bring about its physical destruction in whole or in part; (d) Imposing
measures intended to prevent births within the group; (e) Forcibly
transferring children of the group to another group."

There are numerous critics of this definition. Harff (1985: 11–12)
suggests that the phrase "doing mental harm" should be eliminated because it is virtually impossible to identify such harm and, moreover,
mental harm is not restricted to instances of genocide. She also suggests
that the phrase "bodily harm" could mean too many things and should
be changed to "torture where constituting part of a more general policy aimed at the destruction of a target group."

Perhaps more serious are the numerous borderline situations that, if
not genocide, remain outside the convention. Such cases as China during the "cultural revolution" (1966–76) and Cambodia under Pol Pot
(1975–79) are particularly problematic because, in each case, the state
massacred thousands of its citizens, though not on the grounds specified in the definition. In both episodes, the targets were intellectuals,
professionals, and urban dwellers, chosen on such grounds as their
place of residence, their education, and their occupations, not their ethnicity. These people were deemed to be anti-revolutionaries, whether or
not any of them actually held such views. The killing of people for political reasons is also excluded, so the state murders committed in Latin
America in the 1970s are not covered. Stalin intentionally starved millions of Ukrainian peasants in 1932–33. Was it, as apologists claim, because the peasants rebelled against collectivization of agricultural land
or was it because they had nationalist aspirations? Was it genocide?
The dispersal of numerous other ethnic minorities by the Soviet state
might also be understood as genocides because the victims were shorn
of all their possessions, separated from their families and village neighbours, and sent to concentration camps where survival was rare.

Evidence of the genocide against Serbs, committed by Croatians allied with Nazis during the Second World War in Bosnia-Herzegovina,
was still being unearthed during the 1990 Bosnian crisis (Burg, 1997).
The full extent of that crisis, along with the genocide of Bosnian Muslims by Serb forces, is still only partially known. After the declaration
of India's independence, genocides were committed by both the Paki-

stani and the Indian governments against Hindus and against Muslims, respectively, while the entire subcontinent was caught up in the massive movements of people from one region to the other.

More recently, genocidal outbreaks occurred in Bosnia-Herzegovina in 1992–95 and in East Timor in 2000. In both Iraq and Turkey against Kurds, and in Afghanistan against several ethnic and religious minorities, genocide seems to be the appropriate designation. Events in the Democratic Republic of the Congo, formerly the Belgian Congo and then Zaire, probably include genocide, though knowledge of what is occurring in the early twenty-first century is anecdotal because the entire Congo River basin is engaged in several internal and interstate wars at once.

Rigorous definitions are useful for the development of effective civil rights and the legal enforcement of rights. Overly general and all-inclusive definitions of such terms as genocide defeat the possibility of prosecuting perpetrators in even a limited range of episodes. Still, the narrow definition of genocide is not very helpful, and because the reality is so much more complex and varied than the definition, many scholars object to the UN definition. They would prefer a less restricted one that includes destruction of cultures, languages, or religions, or various forms of mass violence such as pogroms, or accidental events such as Bhopal and Chernobyl. Others have suggested the inclusion of the killing of civilians during wars or the continuing blockage of indigenous peoples' aspirations for self-government and expanded territory. And most scholars would include the killing of people because of their beliefs or political behaviour.

The defence of the UN definition is that, while many historical events have been crimes against humanity, the restricted use of the term "genocide" is essential if legal proceedings are to be carried out. However, legal proceedings are rare. The convention exists primarily at a symbolic level, and the actual explanation for its vague definition is that it was created by the victors of the Second World War, who, already on the brink of what became the Cold War, preferred a weak definition over no statement at all. By the end of the twentieth century, two-thirds of member states of the United Nations had ratified the convention. The United States did not sign until the late 1980s, and then after lengthy debates. As of December 2002, 133 countries were parties to the convention. Among the fifty non-signatories are Indonesia, Japan, and Nigeria (Prevent Genocide International, 2002).

For those who want a broader definition, there is solace in the development over the twentieth century of national legislation that defines genocide more expansively and in other conventions that affect a wider range of perpetrators and victims. Moreover, some of them have strong legal teeth. Spain, for example, has created a wider definition within its national legal framework. Important as these national developments are, the problem is that national courts may be reluctant or unable to take strong action against previous regimes because of fear of retaliation, continuing army disaffection, and personal and group affiliations with former comrades. For this reason, the original drafters of the Convention included reference to an International Criminal Court, but in the Cold War context such a court was not established.

It was not until 1993 that the first of the ad hoc tribunals was established by the Security Council to deal with genocide, crimes against humanity, and war crimes. In 1998 the Rome Statute for an International Criminal Court (ICC) was enunciated to deal solely with the crime of genocide. The statute entered into force on 1 July 2002, after 66 countries had ratified it. By the end of 2002, 139 states had signed the statute and 87 had ratified or acceded to it. Ratification means agreement to be bound by the statute. Signatory states can ratify a treaty until it comes into effect and, thereafter, they can accede to it. So far, only 15 of the 87 states have adopted comprehensive domestic legislation, but the number steadily increases. Canada ratified the statute in 2000. The United States signed in December 2000, but President George W. Bush withdrew in May 2002. This decision puts the United States in the company of Iraq, Libya, and China as non-participants, though China and Libya and currently considering accession. Since withdrawing its signature, the United States has embarked on a global campaign to obtain immunity for US citizens from the ICC's jurisdiction. In August 2002 President Bush signed the supplemental appropriations bill, which prohibits any US agency from cooperation with the ICC. The bill also restricts US participation in UN peacekeeping operations. The ICC is referred to as the "Hague Invasion Act" (International Human Rights Law Institute, 2003).

Other Definitions of Genocide

Many social scientists and writers in other areas have suggested alternative definitions of genocide. For example, Irving Louis Horowitz (1980: 18) defined genocide as a "structural and systematic destruction of innocent people by a state bureaucratic apparatus" and a "systematic effort over time to liquidate a natural population, usually a minority." He argued that its function is to induce "conformity and participation by the citizenry." Helen Fein proposed a sociological definition (1990: 24): "Genocide is a sustained purposeful action by a perpetrator to physically destroy a collectivity directly or indirectly, through interdiction of the biological and social reproduction of group members, sustained regardless of the surrender or lack of threat offered by the victim."

This definition would allow perpetrators to be groups other than the state. It does not exclude political reasons for the actions, but neither does it include actions designed to prevent propagation of ideas rather than physical reproduction of persons. Rather, it requires that there be a collectivity, which may be the case for ethnic, religious, or national groups, but is problematic for urbanites, unorganized groups of students or workers, or individuals who are not organized but who may share similar ideas. It has the merit of excluding accidental deaths or single massacres.

Chalk and Jonassohn (1990: 23–8) propose a more limited definition and urge that the term "ethnocide" be more widely applied to suppression or destruction of cultures. In their definition, genocide is "a form of one-sided mass killing in which a state or other authority intends to destroy a group, as that group and membership in it are defined by the perpetrator." Instead of trying to come up with a definition of the victims, Chalk and Jonassohn suggest that the perpetrator's own ideological identification of them be the guide. The word "form" denotes that there are other forms (e.g., war) not under consideration.

The ad hoc international war crimes tribunals established for dealing with the Rwandan and Yugoslavian cases reinterpreted the convention to mean "stable" groups, "constituted in a permanent fashion and membership of which is determined by birth, with the exclusion of the more 'mobile' groups which one joins through individual voluntary commitment, such as political and economic groups" (Schabas, 1999, 3). This definition overcomes the problem faced by these particular tribunals, since they could not assert that Tutsis or Bosnians were identifiable and distinctive ethnic groups, unlike the Hutus and Serbs who persecuted them. But it does not overcome the problem of crimes committed against groups whose extinction is predicated on the perpetrators' identification of them as political or class enemies. The court dealing with the former Yugoslavian case also has to determine whether "ethnic cleansing" is the same as genocide. If the prosecution cannot show that the ethnic cleansing that occurred in that war constituted genocide, the court could dismiss the case. The defence argues that ethnic cleansing is an attempt to force inhabitants to leave a territory, rather than a deliberate attempt to eradicate them. The definition of genocide, therefore, is crucial to the legal proceedings.

Other definitions are embedded in theories, reviewed in the case studies that follow. Many approaches to these questions make no distinction among genocide, politicide, and ethnocide (as defined below). It is, in fact, not clear that the distinction is necessary for purposes of theory, but because the apparent motivations of the perpetrators and the nature of victims are generally different, the distinctions should be noted.

Politicide

There is no convention regarding politicide – indeed, the word is of recent vintage and was coined so that the word "genocide" did not have to be infinitely expanded. Politicide occurs when governments, or others holding a high degree of independent power, authorize the kidnapping, torture, murder, or other grave human rights abuses against people who hold, or whom they believe might hold, dissident ideas, or whose economic and social class situation is deemed to be anathema, or whose lifestyle is deemed to be impure or objectionable for whatever reason, when such identification is not subject to proof, evidence, or open trial.

Since ideas and even class situations are not held exclusively by any easily identified collectivity, the victims of politicide may include not only persons who are armed subversives but innocent persons who happen to live in a particular area, attend schools or universities, have certain occupations, or appear in the "wrong" company or have their names in an address book belonging to others believed to be subversives. In several instances, age becomes an identifier: in Argentina of 1976–83, anyone appearing to be younger than thirty was a suspect. Typically certain groups are targeted: journalists, social workers, labour lawyers and union leaders, professors, students, and intellectuals more generally. However, bureaucrats and wealthy people might as easily be targets if their opposites hold power, as was the case in China during the cultural revolution, and in Cambodia during the Pol Pot revolution. Typically the perpetrators claim to believe that the subversive ideas their designated enemies might disseminate would destroy civilization and all they hold dear.

One of the objections to including political victims in the definition for genocide was that every state has political opponents, some of whom are armed subversives. Assuming it is legitimate to attempt to capture and disarm such persons, any definition that treats all political acts as genocide would not be accepted even by the most liberal democratic states. However, liberal democratic states are obliged to bring such individuals to trial and to produce evidence of illegal acts; a definition of politicide that clearly states the absence of such protections would be necessary.

Politicide includes what might otherwise be categorized as "class crimes" or crimes committed against individuals because they are, or are perceived to be, members of a class. A class would consist of families who share a position in the economic and social spectrum of the society. The measurements of positions are generally rather crude, such as owning/not owning land or industrial and commercial establishments; living in rural or urban regions; or being employed in manual versus non-manual labour. Because ethnic groups are often discriminated against and ranked within multi-ethnic societies, persons who fall into crude class categories may also share ethnic origins. Armenians and Greeks in the Ottoman Empire, Indians in Uganda, and Jews in much of Europe were disproportionately engaged in commerce: their ethnicity and their occupational niches were so intertwined that crimes against the ethnic group and class were one and the same.

Incidence of Genocide and Politicide

The crimes of genocide and politicide have occurred on every continent and throughout historical time. For the period between 1945 and 1993 alone, Fein (1990) identified nineteen cases of genocide or mixtures of genocide and politicide. Others (e.g., Kuper, 1981; Harff and Gurr, 1988; Ezell, 1989) have identified further cases. The list for the second half of the twentieth century, using diverse sources, includes instances from the Soviet Union, Bulgaria, Romania, Hungary, East Germany, China, Indonesia and East Timor, West Papua, Cambodia, Pakistan, Afghanistan, Iran under the shah and then under the mullahs, Iraq, Bangladesh, Sri Lanka, Ethiopia, Uganda, Zaire, Burundi, Rwanda, South Africa, Brasil, Argentina, Peru, Bolivia, Chile, Uruguay, Guatemala, El Salvador, Nicaragua, the former Yugoslavia, and yet others.

The sheer range of outbreaks of such violence makes it clear that the problem is not confined to one particular country, one ethnic group or ethnic group mixture, one clash of religions, or one political epoch – although in the case of political epochs, the period of the Cold War has a plenitude of examples. Each case has a particular history: this occurred, that leader came to power, that group gained ascendancy, another group became subservient, a particular incident sparked off riots that were met by massive repression, and then, silently at first but with growing public recognition, a genocide or a politicide occurred. The question is, do the countries that have witnessed these separate historical incidents have anything in common? If so, what is the explanation for the frequent occurrence of these violent episodes?

Deliberate genocide and politicide are not typical events in states where indenture and servitude are common conditions; at least, genocide is not committed against the same citizens as those who are obliged to serve. The reason, presumably, is that this group is viewed as necessary labour. Their death would be inconvenient, though if they cause disturbances they may be killed to avoid further nuisance. Servitude, then, is somewhat different from state terror or the horrors inflicted on people during an internal war, yet it stems from the same impulse to use force against other human beings. Whether the objective is to eradicate an ethnic group, eliminate a set of beliefs, destroy a class or a way of life, or enslave others, the basic impulse is to gain absolute control over other people. If we assume that we are all capable of killing others, we might also assume that wanting to control others is well within the normal range of human desires. Again, the question is, under what circumstances is that impulse given free range, or, alternatively, under what circumstances is it reined in?

Ethnocide

The term "ethnocide" was first used in reference to the destruction of a culture rather than the killing of its bearers. We use the phrase "cultural genocide" for this same phenomenon, but it stretches the definition of genocide to include cultural destruction as equal to the mass murder of group members, unless it ultimately leads to the extinction of the group. Ethnocide might include such acts as the forcing of children in indigenous cultures to attend residential schools or the placement of indigenous peoples on reserves where there is insufficient food for their survival. While less overtly brutal than other crimes against humanity, if the intent is the attempted elimination of a people then it is genocide.

Intent and Motivation

The legal definition of intention to commit genocide refers to actions that have the foreseeable consequence of harm or destruction, whereas motivation is the reason for such actions. This definition presents something of a conundrum for the theorist, since it lumps together those who deliberately set out to eradicate a civilian population and those who destroy a population incidentally and without deliberation. Imperial powers throughout the nineteenth and twentieth centuries destroyed indigenous people wherever they took over territories. In some instances they intended to eliminate those who already inhabited the land they wished to conquer, and those were clear cases of genocide. However, more ambiguous are the instances when, motivated by greed, they engaged in searches for resources and profits that incidentally destroyed habitat and inhabitants in conquered territory. Sometimes they used these people as slaves or indentured labour, and the slaves died of exhaustion or hunger. Some conquered people died from diseases brought by the conquerers, and others during wars between conquering groups or during the process of settlement by outsiders. Insofar as the imperial powers could foresee a disastrous consequence of their actions, they were committing genocide. Some theorists would prefer to include all such instances in the tally. I am not inclined to take this stance because the situations, even where equally cruel, are sufficiently different for it to be useful to restrict the term *genocide* to those where both the intent and the motivation to eradicate people are present.

Terror

Terror is a strategy designed to induce fear in the minds of civilian populations by deliberate acts of violence against some of its members. It is used by states where the objective is to frighten citizens so they will not sympathize with or shield selected victims. In many cases, the state imposes punishment for crimes committed by civilians, but the crimes attributed to the victims are so varied and arbitrary that others are unable to predict the potential responses to their own actions. They are constantly frightened of being caught, even though they are unsure which of their own behaviours might constitute a crime in the eyes of those who have the power to harm them. State terror is not a spontaneous violent outburst; on the contrary, it is a carefully planned, organized system that requires the coordinated contributions of agencies engaged in the gathering of information; the sleuthing and stalking of potential victims; abduction or capture, incarceration, torture, and murder of victims; and the disposal of corpses. It occurs over a lengthy period of time and involves the participation of numerous agents in diverse capacities.

Terrorism

I use the phrase "state terrorism" for acts of government designed to instill extreme fear in a population, but the literature in social science disciplines of political science and international relations reserves the term "terrorism" for acts of anti-state groups. Such groups attempt to frighten a civilian population by selective violence of a symbolic nature. The destruction of the twin towers of the World Trade Center is the outstanding example. The kidnapping of corporate executives of foreign companies and the murder of some politicians by the Montoneros in Argentina before the military coup is another example. Violence of this kind is not designed to eradicate a population but to frighten people in the hope they will pay attention to the consequences of state and corporate actions that harm the populations on whose behalf the terrorists act. In my opinion, states also use terrorist tactics, and the term is appropriately applied to such states.

2

Racism and Identity

State crimes against humanity are actually crimes against civilians who occupy low-status positions and who are perceived by higher-status compatriots as real or potential threats to the stability of the existing hierarchy of relationships. In revolutionary states those who have taken control of state institutions perceive proposed victims as potential threats to the stability of a still-evolving hierarchy of relationships. The essential task of the state is to preserve, not necessarily in precise detail but in general form, the system in which these inequalities exist so the system can operate. A slave society must have slaves, a feudal agricultural society needs peasants, an industrial society needs workers: crude as such an observation may be, it is at the heart of social organization. What is variable is which groups become the slaves, the peasants, and the workers at the bottom of the industrial hierarchy. When inequalities cannot be sustained, especially when the carrying capacity of the land and the available resources cannot support the whole population, selective extinction is considered as a more extreme form of inequality.

The status of different groups usually has historical roots in conquest, regional divisions, traditional land ownership, or occupational niches. Ethnicity may be a primary determinant of status, generally combined with other attributes of class position. Class, which by definition denotes inequalities in the distribution of power, wealth, and social opportunities, may rest on ownership of the means of production as defined by Marx. It may also rest on the more subtle gradation of power differentials found in contemporary corporate capitalism, with its use of collective investment funds. Societies divide their populations by age, and this division can turn lethal – when the young kill off their elders, for example, or the generals kill off young warriors or potential revolutionaries. Gender is always a division, though its significance is highly variable.

Class differences, by their nature measures of inequality, may be separate from ethnic dimensions or may overlap with them. Geographical and geopolitical locations of residence may also be dimensions of inequality where persons residing in a dominant society, or in a dominant region within a country, have substantially greater power, opportunity, and wealth than persons residing elsewhere. Whatever their respective weights, all societies are fraught with these divisions and rankings. The effects of state policies are generally, though not invariably and necessarily in specific detail, the means of retaining the inequalities over time.

ARMENIA AND NAZI GERMANY

This chapter will explore themes related to ethnicity and religion in the examples of the deportation of Armenians by Turks in the Ottoman Empire and the Nazi eradication of Jews, Gypsies, and others in Germany. The themes will subsequently be considered briefly with reference to the different cases of the Eastern Ukraine in the USSR, Burundi and Rwanda, and Yugoslavia.

Race and Racism

Existing theories of genocide rely heavily on concepts of race, racism, xenophobia, ethnicity, and tribalism. Most theories of the Nazi Holocaust, for the leading example, focus on the anti-Semitism that was rife throughout Europe for many centuries before the 1930s and 1940s. There can be little doubt that genocide is linked to racism in one form or another; indeed, by definition under the international convention, it is a crime perpetrated against a group identified by race, ethnicity, or religion. But if the theory introduced in chapter 1 is valid, ethnicity is best understood as one possible dimension of inequality rather than as a primary cause of state crimes against citizens.

Race is a problematic concept because there are no "pure" races, and what often passes for race is nothing more than skin pigmentation. Racism is an ideological stance based on beliefs and perceptions about race. Ethnicity is a more comprehensive term, including whatever genetic components are perceived to be common to groups together with group cultural attributes such as religion. In most societies, both contemporary and historical, ethnic groups within a population are ranked, overtly or subtly. These rankings place severe strains on inter-ethnic relations, and even more severe restraints on the freedom of the groups at the bottom of the hierarchy. The reasons for the rankings differ from one society to another. In the cases selected for study here, ethnicity was an important criterion for determining victims in Armenia (1915–16), Nazi Germany (1933–45), Burundi (1972 and later), Rwanda (1994 and later), and Yugoslavia (1990–95). Differing religions were crucial in the Ottoman Empire. Nazi Germany is more complex, since religion and numerous other criteria defined the victims. In Burundi, Rwanda, and Yugoslavia the ranking itself was the issue, as one self-defined ethnic group vied with another or others to come out on top of a hierarchy in the making. Ethnicity might have been a criterion in the case of Eastern Ukrainians, in the USSR, but this example is more ambiguous. None of the other cases examined here rest on ethnic divisions as potential causes in state crimes against their own citizens.

The Nazi case is generally cited as the primary example of genocide because of the long-standing discrimination against Jews and Gypsies. The most frequently cited explanation for the killing of the Jews is simply that Germans were hostile to Jews throughout their history, and Hitler's demagoguery incited them to act out their hatreds. Daniel Goldhagen's controversial account of ordinary Germans (1996) before and during this period is a chilling testament to long-standing stereotypes and racism. Yet the explanation – anti-Semitism, anti-Gypsy – is problematic on several counts. One is that the victims were not all Semites and Gypsies. They included Germans, Poles, Slavs, and others selected on diverse grounds, some because they were low on the still-evolving ethnic hierarchy, but others because of sexual orientation, and still others because of diverse personal characteristics. They included homosexuals and mentally or physically ill or disabled Germans. What these varied groups had in common were two qualities: they all had low status in Germany and they were all regarded as "impure" on an arbitrary bipolar measure. Those who were "pure" were not only ethnically German but physically and mentally "whole," with no recognized defects.

The relationship of ethnicity to territory is of particular importance in empires and imperialist domains. In these cases, subordinate ethnic groups generally reside on lands they regard as ancestral or that generations of their group have called their own. When the dominant group considers the subordinate group as enemies, they are concerned not only with the population but with its land resources as well. Indeed, it is entirely possible that the resources are the focus of the attack, but the subordinate status of the ethnic group becomes the ideological focus for the army or the other forces used to execute the orders. In empires and imperialist domains the dominant group acts on the presumption that it has the right to organize an assault against a minority group residing on land that the empire has conquered or annexed: this is a sovereign right and, in fact, empires and imperial states were able to sustain their rights to the lands of their subject peoples throughout most of human history. We would now regard many of the genocides committed on regional as well as ethnic bases as interstate wars, and possibly we would invoke international conventions to punish the perpetration of genocide during wars, assuming we were unable to prevent them. Among our case studies are two empires, the Ottoman and the USSR (formerly the Russian Empire). Burundi and Rwanda were no longer extensions of imperialist states, but they were still reeling from the impact of imperialism when they moved into genocidal episodes between 1972 and 1994. Yugoslavia had left its two empire origins behind, yet the lingering legacies of both the Austro-Hungarian and the Ottoman empires were part of its plunge into genocide generations later. Neo-colonialism is involved in the Latin American and Asian cases, as we will see later on in this book.

Xenophobia

One line of reasoning about ethnic divisions is that human beings everywhere, always, fear strangers and, perhaps obeying a genetically based survival instinct, will lash out at strangers even to the point of killing them. At a moral level, one might object to the theory because it seems to excuse people from taking responsibility for their actions by claiming they are genetically programmed. We do not need to take a moralistic stance, however, since we have plenty of evidence that strangers roam the world unharmed and have done so for millennia. Diverse populations have co-existed within empires and states throughout history without resorting to mutual destruction; the fact that they sometimes end up on the killing fields is not proof that they do so for genetically predetermined reasons or that xenophobia is a cause. Tourism is the incorporation of strangers into the local economy. It is true, of course, that settled populations might fight off hordes of strangers whom they define as enemies, usually because the designated enemies covet their land or other resources. But wars between people over territory are not manifestations of xenophobia.

Any population that is encased within tight confines, unable to interact with other populations or to exchange views with others unlike themselves, or a population under siege by another group over a long period of time might well become so inward-looking that its members regard the rest of the scarcely known world, or at least their proximate enemies, with deep and almost paranoid suspicion. They become afraid of "the other," and "the other" is, in the nature of the situation, a stranger as well as a real or perceived enemy. This condition is not really xenophobia; it is a trained response to a genuinely threatening situation. The key is not a genetic predisposition but a fear of a potentially hostile "other." The "us and them" syndrome is a widespread phenomenon where two groups, each defining itself as unique and different from the other, have hostile relationships.

Ethnicity as Identity

All cultures include definitions of members that provide them with important aspects of their personal identity. We are, even in highly secular, industrialized, urban societies, particular in our inheritance. We are Scots, Poles, Ukrainians, Ethiopians, Palestinians, Iranians, Americans, New Zealanders, Muslim, Jewish, Catholic, Protestant, Buddhists, Sikhs, or whatever else our contemporary culture allows us to choose for our inheritance – and sometimes in spite of the prohibitions our culture imposes on such choices. Personal identity is a powerful force for many people: it differentiates between them, their creed or their tribal group, and the rest of humanity. But there is a fundamental difference between an awareness or even a pride in our ancestry or roots and seeing those roots as sufficiently precious to ourselves that any price must be paid to safeguard the group to which we believe ourselves committed by birth, race, religion, or choice. If our identity is closely intertwined with a group – as large as an imagined "race" or as small as a gang, perhaps – we may be easily led into believing that any perceived threat to the group is a personal threat that has to be dealt with in the strongest possible terms. If it were entirely personal, and the threat were palpable and terrifying, the individual might commit murder. In the cases of interest to us, the perceived threat is aimed at the group, and its

members, if they identify strongly with the group, may be prepared collectively to commit murders against other groups. Much depends on
how strong the bond is within the group for any of its members.

*The more one's identity is tied to any collectivity, the greater the pro-
pensity to experience perceived threats against the group as personal
threats to oneself and one's family.*

Religion is generally connected to ethnicity, particularly for rural
populations. But religion, apart from ethnic roots, can be a force on its
own in the relations between populations. Judaism, Christianity, and
Islam are all monotheistic religions, each claiming that there is no other
God but theirs, no other way of life for humanity but theirs. Other
philosophical systems that might be understood as religions, such as
Buddhism, B'hai, or more polytheistic and animistic beliefs, might also
fall into the category of "heathen" ideas from the perspective of any of
the monotheistic religions. Relations between believers in a monotheistic system and persons outside it, either believers in one of the other
monotheisms or other ideas, have often been tense. In Iran today, for
example, though the three monotheisms are tolerated, B'hai is anathema to Muslims. Their reasoning is that Judaism and Christianity were
accepted as predecessors to Islam by Mohammed, and must be tolerated, but B'hai came after the one true religion was established, so is a
blasphemous belief system. Diverse ethnic groups subscribe to each of
the three monotheistic religions, so we cannot attribute genocidal
events perpetrated by one against either of the others, or against alternative belief systems, simply to racism; religion itself may be the divid-
ing line.

Among the numerous confusions that arise with such divisions is the
fact that individuals may belong to several groups or none, because of
mixed ancestry to which different meanings are attached by others, or
because they do not choose to identify themselves by arbitrary labels.
In Nazi Germany, for instance, many people identified themselves as
Germans, only to be persecuted as Jews because Nazi officials used presumed biological criteria for classifying the population. The salience of
ethnicity for self-identity can vary widely from person to person or
from group to group, and, likewise, the importance attached to ethnicity by states and their agents can be highly variable.

Ironically, where states engage in the killing of specific ethnic groups,
those groups are frequently embedded in the same population of resi-

dents as the majority group doing the killing. The Nazi state (the proto-
type in these explanations) did not target Muslims and Chinese –
neither of which groups had much representation in Germany of the
1930s. It targeted Jews, Gypsies, some Poles, and a few other ethnic
groups that had lived among Germans for hundreds of years, speaking
German and believing themselves to be German. They were not strangers. Palestinians and Jews in the contested areas of the Middle East
hold in common an account of their ancestry that informs them of their
common father figure, Abraham. According to that account they have
different mothers, so are step-brothers and step-sisters, yet at the beginning of the third millennium they are also bitter enemies.

It is not strangers who are "them" compared to "us." Strangers are
outside the realm of recognition and beyond status comparisons. Until
they become relevant to a population, they are neither enemies nor
friends. "Us" compared to "them," by contrast, involves populations
who are neighbours, friends or enemies, but known, identified, put in
their place by the existing system of inequalities. "They" are not our
equal. This "us and them" syndrome is clearly at work in cases of
genocide. Though ethnicity is a highly problematic concept because it
depends so much on subjective classifications either by members of
groups who share a cultural identity or by members of groups who as-
sign an assumed identity to others, human beings have always attached
great meaning to it. Once we divide the world into two groups – those
who are saved and all others – the ground is laid for the self-righteous
exclusion of others. There is one especially intriguing aspect to this exclusionary stance: it is most virulent where ethnic and religious identities are least well established. It is the weak ethnic groups that are most
determined to prove their superiority, to treat non-members as inferior,
and to exclude or even murder them en masse.

*Insecure, more than secure, ethnic identities are associated with the ex-
clusion of non-members by groups that define themselves in ethnic
terms*

The Turkish and German cases are the primary examples of this conundrum whereby the identity crisis was the problem of the perpetrators, not of the victims. Turkish identity appears to have been a pivotal
factor in the planning of the genocide. R. Hrair Dekmejian (1986:
86–93) identifies a "crisis milieux and pathological leadership" in the
Armenian case. He suggests that the convergence of a social crisis, an

ideology, and a pathological leadership are the conditions that lead to genocide. He notes the shallow roots of Turkish identity: many Ittihad leaders were recent converts to Turkism and were descended from the middle and lower-middle classes. The top leaders were a Bulgarian Gypsy (Talaat Pasha), an Islamized syncretic Jew (Javid Bey), an Albanian prince from Egypt (Said Halim Pasha), and a Cherkez/Albanian (Enver Pasha). The ideologues who were most concerned with Pan-Turanism were from Russian regions and were opposed to the Russian Empire. A large part of the implementation was handed over to a force of 12,000 men, specially recruited from imprisoned criminals. In short, the Turks who ordered and executed the genocide were, in Dekmejian's description, marginal to the society. Similar claims have been advanced with respect to Hitler and some of his acolytes. It stretches the point to suggest that this characteristic is a regularly occurring and essential feature of genocidal leaders, but it raises questions about the validity of an explanation based on ethnicity. Why marginalized people would so single-mindedly seek to have an identity other than their own is puzzling, but there is a more general argument on identity that is germane. Mim Kemâl Öke (1988), an apologist for Turkish attacks on Armenians, argued that the Turks were desperately trying to create their own niche in the world, to define Turkishness in a hostile atmosphere where European powers were clamouring to disembowel their territories. The fact that this defence does not constitute a justification for genocide does not, in itself, invalidate the argument: from the Turkish point of view, they were surrounded by enemies and the Armenians were too dangerous to keep in their midst.

In the case of Nazi Germany, the population had been dealt a killing blow when its cultural identity as a superior people was smashed in the First World War. Not only was it defeated by people whom it had been told were inferior but those inferior people had imposed on Germans conditions for peace that humiliated and impoverished them. As people who had never accepted democracy with its egalitarian principles, they were now obliged to live under the Weimar Republic. What Hitler did, above all else, was restore Germans to their sense of selfhood, their heroic model. He used many techniques, including socialization, youth clubs, military parades, extraordinary rhetoric, and a massive verbal assault – before the physical assault – on minorities and all others who failed to meet the criteria of "true Germanic peoples." He attributed failure to all these "inferior" groups. Hitler's rhetoric and his bravado in rearming Germany against the conditions of the Versailles Treaty gave Germans a renewed sense of their importance and power in the world. Thus, in common with the Turks, while they persecuted minorities in their midst, they were simultaneously recovering their identity as *über-mensch*.

Status Inconsistency and Communal Cultures

Long before their forced evictions, Christian Armenians and Greeks ranked at the bottom of an ethnic hierarchy. They suffered considerable discrimination and deprivation of civil rights over a fairly lengthy period of time during the slow decline of the Ottoman Empire. There were several pogroms before the genocide of 1915–16. Their low ranks, however, were inconsistent with their growing economic power. Armenians, and to a lesser extent Greeks, within the empire had become major commercial entrepreneurs throughout the system. Some Armenians, then, were relatively rich and had more economic power than their Turkish neighbours. This inconsistency between their ethnic status and their economic status, according to several theorists, weighed against them when the Young Turks chose to evict them forcibly from their traditional territories under conditions that amounted to genocide (Kuper, 1981; Dadrian, 1999).

Robert Melson (1992a, 1992b) notes that for both the Armenians and the Jews, the victims had cultures that were more communal than the mainstream, and that both minorities had modernized earlier than the dominant majority. These minorities were perceived to be ideologically aligned with external enemies at a time when military and political disasters were affecting the dominant group. This insight is helpful in the German and Armenian cases, but it does not seem to fit other cases. There is no indication, for example, that Stalin thought that the Eastern Ukrainian peasants were allied with external agents, though he may have considered their resistance to the collectivization of farms and their persisting nationalism to be threats to his grand plans for the USSR. Pol Pot's army in Cambodia acted on the assumption that its enemies included foreign forces, but that was not its motivating explanation. Hutus in Rwanda were much less concerned with external influences than with the advances of the exiled Tutsi army. Chilean and Argentine generals assumed, more or less accurately, that the United States and other external forces were with them, not against them.

The argument regarding status inconsistency may have applicability to German Jews, who, like Armenians, were more successful at commercial enterprise than non-Jewish Germans. If Uganda had been included in this study, we would have recognized another instance of this theme in the expulsion of the Asian population, which was notably more successful as entrepreneurs than the African component of that state. In these cases, the issue is not simply that one group is more successful in business than another; it is that the group demonstrating the superior entrepreneurial skill is otherwise defined as inferior. There is no similar response, for example, to the success of the Pharsees of India, since they have not been defined as inferior people; their success poses no threat to the existing hierarchy of ethnic relationships. The takeover of agricultural land owned by "whites" by the Zimbabwe government under Robert Mugabe follows a parallel logic. A revolutionary government, which Mugabe's became, requires an overturning of existing inequalities, a redefinition of the criteria for domination and subordination. Rhodesians of European descent, who had obtained land available only to the fair-skinned, had to be redefined as inferior, and as inferiors they had no right to dominate the society and own the land.

Hannah Arendt contributed insights to status inconsistency, though she used a different terminology. In *The Origins of Totalitarianism* (1958) she observes what she calls a "common sense fallacy" that the Jews were an arbitrary choice as scapegoats. Not so, she argues, we need to look at their specific history to understand why Jews were despised. Some Jews gained power during the age of monarchies, as financial advisers and international financiers to the courts. But as national boundaries became firmer and nation-states become entrenched, financial institutions emerged to supplant the Jewish financiers. As their real power declined, anti-Semitism grew. This interesting reversal of fortunes was first noted by de Tocqueville in his *Ancien Régime*, where he argued that hatred for the French aristocracy grew in direct proportion to its decline in power. A population served by a powerful group that is also wealthy is tolerable; a group that lacks power but remains wealthy is intolerable. Arendt argues that this same fate befell wealthy Jews. Poor Jews, who made up the majority, were simply branded with the same brush. Though nationalism and its attendant institutional development began the process of displacing the Jewish financiers, it was imperialism and the rise of an international bourgeoisie that destroyed the unique power of nation-states. Banks were now imperial institutions and, by the time Hitler came to power, international finance and the German banks were already established, as they also had been before the Dreyfus affair in France.

Ethnic Nationalism

States were created by dominant classes with reference primarily to territory – the extent of territory they could control. Often the population in the territory included more than one cultural group, more than one linguistic group. The borders frequently cut an ethnic population into diverse sections in differing states, or, over time, ethnic populations originating in one state moved to another where they could obtain more land or other benefits. The Turks in the Ottoman Empire shared this record, as did German-speaking people in northern and eastern Europe. For both ethnic groups, the growth of nationalism subsequent to wars and perceived threats to their security took on an added dimension of ethnicity. As the Young Turks began their rule of the Ottoman territories, they began to call for "panTurkism" – annexation of nearby territories in Russia and other states where Turks had settled, and expulsion of non-Turks from the Ottoman Empire. Non-Turks, however, did not necessarily include Muslims of other ethnicities. They were lower in rank than Turks, but well above Armenian Christians. They were encouraged by the Young Turks and, earlier, by the Ottoman rulers to move into traditional Armenian territories (Dadrian, 1999). These minorities helped to perpetrate the dispersion of Armenians, on the promise of land redistribution in their favour.

A similar movement emerged in Germany, captured and expressed in shrill terms by Hitler in the aftermath of the First World War. The demand for *lebensraum* was a slightly disguised way of proposing the annexation of much of Poland and parts of other states where Germanic peoples had settled. Like the Turks, Hitler's administration envisioned the growth of the German ethnic nation to involve the relocation, and eventually the elimination, of non-German populations. In both the Turkish and the German cases there was a religious dimension to ethnicity: the Turks wanted to be rid of Christians; and the Germans, of Jews. In the German case, however, not all the populations to be displaced were Jews; the roster included other ethnic groups (Gypsies, Poles, Slavs) and even Germans who did not meet arbitrary standards of physical and mental perfection.

Arendt regarded the pan-German and other similar movements as non-rational emotional outbursts that displaced political parties and transformed national populations into unthinking masses. Of the victims who were rendered stateless in the process of resettling German outsiders, she said:

The calamity of the rightless is not that they are deprived of life, liberty, and the pursuit of happiness, or of equality before the law and freedom of opinion – formulas which were designed to solve problems *within* given communities – but that they no longer belong to any community whatsoever. Their plight is not that they are not equal before the law, but that no law exists for them; not that they are oppressed but that nobody wants even to oppress them. Only in the last stage of a rather lengthy process is their right to live threatened; only if they remain perfectly "superfluous," if nobody can be found to "claim" them, may their lives be in danger. Even the Nazis started their extermination of Jews by first depriving them of all legal status (the status of second-class citizenship) and cutting them off from the world of the living by herding them into ghettos and concentration camps; and before they set the gas chambers into motion they had carefully tested the ground and found out to their satisfaction that no country would claim these people. The point is that a condition of complete rightlessness was created before the right to live was challenged. (1958: 295–6; emphasis in original)

In the Ottoman Empire the religion of the new rulers was exclusionary and absolutely forbade the sharing of power with non-believers. This stricture reflected a hard fact about the religious culture of the empire. The Young Turks knew they could be successful only if the population saw them as legitimate replacements for the sultan, who was regarded as the direct descendent of Mohammed. The usurpers needed to convince the population that they would defend Islam to the death. In the early twentieth century, with their call for Pan-Turkism, they were prepared to go beyond the ambitions of the Sultanate. This stand assured the Turks, who were a major ethnic group but not a numerical majority in the country as a whole, that they would remain in the dominant position vis-à-vis other ethnicities; and it assured other Muslim ethnic groups that they would remain dominant over non-Muslims. Kuper (1981: 114–16) argues that the dominant Turks fanned existing hostilities towards non-Islamic minorities to give the appearance of spontaneous mob action, which allowed for the plundering and massacring bands of Islamic Kurds and Circassians to play out the final chapters of the event.

"Religious hatreds played their part, with terrible atrocities against priests, the desecration and destruction of churches, and forced conversions." The primary targets of the genocide were not Armenians who lived in the predominantly urban, Turkish, or core regions, but those in rural areas where they were numerous.

Subordinate Groups as Threats to Security

Inequalities may be recognized and obeyed in a relatively passive way by those in both dominant and subservient positions, in which case the state has the simple task of shoring up the status quo. But from time to time, under diverse circumstances, a subordinate population objects. Objections may take the form of requests for improvements in civil rights, demonstrations against discrimination, demands for social change, collaboration with outside powers, or active organization of revolutionary forces. These objections create a different situation for the state, which must not only sustain and reproduce inequalities but also cope with direct threats to the status quo. In considering any of these inequalities, we want to distinguish between the passive condition and the condition of threat. At the same time, we need to appraise the nature of threat, since in all these cases the perception of threat from a subordinate group considerably exceeds the capacity of the groups in question to destabilize or otherwise severely harm the dominant group. The problem, then, is one of perception based on exaggerated fear, and the fear is that the subordinate group might develop the capacity to overturn the hierarchy.

Where a subordinate group is targeted for extinction, the dominant group typically argues that it has become a threat to national or religious security. This reaction is not peculiar to the case of ethnic minorities: the same argument is regularly applied to political opponents who are designated as subversives. In some cases the threat is valid. In the Armenian case, for example, there was an international outcry for a brief period, and Armenian leaders called out for international intervention; moreover, the threat of intervention was real, if not so much on behalf of the Armenians as the voracious appetites among neighbouring European states for additional territory. Like vultures awaiting a death, European powers were planning the division of Ottoman lands. The Turks had reason to distrust the Christian minorities, who were vulnerable to influence from abroad because of their own attempts to persuade external powers to facilitate their departure from the Ottoman Empire. In the Armenian case the persistent agitation for reforms, civil rights, equal opportunities, and security exacerbated the already tense relations between Turks and this low-status yet proud subnation. Here was a relatively powerless minority, defined over a long period as unequal to the dominant group in terms of class and regional location as much as ethnicity, who not only proclaimed itself equal to the dominant group but appealed to external powers for recognition of its rights. Demands for civil rights were defined by the Turks as political agitation and were met with hostility and violent crackdowns. When the reform movement failed, young Armenians, together with youthful members of other minority groups, became militant. Though the revolutionary groups never encompassed large numbers of Armenians, they competed with the clergy and other groups for the allegiance of ordinary Armenians. "The resulting dissentions, schisms, factionalism, and attendant mutual enmities seriously impaired an already weak, fractious, and vulnerable community" (Dadrian, 1999: 133–6), but, from the perspective of the Turks, the Armenians as a whole were contentious, subversive, and rebellious: in short, a threat to Turkish control. In other cases the dominant group invents a security threat with less substance, but, either way, the general rule holds that wherever a group is victimized, the dominant group will provide for external eyes or for its own population a rationale that involves threats to security.

In the case of Nazi Germany, Jews, Sinti, Roma, and the several other groups targeted for extinction by the Nazis were not homogeneous or organized and could not have mounted an effective rebellion, even had they wished to, before the onset of overt acts of violence against them. Jews were known to be suffering discrimination, and the particularly oppressive conditions in Germany were the subject of external handwringing, but there was less overt pressure on Germany to cease and desist than there had been on the Turks with respect to the Armenians. This unconcern probably resulted from the shared prejudices throughout Europe and Europe's colonies against Jews. The Jews did not threaten the stability of the Nazi state. They did not proselytize and were not interested in gaining converts. Their most serious potential crime would have been miscegenation, but because neither they nor the Germans approved of intermarriage, this threat hardly counted. However, the lack of substantive threat is not the only measure: what matters is whether the dominant group believes that the subordinate one poses a threat. It is a matter of perception, and whether in fact or by virtue of incessant propaganda, Germans were of the opinion that Jews (and possibly, but not certainly, others) posed a direct threat to the nation. According to the propaganda, Jews, by conspiring with external powers, had brought about defeat in the 1914–18 war. They had "stabbed Germany in the back" and they constituted the "internal enemy."

Subordinate Groups as "Outside the Universe of Obligation"

Helen Fein (1990: 71–2) argues that in the Armenian and German cases, there were predisposing and facilitating conditions: the victims were previously defined as "outside the universe of obligation" of the dominant group, as aliens; the state had recently suffered defeat or similar destabilization; an elite emerged with an ideology that glorified the dominant group and blamed the alien group or groups for the defeat; and some external event, such as war, inhibited international awareness of violence against the minority. This organization of contingencies is a reasonable rendition of what happened in these cases, though its applicability to other cases is limited. Perhaps we could add to Fein's description that the elite quickly centralized power, came to terms with the existing army, and created its own paramilitary forces for purposes of committing genocide and other crimes. The external wars may have enabled both the Turks and the Nazis to commit genocide, but not all genocides are preceded by wars, so the importance of this factor for a general theory is not established. However, the concept "outside the universe of obligation" is helpful in understanding how a dominant group can victimize a subordinate group without experiencing any crisis of conscience. It simply does not recognize the subordinate group as within the realm of human relations with which it needs to concern itself. That attitude is the essence of racism.

In summarizing the cases of Armenia and Nazi Germany, we have identified these similar conditions:

• For the perpetrators, an insecure collective identity following defeat in wars.
• For the victims, long-standing discrimination: for Armenians and Jews, a low ethnic status based on religious difference and some status inconsistency based on entrepreneurial commercial success; for Gypsies, Poles, and "imperfect" Germans, a low status, but not one related to religion or commercial success.

- In both cases, pan-Turkish and pan-Germanic movements creating demographic pressures and demands for territorial redistribution and displacement of minorities.
- Again in both cases, fear of external intervention and perception of minorities as potential or actual saboteurs.

These are salient conditions for genocide, but we still need to identify their connections. The ethnic tensions and discrimination in both cases had been present for many generations: Why did they become intolerable for the dominant group at those particular times? Defeat in recent wars is a possible explanation in conjunction with the issue of ethnic identity. But perhaps we can go even further: the demand for territory in both cases is another potential explanation for the timing.

Territory or Other Material Properties

In the cases of the Armenians and the Jews, the dominant groups – Turks and Germans – had material interests in land or other properties held by the victims. In the Armenian case it was a substantial region traditionally occupied by Armenians. In the case of Germany, it was all the real estate and other property (paintings, artifacts, jewellery and other valuable goods) held by Jews that could be appropriated by the dominant group or used by repatriated Germans under the Pan-Germanic policies of the Reich. The areas occupied by Armenians had been in contention for several generations, and non-Turk Muslim populations had been deliberately moved into these regions for some period before the genocide. The German case is less obvious because the "final solution" was not, in fact, put forward until 1942, some time after the repatriation policy had been introduced and while defeat was imminent on the Russian front of the war. Repatriated Germans were provided with real estate and other properties of Jews, especially in the areas traditionally occupied by Jews in Poland. The racist case against Jews was introduced much earlier, but until the enunciation of the "final solution" the idea of eradicating Jews from Europe took the form of a plan for forced migration to Madagascar (and, earlier, to other areas). The case against the mentally and physically ill or the disabled was more explicitly stated: they were using space, food, and other life supports that healthy Germans required. That logic was also applied to Gypsies and vagabonds. In all these examples, we might argue that the real motivation was material (to take over property belonging to the victims) or that the argument in favour of such takeovers was an ideological rationale for actions that were, basically, racist and inegalitarian. In my opinion, the ideology is both the racism and the idea that sick people, or people who do not lead what the dominant group decides are healthy lives, are dispensable. Underlying the actions, there was a material ambition to obtain territory, real estate, and goods, or at least to displace others from controlling or occupying space and goods. Readers of the case studies in Part Two of this book may argue otherwise, though the more general argument would be similar.

When certain groups (ethnic, religious, but also other groups in the case of Germany) are defined as inferior, the dominant group is threatened by them for such reasons as status inconsistency, demands for equality and civil rights, and their perceived relationship to external powers. The dominant group attempts to increase its power by bringing in new, culturally acceptable populations or by attempting to annex adjoining territories, or both. The property or traditional territory of the low-status groups is coveted, and genocide becomes a means of obtaining additional land and property while simultaneously eradicating a real or potential threat to the dominant group.

OTHER CASES

The conditions found in the Ottoman Empire and in Nazi Germany are not apparent in any of the other cases under study. Ethnicity, on close inspection, fails to materialize as an adequate explanation for events in the Ukraine, Central Africa, or Yugoslavia, even though in each of these cases some form of ethnicity or ethnic nationalism is prominent. We will need to probe more deeply for explanations.

The Ukraine

In the case of Eastern Ukrainians, located in another empire, the victims were farm labourers and farmers (owners of small plots who supplied their own labour), otherwise collectively known in the USSR, as in Czarist Russia, as peasants, a class position they held in common with most rural people throughout the Soviet Union, including many Russians. Although urban dwellers discriminated against the peasants, this bias was not an ethnic division. Peasants were serfs in Czarist Russia until some seventy years before the 1917 revolution, and the USSR continued to regard them, as had the previous bureaucrats, as irresponsible and ignorant people. Marx had offered a similar opinion, suggesting in *The Communist Manifesto* that they, along with small business owners, were conservative and reactionary forces likely to oppose the socialist revolution. In his opinion, only the urban proletariat could form a revolutionary force.

One argument supporting the idea that ethnicity was of primary importance in this case is the fact that the Ukrainians were increasingly nationalistic and were pressing for reforms – in some cases for a separate state. Ukrainian nationalists participated in the 1917 revolution and declared their territory, including what later became the Western Ukraine, an independent country. Under the Treaty of Brest-Litovsk they were to be dealt with as an independent country by both the Central Powers and the new USSR. But those agreements were dismissed when Ukrainians of different regions were unable to reach a consensus on government and, after a brief period of German control, anarchy became pervasive in the Ukraine (and was present elsewhere in Greater Russia). In 1922 the Bolsheviks gained control of the government and the territory.

But nationalism was far from defeated. Indeed, Ukrainian culture reached its high point during the mid-1920s before Stalin's ascendancy to power in Moscow. There is no indication that Ukrainian nationalism was seen by Russia as a fifth column likely to aid external powers in any attack on the USSR at the conclusion of the war, but there was a potential threat to the unity of the lands inherited from the Tsarist period. The separation of the largest single minority, and also the largest wheat-growing region, would have signalled the possibility of separation for numerous other minorities and weakened Moscow's control of the whole territory.

Miron Dolot, a survivor of the 1932–33 famine in the Ukraine, questioned why his village was being cruelly subjected to starvation and concluded: "Now it began to dawn on everyone why there wasn't any food left in the village; why there weren't any prospects of getting any more; why our expectation that the government would surely help us to avert starvation was naïve and futile; why the Bread Procurement Commission still searched for 'hidden' grain; and why the government strictly forbade us to look for means of existence elsewhere. It finally became clear to us that there was a conspiracy against us; that somebody wanted to annihilate us, not only as farmers but as a people – as Ukrainians" (1985: 175). In addition, Stalin vigorously persecuted other minority groups whom he regarded as nationalistic. The starvation of the Ukrainians in 1932–33 may be viewed, then, as consistent with a larger policy against minorities, yet the nature of the persecution and the number of victims exceeded even the most vicious of the previous and later attacks.

In other respects, however, the Ukrainians were not like the Armenians, in that they were not the butt of long-standing animosities among Russians, the dominant ethnicity. They shared the same Catholic orthodox religion (though by the time Stalin took control, religion throughout the USSR was under attack) and the same alphabet (with minor exceptions) as the dominant group, their language was closely related, and in other respects they were similar not only to Russians in rural regions but also to many other ethnic minorities. They were the largest ethnic minority in the former Russian Empire, and it is possible that Stalin perceived their obstinate stance against collectivization as a problem in part because of their numbers: if they were permitted to evade collectivization and factory farms, others would soon demand similar exemption. The Ukraine was also the breadbasket for the empire, and its produce was essential for the feeding of urban workers and external trade. The case is thus ambiguous: the nationalist movement marked them as an oppressed ethnic group trying to remove itself from Russian domination, but class and territorial concerns weigh heavily in this case. We will consider these other arguments further in chapter 3.

Burundi and Rwanda

The cases of Burundi and Rwanda are instructive less with respect to ethnicity than to racism – to beliefs about racial origins. As we see in the case studies in Part Two, the ethnographers who have intimate knowledge of these African societies argue that the Tutsi and Hutu were not regarded as distinct ethnic groups before the colonial period. The terminology was used to describe occupational niches rather than ethnicity. Recast by the Belgian administrators after the First World War, the Tutsi became an overlord race of herders presumed to have derived originally from Ethiopia, while the Hutu were classified as relatively unimpressive and unimportant farmers. By the time the colonial powers turned government over to local people, their versions of ethnic origins had become embedded in the psyches of both groups. History had been reinterpreted, each group imagining its past in terms that made the other group less attractive. Hutu now recalled how mean and arrogant the Tutsi were when the Tutsi were favoured by the colonial governments, and they clung to the idea that they, unlike the Tutsi, were the original inhabitants of the land. The Tutsi imagined themselves as the natural rulers, displaced in Rwanda by upstart Hutus. The hostilities that emerged during the post-colonial period had many other sources, but the persistent theme emphasized by both groups was their ethnic divide. Ethnicity had become "real" and was the basis for two warring identities.

The wars in Burundi and Rwanda cannot be reduced to the imagined ethnic differences between Tutsi and Hutu. As important to an explanation of the events is recognition that, within both states, the ruling parties were divided between factions within their own "ethnic" group. It was because of the conflict between differing Tutsi elites in Burundi and differing Hutu factions in Rwanda that the opposite "ethnic" group used this moment to attempt a takeover of the respective governments. Ethnicity itself, then, even had it been a valid construct to begin with, is not a sufficient explanation for the genocides.

Yugoslavia

In the former Yugoslavia, where the three major self-designated ethnic groups engaged in bitter disputes over control of the federation, over the right to self-determination and separate regional governments, and, above all, over territory, ethnic identities were pronounced and persistent, even though all the groups had originated in the same ethnic stock centuries before and the Yugoslav federation under Tito had held them all together for half a century. The tenacity with which ethnicity was held to be central to identity is due in part to the viciousness of pre-federation interactions, and, possibly, to the uncertainty with which any one of the identities that had since been forcibly merged into the idea of Yugoslavia could now be recreated. The war against others was, arguably, a war to assert differences.

Lenard Cohen (1993: 265–6) argues that the failure of the Yugoslav federation was due to political leaders who could not agree on a revised model of political and economic coexistence. Inter-elite mistrust and elite-led ethnic nationalism prevented calm negotiations for a redesigned Yugoslavia. The cause of the barbarism with which the dissolution occurred rests, he suggests, with three factors: the persistence of long-standing animosities; the continuing desire to redress grievances that arose during the Second World War; and the failure of the communist regime's policies to resolve outstanding inter-ethnic grievances and to engender inter-ethnic tolerance. These conditions contributed to elite intransigence and unleashed the violent inter-ethnic conflict. Aleksandar Pavkovic, a professor of modern languages in Australia, offers a somewhat divergent interpretation. He begins his study of the Yugoslav breakup with the statement: "The conflict in the former Yugoslavia which erupted in 1991 ... was essentially a result of competing national ideologies laying claim to one and the same territory for their respective national groups" (1997: ix). This interpretation reduces the conflict to an economic struggle over territory and resources.

Regionalism and greed for territory were, as Pavkovic asserts, fundamental to the conflict. The parts of Yugoslavia had never fully emerged from their status as states in competing empires. Croatians, Serbians, and Croat-Serbian Muslims were, in origin, the same people, yet in the course of empire history they had established different "ethnic" cultures. Over those years, as well, one of the groups, Serbs, had migrated into the other regions, where they established enclaves. Much of the war was over these enclaves or, better stated, over fears among Serbs that those in the enclaves would be evicted, or, among others, that the Serbs would use the enclaves to oust Croatians and Muslims. The regions where the fighting was greatest were not the poorest areas of Yugoslavia, though there were regional inequalities due to both available resources and the history of economic development. All that was needed to bring the house down was leadership and ideologies, and these fell into place with remarkable speed before the opening of hostilities in 1990.

Yugoslavians had an identity as Yugoslavians for a half-century, with feebler attempts at developing that identity earlier in the century. But because of their bitter relationships, ineradicable memories, and long histories as separate peoples, that identity did not stick even among young people socialized in state schools to think of themselves as a single, federated national society. Religion was not a predominant factor here: none of the groups was intensely religious, including the Muslim population. But memories, both long-standing and more recently revitalized under intense propaganda efforts by the Serbian and Croatian governments and armies, were the major components of the ethnic nationalism.

Smilja Avramov (1995: 2), whose telling of Yugoslav history began with the genocide of the early 1940s, provides the story from the Serbian camp: "Denazification was never carried out in Croatia or in

Kosovo. And this is the main reason why, fifty years after the tragic events in Croatia and Kosovo, a new round of genocide of the Serbs has begun." She then goes on to say that the 1940s genocide in Croatia and in Kosovo had independent roots apart from the Nazi occupation and that Serbophobia existed in Croatia, connected as much to the Comintern as to ethnonationalist leaders, religious fanaticism, and glorification of Croatian history. The Comintern, in her opinion, derided the Serbs as "hegemons" and turned Croats against them. Finally, she concludes, "The Serbs have been subjected to mass extermination simply because they are Serbs, regardless of their political beliefs" (437). Avramov is singularly helpful in enlightening a puzzled reader about the mindset of Serbs in the 1990s, not necessarily about a reality but certainly about beliefs that created the new reality.

In stark contrast to Avramov's version, Anthony Lewis, columnist in the *New York Times*, argued most strongly against the view that the horrors in the former Yugoslavia were caused by "ancient hatreds." In one column (reprinted in the *Vancouver Sun*, 8 January 1996), he argued: "But it was not 'ancient hatreds' that produced ethnic cleansing, rape and concentration camps. It was men: ambitious men who stirred up extreme nationalist emotions as a way to power. It was one man above all, Slobodan Milosevic of Serbia." On this score, many other writers concur. Milosevic has much to answer for, and, as this book is in press, the United Nations Tribunal is trying him on several charges of "Crimes against Humanity" in the Hague.

The conflict between Croatia and Serbia was of such lengthy duration that the neglect manifested by the world might be excused: a pox on both their houses, the more so because their respective leaders, Franjo Tudjman in Croatia and Milosevic in Serbia, were regarded as equally ruthless. The war against Bosnian Muslim civilians was of a different kind. Thomas Cushman and Stjepan Mestrovic, and the contributors to their book on the Bosnian crisis (1996a), take the position that the Muslim civilians were "at the mercy of crazed Serbian Chetniks." They argue that British policy supported the Serbs. They also accuse many reporters of having created the myth that all sides in what they described as a civil war were equally culpable and that intervention would be useless.

A more nuanced version turns up in an unexpected source, an ethnographic account of Muslim life in a Bosnian village in the late 1980s and early 1990s. Author Tone Brinka was just about to leave for Cambridge to write up her study when the 1992 war broke out. She writes:

During most of that year, people in the village believed that the only way they could be directly involved in the war was if "outsiders" entered and start provoking them. Even when Bosnian Croat (HVO) and Croat army forces clashed with Bosnian government forces (mainly Muslim) elsewhere in central Bosnia, the Muslims and Catholic Croats in our village continued to live together side by side in peace. In the end what was so painful to most Muslim villagers and to many of their Croat neighbors was that the attackers were not only "outsiders." When HVO started shelling and killing Muslims and burning their houses in the village, some of the Muslims' Catholic Croat neighbors joined in, although the attack had been planned and initiated by people far from the village. Starting out as a war waged by outsiders it developed into one where neighbor was pitted against neighbor after the familiar person next door had been made into a depersonalized alien, a member of the enemy ranks. (1995: xvi)

Brinka revisited the village in May 1993 and discovered that all Muslim houses had been destroyed and all the Muslims were gone. In her attempt to understand what happened, she observes that neither the idealized version of Bosnia portrayed during the Sarajevo Olympics nor the media coverage that talked of ancient hatreds fit the Bosnia she had lived in and studied for several years. Instead, she said, "There was both co-existence and conflict, tolerance and prejudice, suspicion and friendship" (3).

In fact, none of these accounts provides an explanation of the war against Bosnian Muslims. None explains why Serbs initiated the war, why Croats living within Bosnia-Herzegovina joined the conflict against Muslim civilians, or why the twilight war was so vicious, so barbarous. Cohen translates and quotes Nobel prizewinning author Ivo Andric:

Adherents of the three main faiths, they hate one another from birth to death, senselessly and profoundly ... whenever the established order of things is shaken by some important event, and reason and law are suspended for a few hours or days, then this mob or rather a section of it, finding at last an adequate motive, overflows into the town ... and, like a flame which has sought and has at last found fuel, these long-kept hatreds and hidden desires for destruction and violence take over the town, lapping, sputtering, and swallowing everything, until some force larger than themselves suppresses them, or until they burn themselves out and tire of their own rage. (Andric, *Gospodjica* [Zagreb: Mladost, 1961]: 77)

Ethnicity, religion, and ethnic nationalism are targeted in this quotation, as in much of the literature, as the causes of the genocidal episodes. But these explanations fail to take property and territory into account, and there is no doubt that the drive to gain territory was paramount in Serbian army motivations. They also ignore the preceding conditions: the breakdown of the central government; the loss of control by civil authorities of the army; the exclusion or voluntary removal of army personnel from Slovenia, Croatia, and Bosnia; and, finally, the takeover for all effective purposes of government by the Serbian armed forces. They omit consideration of the territorial issues in Croatia and Bosnia. They focus so entirely on ethnicity and religion (even though religion was relatively unimportant) that they ignore the underlying issues of inequality: the Serbs persistently had greater power than the others. With the breakdown of government, the hierarchy of power had to be reformulated, but since the other ethnic-regional groups were unwilling simply to concede to Serbian superiority, the determination of a new power distribution became an open and violent war.

CONCLUSIONS: ETHNICITY AS A CRITERION

Ethnicity is obviously a vital division between populations within the same state territory or subject to the same empire or imperial state. It is one, and often a major, determinant of the overall status hierarchy: those at the bottom, those at the top, each an ethnic group occupying its niche relative to others. This is the case with relatively superficial ethnic divisions, such as in Burundi and Rwanda, and in long-standing arrangements, as in Germany and the Ottoman Empire. As long as the divisions are generally accepted and obeyed, the status quo is maintained. There is no need for genocide when there is no threat. But when an inferior group challenges the status quo, the dominant group or groups gird themselves for action. The conclusion here is that it is insufficient to attribute to ethnicity, racism, tribalism, xenophobia, or any combination thereof the causes, as contrasted with the "reasons," for genocide. Whatever the tensions between ethnic groups, the fundamental cause is their unequal relations and the attempts of states or dominant elites to sustain the system of inequality in which they are embedded or to obtain greater property rights or other privileges by excluding or even exterminating subordinate groups.

3

Class and Territory

Class distinctions are similar to ethnic labels: they are created within a social fabric; may persist for many generations; and involve inequalities of power and, usually, of wealth and opportunities. They are unlike ethnic labels in that they are never neutral; there are no equalities between classes and there is no equivalent to "multiculturalism" governing class relations. By definition, classes are unequal. Even so, the chasm between those at the top of the class hierarchy and those at the bottom is variable. Some societies, such as the Scandinavian societies at the turn of the twenty-first century, have relatively small gaps between top and bottom. Those at the top accept a system in which they tax themselves so that those further down the hierarchy can have education, medical care, and other public services. Other societies have huge gulfs between the classes, and their middle class is sparsely populated. Often ethnic and class attributes overlap, with most members of an ethnic group labelled as lower class and most members of another ethnic group called upper class.

Some mass slaughters can be attributed to classes that rise up against their oppressors, as in Cambodia in 1975–79. Revolutions, successful or otherwise, tend to be bloody events, and some turn into massive killing fields. Many more slaughters of history can be attributed to oppressors pre-empting a revolution by killing off their designated inferiors – as in the majority of the genocides and politicides of the past century. Karl Marx anticipated that industrial workers (the proletariat) would eventually rise up against the capitalist owners (the bourgeoisie) and stage the final revolution of human history. No such event has yet occurred, though there have been many rebellions and some revolutions. The French Revolution of 1789 was staged by the rising bourgeoisie against the landed aristocracy and the monarchy, when the former had gained economic power and wanted the political power that matched it (Lefebvre, 1962, 1964). The second French Revolution in 1968 was an attempt by student activists and some organized workers to stage a revolution against both the bourgeoisie and the political elite: it failed, though the attempt became a model for Argentines and many other students around the world who shared the ideals of the would-be revolutionaries. This revolution failed in large part because the students and workers were unable to gain a sufficient following to sustain the momentum, and they lacked a plan for taking over government even if they had maintained it (Seale and McConville, 1968).

The Russian Revolution of 1917 was staged by middle-class intellectuals and urban workers, but in a country that was not yet industrial or capitalist. The rebellions that confronted the Bolsheviks when they gained power were staged as often by a rural peasantry as by dislodged aristocrats. The example we investigate here has a rural peasantry in the Ukraine challenging and being savagely beaten by a government acting in the name of the proletariat. Revolutionary governments have the same task as their predecessors: to sustain themselves and the system of power relations they created.

Although there are no instances of an industrial working class mounting a revolution against an established bourgeoisie, there are examples of more nuanced class struggles throughout the century. Middle-class students, intellectuals, and professionals are frequently the leaders of attempts to change the system, often projecting themselves as the vanguard of a revolution on behalf of the working class, the impoverished, or minority ethnic groups. People are not always as class conscious as the French students of 1968 or the Argentine students whose lives were snuffed out by the military junta after the coup of 1976, yet they may act out class grievances or seek changes in the state that are basically about unequal conditions and opportunities. In the Argentine case the students were opposed to continued military rule and the bourgeois capitalist state, but we cannot assume that the military forces were defending the bourgeoisie when they began their criminal activities. The bourgeoisie was fractured: by no means was it consistent or homogeneous in its economic interests, let alone in its ideologies and wishes. And the military forces had their own agenda. Class, then, is not a simple hierarchy: armies are not merely functionaries on behalf of the dominant economic class, and they may become dominant in their own right. A similar development may be traced for

Chile, where a nascent revolution was cut short not by a concerted effort of the bourgeoisie but by the armed forces supported by military and financial aid from the United States in defence of its corporate extensions on Chilean soil.

There are also examples of class struggles that Marx did not anticipate because he assumed that the feudal system would wither away with the advent of industrialism. Yet in three of the most damning genocidal episodes of modern history – the Eastern Ukraine, Cambodia, and Guatemala – the struggle took place between peasants and a state bureaucracy. Peasants did not disappear into history quite as readily as Marx supposed.

Power is rarely distributed evenly across the territory of any state and it is, virtually by definition, uneven in empires, imperialist systems, and states that cover expansive areas. The core region of the empire and the core cities of the state are the centres of power; the economic and political elites of the country reside there, as do the bureaucratic offices of government and the defence establishment. Provincial elites emerge and may have power vis-à-vis provincial populations, but they are no match for the elites at the core. The class system describes the internal relationships of domination, but the degree of real power held by anyone in the society is a function of the society's independence and its power within a global context. A colonial society within an imperial system, or a contemporary society that is heavily dependent on aid or investment from elsewhere, has little power to determine its own directions. Even those at the top are constrained in how much latitude they have in their handling of internal dissension. Among the cases examined here are several where politicides were connected to differentials in power in both class and territory: the USSR versus the Eastern Ukraine (1932–33), Argentina (1976–83), Chile (1973–88), and Cambodia (1975–79). These examples will be analyzed separately under the country headings below because each one provides a distinctive organization of class, ethnic, and regional characteristics.

EMPIRE: THE USSR

Like the Ottoman Empire, the Russian Empire was falling apart long before revolutionaries seized control, and for much the same reasons. Its feudal organization, the huge gap between the rich and the poor, the control of land by a few aristocrats, the failure to feed the population, the inability to maintain the army, and the lack of education and know-how for entering the new industrial age meant that the Russian Empire just did not measure up. Since it failed to change on its own, a revolution finally toppled the monarchy.

The Bolshevik Revolution that created the USSR was even more traumatic and dislocating for large parts of that empire's population than the relatively small coup by army officers had been in the Ottoman Empire. By the 1930s the new Soviet hierarchy was in place, but it still had to cope with the many organized and anarchic discontents throughout its empire. That empire was still reeling from great human losses in war. The sense of defeat, the impoverishment, and the decay of the state engulfed everyone. The Bolsheviks fought their way to the top and promised change, but the change was going to be extreme. There were going to be new elites and new patterns of ownership and production: this gigantic empire embarked on one of the most extraordinary social experiments in human history. The fact that it failed should not obscure the reality that it was an innovative, daring, and imaginative human experiment. No such extreme change could have been undertaken without bloodshed; tragically, this one spilled a great deal of blood and manifested the cruelty of humankind on a scale not hitherto experienced.

As in the Ottoman Empire, the new leaders in the USSR had to watch their flanks. They were not concerned with a divergent religion, but with preventing the return of past privileges, wealth, and regional autonomy. Lenin and Stalin both knew what they were up against and that only the most ruthless response would stifle the resistance to socialism. Moreover, they knew that if socialism required collective production techniques (as they believed it did), those who resisted would have to be forced to accept the new reality. These conditions – the context of an empire, the shock of social change on a grand scale, the determination to eliminate opposition – were fundamental to the decision to commit genocide or, equally applicable in this case, politicide.

The ideology of the new Soviet rulers promoted the proletariat as the vanguard of change, and the ideology was important. But it was not just ideology that fuelled the USSR at that time. The society was backward and impoverished; most of the people were poorly educated; much of the territory was still feudal in its relationships and power structure; and it had barely begun the process of modernization and industrialization embarked on by most of its European neighbours. Social stability could be achieved and maintained only if the state could feed and sustain the army, without which there would have been no revolution. The state also had to provide industrial machinery and work for the proletariat, on whose behalf the revolution claimed to have been staged. It had to maintain a substantial state bureaucracy, much of which was inherited from the czars, but the empire could not have been controlled without it. And it had to feed the urban population. Independent of ideology, the revolutionary government was not in an easy position at that time.

In a similar situation in the early 1920s, the Young Turks, by then under Kemal Ataturk, turned to the external world and invited investment. But even had the Bolsheviks been prepared to go that route, by the end of the 1920s when they had succeeded in centralizing power and gaining control of the empire, the capitalist societies were engulfed in the Great Depression. Those societies were, by then, unable to challenge the growth of the USSR and to help its people survive. So, from the point of view of the Bolshevik government, this tight situation called for the most forceful action against any group that failed to be supportive of state initiatives and demands.

For the Soviet government, the possibility of obtaining the requisite machinery for industrial development by sale of wheat was undoubtedly an incentive for requisitioning quantities of grain from the rural regions in excess of their capacity to produce and still have sufficient food for themselves. Had the peasants continued to resist the obligation to produce the wheat, the central government would have been unable to continue with its revolutionary agenda, since the plan for industrialization and rule by an industrial proletariat would have been thwarted. If the government had backed down, the repercussions would have been felt throughout the entire wheat-growing territories, which extended well beyond the Eastern Ukraine. The situation called for dramatic action once the peasants defied the government and refused to join collective farms.

In these circumstances, there is a cogent argument that legitimacy for the new Soviet leaders rested on material, more than nationalistic, supports. They had to invent industrialism in a backward, feudal empire, and they had to do so at top speed. If they allowed events to mature slowly, their enemies would oust them before change could occur; and if not their internal enemies, then the imperialist wolves at the door. To effect this change, especially in a world deep in a global economic depression, they had to procure large quantities of grain and other foodstuffs to feed the industrial proletariat and the army, and to exchange on capitalist markets for industrial machinery. These surpluses were their means of gaining legitimacy.

In the Eastern Ukraine, a large non-core population occupied prime grain-growing land. Since Ukrainians were about six times more numerous than the next largest minority in the USSR, the drive to integrate them into the party and state apparatus or to exclude them positively was more forceful and determined than for other minorities. The core Russian urban population defined the empire as theirs; others were there on sufferance. The USSR needed the produce of the region, and, if need be, it could obtain it by force. The initial condition here was regional inequality: those at the core of the empire had more power than those at the peripheries.

Many writers seem to be persuaded that the reason for the genocide of this population was that it was nationalistic in its defence of Ukrainian interests. The problem, then, was ethnic conflict. However, as suggested in chapter 2, this interpretation fails to take into account the similarities between the dominant and the minority populations. Both were Christian; their histories were intertwined; and their languages were similar, especially as they used the same alphabet. The Russians did not kill Ukrainians who worked and lived in the Russian territories.

Still, within an argument centred on discrimination and now focusing on class, not only were the victims a group other than the dominant Russians but they were also peasants. In the czar's era, peasants were the lowest form of human life, treated so harshly that landed gentry tossed dice with the transfer of serfs, the not-so-distant ancestors of the modern peasants, as the medium of exchange. Their status did not change with the revolution. They remained at the bottom of the social and economic hierarchy. When the inequality of territory was added to ethnicity and class, this population simply did not matter to either the czars or the Stalinist state. Had it supported collectivization, fine, it would have survived, but its survival was not a matter of concern one way or the other to the state. What mattered was that the region's potential grain-growing capacity be fully exploited, and when the peasants refused to comply with demands for collectivization, they became an impediment to the greater glory of the USSR.

Collectivization was viewed by the Bolsheviks as a means of controlling the peasants, improving the yield of the fields, and releasing some portion of the population for wage-work in factories. In the early 1920s the farmers each had some 15–25 acres under production, some portion of which was planted in vegetables and intended for family consumption. Machinery was virtually non-existent and, even in the communal regions where farmers voluntarily worked together, animals and humans provided most of the energy. The Bolsheviks theorized that if the state collectivized the whole farming area, the producers could be organized to work more productively and there would be advantages in the purchase of modern machinery. But advantageous or not, the farmers were not interested in trading their hard-won independence for collectivized factory farms. Some went so far as to burn their houses and kill their farm animals rather than become wage-earners in the farm factories. Despite extreme measures imposed by representatives of the central state from 1929 through to 1931, some farmers continued to resist. By 1932 few of those farmers were still resident in the besieged villages: they had been deported to Siberia as kulaks, killed outright by government forces, or died of starvation. Whenever a farmer was deported or killed, his family was soon afterwards deported as well. Collectivization, then, was the central theme of this genocide or politicide.

Collectivization might have increased production had it been accepted, but yet wherever it was introduced, the yield declined. The decline must have been due in large part, at least in the Eastern Ukraine, to the brutality of the regime and its starvation policy. By 1932 the seeds for future harvests had either been surreptitiously consumed by starving people or destroyed by vindictive authorities. Moreover, because the people were so hungry and so many were dying every day, human labour was insufficient for the production process. The machinery that was supposed to be part of the arrangement was rarely forthcoming because Moscow did not have the funds to obtain both factory and farm equipment in the early 1930s. Herein lies one of the central dilemmas of this terrible tragedy: if the objective was to force the peasants to work on the collective farms, their starvation was obviously a self-defeating policy. It can only be understood in light of the desperate need to feed urban populations, to obtain industrial machinery, and to sustain the ideology of the proletarian revolution.

Politicide was a response of the centre versus the periphery of an empire, and of a bureaucratic class versus peasants, after a revolutionary reorganization of the entire state and in a context of insufficient food supplies for all populations.

PEASANTS VERSUS URBANITES: CAMBODIA

The conflict between peasants and bureaucrats was re-enacted in Cambodia some four decades after the Eastern Ukrainian episode, but in this case the peasants became a successful revolutionary army and were one of the bloodiest governments ever to rule over a state. This example is similar to the Ukrainian case in that it, too, had an underpinning of scarce food supplies and a dominant class that siphoned off the food. Finally, in both cases, the governing bureaucrats were scarcely aware of the food shortages in the countryside. In Cambodia they did not deliberately impose the suffering on the peasants; they were merely indifferent to it. They were scarcely aware of the reasons for the growth of the peasant army when their cities were taken over, and they had no time to react to the revolution once it invaded their space. They could not organize resistance, and their army was first defeated and then disbanded as well. There was no opportunity to rail against the conquerors. And the conquerors were totally uninterested in fine social distinctions: all urban dwellers were victims, and there was to be no jostling for little privileges in this revolution. In the Cambodian case, as in Iran and Afghanistan, the victorious groups either representing or including peasants have taken extremely puritanical ideological positions.

Michael Vickery (1984) opens his book on Cambodia with anecdotal evidence attesting to the huge difference in customs and mores between the urbanites in cities and the farmers in their immediate rice-growing regions, on one side, and, on the other, the distant forest peoples who subsisted on forest foods more than on agriculture. The latter folk, he argued, were antagonistic towards urban people for many generations before the Pol Pot regime. He claims that "patterns of extreme violence against people defined as enemies, however arbitrarily, have very long roots in Cambodia" (7). Vickery observes that cruel and murderous behaviour was as compatible with Buddhist philosophy as the Inquisition or the Nazi ss were to Catholics: the philosophy/theology was not an impediment to the behaviour. He says that the West's version of Buddhism, all peace with the universe and harmony, is "arrant nonsense" (9). Rather, Buddhism provided an upward mobility path for young men of some material wealth, but was no help whatsoever for the poor. Resentment among the poor was a normal response. Vickery also debunks the notion that village and family organizations were strong in Cambodia. It was virtually impossible for a poor peasant to accumulate wealth or move up the social scale, so families were not inheritors of a person's good deeds, and ancestors were not prayed to as in religious cults. "Corporate discipline over the individual by extended families or by village organizations was weak, and once a person had fulfilled his obligations to the state as a tax or corvee – there was little constraint in his activities. It is thus likely that a paradoxical situation of great anarchic individual freedom prevailed in a society in which there was no formal freedom at all" (13).

The three traditional classes of Cambodian society were royalty and urban elite families, bureaucratic officials, and peasants. They were organized in a system of patrons-clients, each person dependent on the one above him. The ruling class was dependent on foreign overlords in Thailand, Vietnam, and, finally, France. Vickery argues that the mindset of Cambodians at every level was to expect someone else higher in the hierarchy to save them from bloodshed or hunger. They were never trained to be self-reliant. The revolutionaries, many drawn from the non-rice-bowl areas and tribal roots of the country, were trying to create a revolution of the mind as much as of the society.

In addition to passive cultural attitudes, material conditions underscored the revolution. Vickery notes that exploitation of the peasants had increased during the French period, and even more after independence. Rice production was never high in Cambodia because of poor soil and inadequate water supplies. After the war, demands for export rice by urban merchants had become a major problem and contributed to the peasants' resentment of urbanites. In Vickery's view, the revolutionary movement in Vietnam and foreign military intervention were primary causes of the development of a revolutionary movement in Cambodia (15). But he argues that the history of the country has to be understood as a contributing cause, a context that permitted the revolution to occur and to take the form it did. A fact that is rarely mentioned in other texts is that close to a million rural inhabitants were forcibly "regrouped" during the first Indochina war of 1946–54. Further, a plan existed, though it was foregone because of the war and revolution, for the creation of the Mekong Project dams, which would have flooded the territory of half to three-quarters of a million peasants. In short, says Vickery, "for the rural 80–90 per cent of the Cambodian people arbitrary justice, sudden violent death, political oppression, exploitative use of religion and anti-religious reaction, both violent and quiescent, were common facts of life long before the war and revolution of the 1970s. The creations of Pol Pot-ism were all there in embryo."

Both Vickery and François Ponchaud (1989), though differing in many other respects, argued that education in Cambodia lagged behind other Southeast Asian countries before the 1960s, but primary school through to university enrolment expanded rapidly during that decade.

This growth would have been a sign of progress had there been sufficient employment for the graduates. The Chinese, Vietnamese, and some elite Khmer families controlled the commercial sector, and industry scarcely existed. The educational system turned out numerous graduates who could not find jobs in the cities, but were too far advanced to go back to the country. Unwilling to become agricultural labour, and no longer capable of sharing in the ethical and religious beliefs and practices of the rural regions, unemployed graduates became a class of disgruntled young people. They were trapped in the spiral of aspirations for luxurious living that had become, by the mid-1960s, commonplace in the cities. The graduates of foreign universities, now employed in the administrative bureaucracies, became wealthy and set the tone. Their children would inherit their privileges. According to Vickery, this situation affected the whole society. "Everyone aspired to luxuries which neither the individual, nor the society as a whole, could afford, and the result was a generalized corruption and a draining of wealth into unproductive investments" (25).

The military forces under Lon Nol maintained all the class distinctions of Cambodian society. The officers continued to live a luxurious lifestyle in Phnom Penh. The troops were largely country boys who had joined the army as a means of obtaining a daily rice ration. By 1972, however, the beginnings of hunger were apparent in the cities, partly because of inflation and then because food supplies were insufficient. The army was unable to provide adequately for the troops, even while the officers were well fed.

Ponchaud argues that the radical revolution may be explained in terms of Cambodian culture, through which Marxism and Maoism were interpreted. This revolt represented the hinterland against the centre, youth against elders, and indigenous peoples against foreigners. The urban and rural worlds had developed in different ways, largely because of the presence and leadership of the French while Cambodia was a French protectorate. During the French period, the cities had acquired many foreigners – Vietnamese and Chinese particularly – who functioned as intermediaries between the urban and rural markets. Most members of the administrative class were of foreign descent or of mixed blood. They were divorced from the agricultural world in which "knowledge consisted above all in mastering a moral ethic, judged to be indispensable to the collective well-being of the community," and which was intimately connected to the spirits of the earth (154). By contrast, the urbanites were more concerned with schooling, science, and technology. They were less concerned with the moral codes of religion and neighbourhoods, and, by the standards of the rural people, they were debauched. The Cambodian peasants identified with a revolution that recognized cities, foreigners, managers, and middlemen as their enemies.

After independence, according to Ponchaud, the cities were remodeled along Western lines. "The peasants became gradually excluded from the cities: edicts were passed, for instance, forbidding them to walk about the town either barefoot or stripped to the waist wearing sarongs, as had been customary" (156). Other restrictions essentially prevented peasants from interacting with city dwellers. The disdain for traditional culture was endemic in cities. Teachers in the countryside reacted against this urban prejudice and became important carriers of an anti-urban nationalism, says Ponchaud, who also claims that the revolutionaries were the children taught by these teachers. The rural culture was still an oral culture, while the urban centres became ever more oriented towards written communications. The revolutionaries were noted for their eloquence of speech; the fact that many were illiterate was of no importance as far as the revolution was concerned. And, having taken over the country, these revolutionaries managed affairs without the bureaucracies of educated mandarins. They spoke to the people, rather than promulgating laws. But, explains Ponchaud, this practice has another aspect not anticipated in the West: in an oral culture, only the rulers or the cadres speak; underlings are always silent.

Ponchaud provides yet another component of the explanation:

The Cambodian revolution was born in a period when the nation's institutions were blocked: the Westernized official class had lost contact with the people in the countryside and bowed to the exclusive authority of the head of state. Young intellectuals had little opportunity to share even partially in that power. Returning back from a foreign education, and rapidly in breach with the powers that be, the revolutionary leaders fashioned their plan in direct contact with the peasants. Cut off from the outside world, in part even opposed to the Vietnamese and Chinese communists, they developed their ideology to the fullest in their own closed and ingrown world. (177)

Vickery and Ponchaud have differing interpretations, but the difference is more a matter of emphasis and level of sympathy for the revolutionaries than of reasoning. Both argue that the dispossessed of the countryside formed the bulk of the revolutionary force against the prosperous but unproductive urbanites. Neither explanation, however, advances beyond the historical events towards an interpretation of why the revolutionaries used such brutal methods to subdue a population in which, if the accounts are reasonably accurate, a majority had, by 1995, developed some sympathy for the revolutionaries.

The immediate precedents for the internal war included a government too paralyzed to take action while Lon Nol attempted to displace Sihanouk. The long-term neglect of the countryside and the peasantry had brought the country to a point where it was not governable within its age-old cultural habits, class structure, and extreme differences in wealth, education, and opportunities. The urban society that had come into existence was unsustainable, and no government in 1970 could have solved the economic problems of the country. It took five years of struggle, however, for the paralysis to play itself out as internal war, followed by the takeover of government by a party prepared fundamentally and dramatically to alter the structure of government, the culture, and even the physical location of the population.

All the writers on Cambodia emphasize the role of external powers throughout the modern history of the country. French influence, followed by American critical attention and then bombing, had major impacts on the country. The Kampuchea Inquiry Commission in Finland (Kiljunen, 1984) explained the emergence of the revolutionary force with reference to the history of French rule and the rocky relationships with the United States. It noted the cessation of aid from the United States in 1961 and the resulting nationalization of the banks and other financial institutions. These influences were not merely economic and political: the immersion of Cambodian students in French culture and intellectual life were major contributors to their interpretation of the issues in their own country.

In Cambodia, the politicide was a response of the rural periphery against the urban centre of the state, and of rural peasants against the urban bureaucratic class, after the breakdown of the state and the defeat of the army, and in the context of insufficient food supplies.

POST-COLONIALISM: BURUNDI AND RWANDA

While peasants continued to labour in many countries of the world throughout the twentieth century, the age of formal imperialism came to a close towards the end of the Second World War. Imperialism determined the relations between most European countries, the imperial centres, and their colonies in much of Africa, Asia, Oceania, and Latin America, and among the indigenous people of North America and other regions during the eighteenth and nineteenth centuries. As in empires, those who were participants in imperial states were interested in obtaining land for settlement of excess populations, resources, and labour. They were ambivalent in their concerns about transforming local cultures: their missionaries tried it, but their economic agents were generally more interested in obtaining resources. As a consequence, while preachers ranted, indigenous people the world over were turned into packhorses and mining slaves or killed by overwork, disease, or desperation. Villages were destroyed, and cultures were shoved aside in the pursuit of elephant tusks or rubber. In the course of about thirty years, Belgium under King Leopold II caused the death of an estimated 5 to 10 million people in the Congo basin (Hochschild, 1999: 3, 225-34). And while that episode might be the worst of the imperial age, many million others were subjugated or killed not by tyrants or warlords who wanted them dead but, as in the Congo, by adventurers intent on extracting wealth in as short a time as possible. These imperial systems were coordinated by governments. It was not simply the East India Company or the Hudson's Bay Company, to name two of England's most successful companies of the period; it was the governments of Europe, competing with one another all the while, who established the conditions for plunder, set up colonial offices, provided armies, and ensured that some part of the wealth returned to the state's coffers.

The case studies of Burundi and Rwanda demonstrate the after-effects of colonial rule. Belgian colonialists in Rwanda had initially favoured the Tutsis and invented an exotic origin for them so they were regarded as a special race anointed as natural rulers; then, facing pressures from both the Catholic Church and the international community to create more equitable conditions, the Belgians did an about-turn, promoting Hutus and trying to bring about instant equality. When, on exiting, they handed over control to Hutu leaders, they ensured that turmoil would follow. Hutu governments, following a revolution that threw out the monarchy, were never able to establish legitimacy and were regarded as upstarts by both Tutsi and competing Hutu elites. They continued to jostle for control, unable to create an agreement for the way power would be established, shared, distributed, and peacefully transferred. The Tutsi exodus to Burundi, Uganda, and other nearby states locked in the hostilities that had been initially created under Belgian rule. In addition, the migrants had the opportunity to create a revolutionary army on the fringes of their own country, increasingly potent as a threat to the Hutu elites. Demographic pressures, draught, and hunger added to the tensions. While Tutsis remained in power in Burundi, the exodus of their cousins from Rwanda deeply disturbed their peace and encouraged Hutu in their realm to rebel against their rule. The Tutsi response was genocide in 1972, one that increased the credibility of Hutu claims in Rwanda that, should the Tutsi be permitted to return, they would use extreme force to evict the Hutu. So long as both were resident, there were unequal economic conditions between the two major groups in both societies. After the Tutsi fled to Uganda, there was continuing agitation about their losses and their determination to return to Rwanda. In both societies, the issue rulated to whether the incumbent rulers could tolerate challenges from the less powerful groups – from their own as well as from the "other." The potential change should the "other" gain a foothold was sufficient to induce extreme paranoia, even to the point of committing genocide.

An Oxfam observer in Rwanda, David Waller (1996: 5–10), while agreeing that history is "used to serve the particular ends of those who are telling it," cites individual Hutus to the effect that the Tutsi "overlords" during the periods of German and then Belgian protectorates mistreated the Hutu peasants, giving rise to the long-simmering resentment of Hutus to Tutsis. He suggests by way of explanation that "the government was hemmed in on all sides: by a history of mistrust that was particularly marked between the northerners who monopolised power within the country and the Batutsi outside the country who were demanding their right to return; by the inertia produced by 17 years in power without an effective opposition to stimulate debate on policy questions; by the lack of easy solutions to the country's problems; and by Rwanda's growing dependence on its foreign funders – who, inspired by events in Eastern Europe, were increasingly insistent on political change."

In Burundi there were extremists in both groups, but those in the Tutsi camp were better positioned to turn their fanatical ideas into murderous realities. In Rwanda, according to African Rights (1994: 33–4) Hutu extremists, racist, fascist, and genocidal, rooted in the northwestern regions of Rwanda, were organized and cultivated by persons in high government office. These people "had all the state-controlled organs of mass communication at their disposal, and could pay the salaries of ideologues in the universities, ministries and media. These are what made them so powerful." The ideologues persistently fanned extremism by telling Hutus they had been victims of historical injustice and would again become victims if Tutsis were allowed to return. While other analysts emphasize the on-going struggle between northern and southern Hutus, virtually all writers agree that the ideological thrust was central to the genocide, and there is agreement that the racist ideologies were introduced by colonial powers and fanned to genocidal frenzy by a government that used the Tutsi threat to deflect the other cleavages between northern and southern Hutus. René Lemarchand (1997b: 409) argues along similar lines:

It is imperative to explode the myths surrounding the Rwanda genocide. Contrary to the image conveyed by the media, there is nothing in the historical record to suggest a kind of tribal meltdown rooted in "deep seated antagonisms" or "longstanding atavistic hatreds." Nor is there any evidence in support of the "spontaneous action from below" thesis. From this perspective, the killings are largely reducible to a collective outburst of blind fury set off by the shooting down of President Habyalimana's [sic] plane on April 6, 1994. However widespread, both views are travesties of reality. What they mask is the political manipulation that lies behind the systematic massacre of innocent civilians.

Gérard Prunier (1995: 241–2) agrees with the general thrust of this argument. He is particularly strong in his condemnation of French support for the Hutu government and the failure of the French government to provide any help once the genocide began. He notes the pattern of the perpetrators: to attack the victims verbally and deny that violence is occurring, and then to deny responsibility. He lays the blame squarely on the economic and political elite "who had decided through a mixture of ideological and material motivation radically to resist political change which they perceived as threatening."

Lemarchand adds a useful description of the motivations of the troops or, as he calls them, "the grass-roots killers" (2002: 7). He suggests that the threat of sanctions, a culture in which compliance with authority had always been expected and given, extreme poverty, and hatred born of hardships were probable explanations. The sanctions came in the form of the excuse "they will kill us if we do not kill them first." The poverty was so great that "cases were reported of landless

Hutu turning against their land-owning neighbors, irrespective of ethnic identities ... As one eyewitness reported, 'someone could be called Tutsi simply to take away his cow; it would have been illogical to steal his cattle without calling him a Tutsi, and once thus named, his fate was foreordained.' " Of the hardships, Lemarchand says that hundreds of thousands of Hutu were driven from their homes by advanced FPR troops, and they, together with the refugees from Burundi, joined the interahamwe militias "and became enthusiastic genocidaires."

Colonial interests were never absent while all this tension was being generated, even while it resulted in such awful crimes in both former colonies. As the case study indicates, both Belgian and French commercial and political interests were persistently involved behind the scenes. The United Nations was shorn of any capacity to address the genocides when the world's great nations were unwilling to contribute to a peacekeeping force in a situation where their own interests could not be enhanced.

The politicides in Burundi and Rwanda were responses of post-colonial populations, still extremely dependent on external interests, to their inability to establish legitimacy, in the context of external interference, persistent competitive threats, extreme poverty, and inadequate land and food supplies.

CONTEMPORARY GLOBAL CAPITALISM: WORLD SYSTEMS THEORY

Imperial colonies were disbanded in the aftermath of the Second World War, just as many of the remaining empires had been disbanded after the First World War. Two countries emerged as strong contenders for world domination following the war: the USSR (an empire, rather than a state) and the United States (very close to being an empire). With the reconstruction under the Marshall Plan and other aids, European states were rejuvenated. Germany, Britain, France, and other states in Europe, together with Japan, became relatively independent of the two giants over the next two decades. But many of the former colonies of imperial European countries lapsed into semi-peripheral and peripheral status, lacking the capacities, capital, or skills to enter the capitalist marketplace on competitive terms. Most were poor and eager for foreign investment, tourism dollars, or foreign aid. Globalization – in the form of economic penetration by American and European banks and other transnational corporations (TNCs) – moved in where direct colonialization had departed. These symbiotic arrangements may continue uninterrupted for a long time, but not all members of the subordinate populations are satisfied to remain in that situation. And while, in general, military forces are not required to enforce the rules of a marketplace dominated by the core countries, when subordinate populations threaten to take unwelcome action, external force is often applied. Its potential is never absent.

World Systems Theory (Wallerstein, 1979) and prior dependency theories are both explanatory frameworks that posit a global economy in which one or a few states are at the core of an empire or an imperial system, while other societies radiate out from that core in descending order of independent capacities and economic well-being. At the peripheries, states are scarcely capable of mending their own fences, let alone initiating economic or political development, without the express agreement and financial aid of core states or their agencies (the World Bank or the International Monetary Fund [IMF] for prime examples). Many of these states are former colonies within imperial systems. The aspect that is pertinent to our present enquiry, elaborated particularly by Guillermo O'Donnell (1988), is an argument that when global capital, especially in the form of TNCs, becomes embedded in relatively underdeveloped economies, all other economic units are affected by the changed context of operations.

After the Second World War, Latin American countries lost much of their economic vitality when primary product export ties to the world capitalist centres became increasingly subordinated to the organization of TNCs. Subsidiaries of TNCs domiciled originally in the European and North American core countries were dependent on parent companies for many of their products or parts. They did not produce their own technologies or provide incentives to domestic companies to produce parts or services. The subsidiary's balance of payments was negative even if the country's balance of trade was positive; its domestic capital markets were poorly developed. TNCs were the largest and fastest-growing private economic units; the range of goods and services mirrored those in core capitalist countries, but the distribution system of all resources (including cultural resources) was extremely uneven. Some economic units became linked to the TNCs, providing them with communications, transportation, financial, or numerous other services and goods. Others lost vitality because what they had produced in an earlier context had ceased to be economically viable, given the range of products the TNCs produced for the domestic economy. Still others competed unsuccessfully for labour when TNCs produced goods either for export or for domestic markets. Argentina and Brazil were more advanced capitalist countries in Latin America, and O'Donnell argues that because they had larger production capacity and market demand than other countries in Latin America in the 1960s and 1970s, they were particularly affected by the early waves of globalization. However, like their other neighbours, their economies were characterized by ."pronounced fluctuations" in economic growth and in leading sectors, "large intersectoral transfers of income, rising inflation, recurrent balance-of-payments crises, capital outflows and reduced external investment, diminishing private investment, and large fiscal deficits. In O'Donnell's reading, then, all these countries were in or were rapidly moving towards economic crises – Argentina and Brazil most prominently.

This theory is useful for understanding the linkages between core country economic expansions and economic conditions in host but dependent countries. However, empirical conditions seldom follow the trajectory anticipated even by very good theories. Brazil moved into the phase of crimes against humanity in the 1960s, but never on the scale experienced later by Argentina and, relative to population size, Chile. Bolivia and Uruguay, and in differing degree, Peru, suffered similar atrocities in the same period. All these South American countries had some foreign direct investment and some experience of IMF demands against social spending. This contact does not invalidate O'Donnell's thesis, but it obliges us to treat the economic linkages as one, rather than the deterministic one, of several conditions leading to these events.

Argentina

American intervention was not manifest in Argentina as it was in Chile. Argentina had not democratically voted into office an avowed Marxist, nor was there any likelihood of such an event. American corporations were present, together with European companies, especially in the automobile sector, but neither the Peronist nor the military governments were interested in nationalizing them. They were not high profit-makers, nor were they tapping rich and unique resources, as were the copper corporations in Chile. The TNCs affected the society along the lines suggested by O'Donnell, yet there were other strands to this particular tapestry.

The crisis in Argentina was still in the future when the populist government of Juan Domingo Perón was elected to office in 1946. Perón's immense popularity was based on his recognition that the growing labour force was the source of electoral power. Though he came into office as the labour minister in a military government, he soon antagonized the military by his intimacy with unions, which he organized so they bargained not with capital directly, but through the mediation of the state. Their share of the growing economic wealth in the immediate postwar period dramatically increased, but the trajectory turned downward by the mid-1950s. For domestic capital, the capacity to meet union demands decreased operating longevity. For international capital, the demands became a signal that Argentina was no longer capable of providing a significantly cheaper labour force than competitive regions, even though it could, and did, provide a highly skilled labour supply. By the mid-1950s, as the armed forces plotted a coup to depose Perón, foreign investment was no longer growing and industries in Argentina were no long expanding.

While they were sponsored by the state, however, members of the urban working class demanded greater inclusion and equality in the economy. Their demands threatened the urban bourgeoisie, already experiencing some dislocation because its own share of the economic pie was shrinking while the more dynamic sectors of the economy, connected to the TNCs, was growing. The transnationalization process created a demand for new forms of consumption. As O'Donnell (1988) writes: "This is socially absurd in societies marked by inequalities much more profound than those of the central capitalist countries, and the tensions that result from such patterns of consumption have important political consequences"(13). The political impact intensified as new foreign investment declined, yet the state was expected to save the day. In what Marx called "the executive looking after the long-term interests of the bourgeoisie," the state is supposed to transcend the immediate situation and restore conditions for improved capital accumulation. According to O'Donnell: "In a crisis triggered by an economy of plunder that has gone 'too far,' the foundations of the class structure and the domination implicit within it are unavoidably shaken. At this point the crisis engulfs the whole state, which, far from being the foundation of order, is caught up in, and aggravates, the crisis. This gives rise to efforts to restore the state to its role of effective guarantor and organizer of social domination and normal patterns of capital accumulation" (22).

In terms of the theory presented here, the net result of popular demands for services akin to those in the advanced economies – unemployment insurance, social services, welfare provisions, education, child care, and so on – for a working class that includes both sexes and double-worker families vastly exceeded the capacities of a dependent state. Such states are caught in an impossible situation. They cannot serve or service the domestic upper class because it is already an anachronism; they cannot meet the requirements of the external corporation's local bosses because they have no resources to do so; they cannot replicate the former working class, which now demands consumer products and state services the state cannot possibly provide. O'Donnell argued that, in this crisis, the state establishes a form of organization he dubbed "bureaucratic authoritarianism" with these characteristics (23–32): it is a response of a transnationalized urban bourgeoisie where the economy is organized into oligopolies formed by transnational corporations; military forces (what O'Donnell calls "specialists in coercion") have decisive weight, and their task, together with that of economic actors who attempt to re-establish profitable economic conditions, is to deactivate the popular sectors (i.e., the working class) through coercion, withdrawal of citizenship and democratic rights, and exclusion of their organizations (i.e., unions); promote the oligopolistic units or private capital and some state institutions, thus intensifying inequalities; and depoliticize social issues by closing democratic channels for dissent. O'Donnell argues that this set of characteristics distinguishes a form of authoritarianism peculiar to a stage of capitalism.

From the standpoint of the dominant classes, both domestic and external, the economic and social crisis in the countries in which the BAs (Bureaucratic Authoritarian organizations) emerged involved more than the absence of the general conditions for normal economic functioning. It also raised the possibility (more or less imminently, dependent on the case) that capitalism itself would be eliminated. This perceived danger – the most pessimistic of predictions – was a key factor in the decisions that led to the implantation of the BAs.

The repression of the 1960s became, after a brief and bloody interlude while Juan Perón returned for a short tour of duty as ailing president followed by the street battles that characterized Isabel Perón's presidency, the terror and politicide of the 1970s. Now not only the working class was repressed but much of the population was reduced to an atomized mass of the kind that Hannah Arendt would have identified. Fear was pervasive, especially among young people and people in the liberal professions. The extreme force retaliated against the emergence of organized opposition. Spurred on by the attempted revolution in Paris and the global opposition among young people to American intervention in Vietnam, and also in awe of an idealized Che Guevara's exploits in Cuba, young middle-class students in Argentina organized resistance to military government and repression. Though the organized working class was not their ally in much of the country, caught off-guard by their demands and still making demands of its own, the two spearheads of revolution frightened the established bourgeoisie and the army.

The violent history of Argentina is a part of any explanation of what occurred there. This is a history, moreover, in which the military forces had frequently defended the arbitrary demands of an agrarian oligarchy during the earlier years of the country, and the agro-business and other elites during the latter periods. A civil society never emerged; immigrants with wealth tended to avoid citizenship, preferring instead to belong to their countries of origin so that they could escape if needs be. None of the major institutions of the country was entirely autonomous: the Catholic Church became in all but name a state church; universities were frequently intervened by whichever powers held the strings of government; agrobusiness was embedded in the state; and small businesses were always under the thumb of the state. Unions under Perón had become extensions of the state, and political parties were never well developed, autonomous organizations. Even the courts and the legal system were weak organizations, and the mass media were so intimidated by one government after another that only the foolhardy managed to express independent opinions – and they never survived. This constellation has to be appreciated in order to reach an explanation, because it shows why control of the state was so vital to the revolutionaries, the unions, the military, business, and political parties such as they were. Only by controlling the state could they achieve their other objectives. Even more important, if the state were controlled by any of the other institutions, or any combination of them, all other groups became potential victims.

Four possible explanations for the state terror that followed the coup were suggested by informants to the study by Patricia Marchak (1999). These reasons were that

- this violence was a holy war, a crusade against supposed Marxists by the military and their supporters (primarily the church);

- the objective was to impose economic restructuring, and the neo-liberal agenda was at the base of it;
- the terror was a displaced war between the United States and the USSR of the Cold War period; and
- it was a struggle for power between factions of the middle class for control of the state.

The anti-Marxist crusade was clearly part of the picture. It was, certainly, a holy war, with the military seeking the purification of the citizenry. The interview data clearly indicated that the military and church spokespersons saw the war as one of ideas, not merely of people and arms. They were determined, at any cost, to destroy Marxist ideology – and they believed that all dissidents were Marxists. However, the military forces had actually destroyed the only genuinely revolutionary force (the ERP) a year before the coup, and if, as much of the evidence suggests, the Montoneros were led by at least one and possibly others in the employ of the intelligence services of the military, their holy war had much to do with their ideological position and little to do with reality.

One of the military informants suggested that external powers had used Argentina as a testing ground for a third world war. Since there is no evidence to support this theory, it will be dropped from further consideration. However, it should be noted that conflicts throughout the Third World were often merged with Cold War strategies of one or the other of the major powers, so the suggestion was not outrageous.

Finally, there is the theory of intra-class power struggles, within the context already established of political paralysis and a crisis of accumulation. Essentially the argument is that the various sectors of the middle class contended for control of the state (Marchak, 1999: 329–31). These sectors included the military forces, the priesthood, the academic establishments, the substantial public service bureaucracy, independent professionals, small business, and a layer of union bureaucrats. The class was organized around or in the state itself, and a large part of it was employed by the state. The military forces that had governed the society since 1930 had prevented elected governments from working with capital and labour, as had occurred in other European settler societies such as Canada, and instead determined to control both forces within the state. By the 1960s the whole operation was stuck. Unions blocked the demands of the military, and both unions and the military were threatened by American-style unions in the huge automobile industries. Marchak argued that the students came later in the struggle between unions and military. They moved into a political vacuum where neither of the other contenders could control the population and where neither global nor domestic capital was capable of controlling the military and the unions. She concluded:

Argentina was a semi-modern, unevenly developed society which, through decades of military rule, had come to an economic standstill. The economy was not only failing to grow; industrial wealth was retreating from its factories. Reconstruction was essential, but there were opposing views on how and in whose interests it might be undertaken. Private capital was not well organized, and much of it was so externally oriented that its owners were unwilling, and possibly unable, to attend to the problems of their own society. There ensued a power struggle between the major institutionalized fractions of the middle class, each armed with a powerful and all-encompassing ideology. At that moment in history, the military won with its superior weapon – state terrorism. (330–1)

The politicide in Argentina was a response of a military force against an organized movement of middle-class students and militant unions, where the wealthiest class was fractured and real wealth was leaving the country, following the breakdown of the state and in the context of a crisis of capital accumulation.

Chile

Guillermo O'Donnell focused on Brazil and Argentina, both large territories with a middle class and a skilled labour force. He excluded other Latin American countries from his analysis on the ground that they did not meet the same criteria, but some of the problems that he noted for the larger societies were also evident in Chile. The northern half of its narrow strip of land, cuddled up to the Pacific Ocean, was dominated by North American mining companies. Related manufacturing companies and consumer goods subsidiaries of American and European parent firms, including Bata shoes and Coca Cola, were established. The southern half of the strip remained largely agricultural in the 1960s, still under the control of estate owners who ran semi-feudal farms and ranches. In some areas, absentee landlords continued to control land that was not used for food production. Gradually over the post-war period, the mining sector had transformed the north and Santiago; the southern regions had not progressed, even though the landed families had lost much of their power.

The Chilean episode is almost a textbook case of a society torn between those who were determined to sustain the existing relations of domination and subordination and those who were equally determined to topple the hierarchy. The whole edifice of democracy had been sustained by a conservative bourgeoisie that allowed the *estancia* owners to maintain their privileges and quietly kept the urban riff-raff out of electoral politics. But, inevitably, the country changed. The foreign-owned mining sector of the north gave rise to strong unions; other unions moved into construction and trucking. The poor and disenfranchised demanded entry into the system. The land monopolies became an impediment to changes that even the urban bourgeoisie saw as necessary, but the landed agro-oligarchy was unbending in its control of agricultural land. The small businesses were opposed to any form of sharing that reduced their already tiny share of the country's wealth. The truckers, too, when the chips were down, were not willing to support land-reform and redistribution policies that were not in their immediate economic interests.

Liberal and left-wing governments were unable to satisfy all the demands. They were besieged by their own extremities and by right-wing unions, as well as by organized conservative interests. One after another they succumbed to paralysis, resting on extreme inequalities of power, wealth, opportunity, and education. As long as governments worked within democratic controls, they could not reduce the extreme ideological polarization of the population, and without a higher level of popular support for their policies they could not resolve distributional issues peaceably. They also had no real alternatives because the unorganized working class was not willing to passively accept inaction on its agenda. It had brought the Popular Unity government to power in 1970, and it demanded that reforms be enacted – indeed, that more be given than even its president, Salvador Allende, was willing or able to deliver.

The pattern detected for Chile is similar to that found elsewhere. The preconditions, occurring over a lengthy time period, culminated in political paralysis. The country did not have the institutional strength to cope with the tensions, conflicts, and contradictions inherent in the society. Alternative institutions capable of reducing the strain were not available. Violence was occurring on a random and occasional basis and threatening to increase. The population wanted a solution, wanted the tension to end, but also wanted its subsistence guaranteed. These demands are the structural preconditions of state terror in capitalist, democratic states. Not all societies in this bind have the military and financial support that the United States provided to the armed forces by way of getting rid of Allende, nor the financial support after a right-wing revolution to keep a government based on force in power. These factors were special characteristics of the Chilean episode, but they were not the fundamental causes of the paralysis.

Before the coup, Chile was already a polarized society, with extremists on both the right and the left preaching violence. Confrontation was inevitable. The Popular Unity government under Allende attempted to bring fundamental reforms to the country at rapid pace. Moreover, according to many of its own supporters, now speaking with hindsight, the government was somewhat high-handed, even arrogant, in ploughing ahead despite opposition. One of its members said retrospectively during an interview that "the Popular Unity government was politically utopian and even irresponsible. We thought that history was on our side."* It attempted to do everything at once, and, self-righteously, thought that the gods would ensure that justice and mercy would ultimately win out. The revolution in Cuba was an inspiration, and many Chileans anticipated a similar revolution in their country. However, opposing forces, led by the army and fuelled by numerous though divergent grievances, had vastly greater military power than the government and its unarmed supporters. And the opposition within the army was equally self-righteous, equally sure that its interests coincided with the "national" interest. Businessmen, including the owners of large and medium-sized enterprises, and American corporate managers backed General Pinochet's counter-revolution. The media, particularly the two newspaper chains, *El Mercurio* and *La Tercera*, supported the counter-revolution. Adding to their voices and strength were the Confederation of Manufacturing and Commerce, bringing together all organizations of farmers, miners, industrialists, and tradesmen. Once the counter-revolution began, the defence of Allende's revolution disintegrated. Its supporters had no arms, no army, no independent sources of wealth, and they were on the wrong side of the United States and its mining corporations.

---

* Quotations are from interviews with Chilean citizens conducted by Patricia Marchak and William Marchak in 1997 and 1998. Interviewees are not named, as a condition of granting the interviews. This fieldwork has not been published elsewhere.

The role of the United States and its mining and other corporations included substantial funding of strikes by unionized labour, especially in the trucking industry, which was essential for the distribution of food in a country that could not provide sufficient food from its own farmland. It also included blockades of exports, particularly copper, which was essential for sustaining the economy and purchasing imported food. It involved funding of anti-Allende groups, organizations, and the leading newspapers, along with repeated attempts to assassinate Allende and the murder of General René Sneider (Spooner, 1994; Hersh, 1983; U.S. Senate Select Committee on Intelligence Activities, 1975a, 1975b). The interests of the United States military, the CIA, and the Nixon administration were partly economic – the mining companies that had been nationalized were primarily American-owned, as were many other subsidiaries of American companies. The fear of communism – or of any equalization that might reduce the power of the United States and its capitalist class – was extreme in the early 1970s. Seymour Hersh (1983: chs. 21–22), in a trenchant analysis of the activities sponsored by Henry Kissinger, then national security adviser, and US president Richard Nixon with respect to Chile, argues that while Nixon acted on behalf of the corporate interests of his benefactors, Kissinger acted out of an overwhelming fear of the spread of communism. The fear, however, was less about the potential for Allende to destroy democracy than about the greater potential that he would respect it, thus showing that socialism and democracy could be compatible.

Politicide in Chile was a response of the military, acting on behalf of, but not necessarily at the behest of, diverse fractions of the dominant economic class, to the perceived threat of revolution by workers, the poor, middle-class students, and others speaking on their behalf, following the breakdown of government.

SUMMARY OF DIVERSE CASES

Class and region are basic divisions within large populations. Ethnic divisions may overlap with them or add cleavages to the basic structure of inequality created by class and region. If, as argued, a basic function of the state is to sustain the system of inequalities, any situation that threatens to alter class relations or disturb the relationship between regions (domestic and global) becomes an unsettling event for the state.

A crisis of food production, a capital accumulation crisis, the displacement of a domestic bourgeoisie and labour hierarchy by external capital investment and development, as much as wars, can fundamentally discombobulate the whole society. The transition to new modes of governance was violent in all cases – not on ethnic, but on political grounds. These episodes were all class and regional conflicts.

4

Culture and Ideology

Societies moving towards crimes against portions of their own numbers are divided. Their social polarization always has two aspects, material and ideological. Some portion, contentious and already targeted as potential victims or their allies, demands change; its members may even organize resistance or call for revolution. They speak on behalf of those who are beleaguered by poverty or racism or other outcomes of unequal conditions. Theirs is the culture of the oppressed or the champions for the oppressed. Another portion, powerful, in possession of privileges, seeing itself as the cream and leaders of society, is afraid only that the subversives in its midst could fundamentally alter the direction of the society and remove its privileges. It speaks on behalf of the nation, the true god, history, and "all that we hold dear."

There are societies where the potential victims are a minority; the majority agrees with their oppressors. There are societies so torn between the two that there is scarcely any occupied middle ground; everyone is caught up in the vortex of the battle between perceived good and evil. The Ottoman Empire before the deportation of Armenians is an example of the society where a minority is the victim of a majority. In such societies, the minority is generally visibly different from the majority or has attitudes and behaves in ways that are visibly different. By contrast, Chile before the military coup of 1973, an example of a highly polarized society with no middle ground, rarely provides visible minorities; its victims look the same as its oppressors, though they act differently.

There is another difference between these two kinds of society; in the Ottoman Empire and other racist societies, the objective is to eradicate the entire minority, not just their ideas but their bodies as well. In the case of a polarized society, the objective is to eradicate the enemy ideas and enough of its leaders to terrify followers into abandoning those ideas. Though these objectives are very different, and the outcomes are different, the stated rationale from those who are engaged in planning, executing, or explaining genocide is often similar. The victims are "vermin" who contaminate the society. The protagonists are "saviours" without whom the society would surely have disintegrated or turned into an animal farm. This mode of explanation reflects a basic fact of all genocides and politicides: they are fundamentally political events, irrespective of the identification of victims, whereby one group defends its privileges against real or imagined threats. Ideology is the bridge between the material interests and the acts in defence of them. Culture is the cushion whereby both material interests and the battle of ideas are mediated, absorbed, ritualized, explained, and transformed. A culture is effective to the degree that it transforms inequalities into acceptable differences, so neither the privileged nor the poor are threatened with extinction – and that task, too, is largely ideological.

Ideology is a set of assumptions, shared beliefs, values, norms, and habits of mind that provide "rule of thumb" explanations for the nature of the world and its inhabitants. The community of believers can understand one another's actions and reasoning because they start with the same assumptions. Ideologies may mask behaviour, rationalize it, or excuse it. They may be imposed on others or used to misinform or disinform others. They are especially critical to the formation of cultural identities; they provide the basic rationale for why a group (ethnic, national, religious, tribal, and, in the Chilean case, class and occupational) is superior to others and who a member is, in relation to others.

History may belong to the victors, but cultural groups interpret their own history, often seeing themselves as the victims whose claim to heroism is buttressed by years of burnishing the myths and legends of long-gone battles between good and evil. What we believe about our ancestral past is invariably an outcome of a long history of actual or imagined events misted in interpretation and reinterpreted through the veil of later events and new interests. Often ideologies become exclusionary, informing believers that they have a monopoly on truth and that others are excluded from the realm of the select.

Beliefs and interpretations are not necessarily based on demonstrably evident facts: they are always screened through the ideologies held by groups (and, by extension, individuals within the groups). It is not truth but objectivity that may be absent. To cite an interesting example that is engaging biblical scholars and archeologists at the time of writing, there may or may not have been an exodus of Jews from Isreal as the Old Testament describes. What matters, apparently, is not the factual truth of that event, but the belief among contemporary Jews that it occurred and that it had, and still has, religious significance. The majority of Jews who believe in "the exodus" attribute a political meaning to that event in the twenty-first century as the state of Isreal stakes out its claim on contested territories. Was there a city of David? Some outstanding archaeologists suggest there is no evidence for it (Lazar, 2002). But does it matter? Not to those who see that city as the legitimation of the claim that Isreal has a right to occupy lands also claimed by Palestinians. The point here is not to argue the case for either Isrealis or Palestinians, but to illustrate the argument that what a people chooses to believe can have profound implications for its behaviour – including, if necessary, the excessive use of force or the resort to suicide bombing where other forms of force are unachievable.

Ideologies may be benign ways of coping with the uncertainties of life, but the ideologies of concern here are absolutist and exclusionary in character: they are not benign coping mechanisms, but, rather, channels of hatreds that permit a group to be self-righteous. They are claims to absolute truth which allow no other claims to be sustained; they are claims that only those with the absolute truth are pure and worthy of respect – indeed, of continued survival. Anyone who fails to meet the test of purity – however it may be defined – is less than human, to be degraded, spat upon, or killed in the name of a higher good. Such ideologies may be religious in nature, as when a society defines itself in relation to a god and directs its behaviour to praise or please the god. In this case, infidels are the enemy, and infidels include atheists as well as believers in other faiths. The crusaders of the twelfth century, armed with the belief that Muslims and Jews were infidels, justified their military and (not so incidentally) economic ventures as necessary acts on behalf of Christianity. Both state and non-state terrorists of the late twentieth and early twenty-first centuries have justified their violence as protection of Islam, Judaism, and Christianity, depending on their home-base location.

Beliefs may also be nationalist: indeed, religion and nationalism are frequently combined as rationales for terrorism, whether directed against external or internal enemies. Ethnicity, class, status, political affiliations, or interest groups with other bases can also become the anchor for ideologies that threaten those who fail to belong to the preferred groups. In all cases, god, nation, race, class, or other affiliations may serve equally as causes larger than a human life, causes that justifiably call forth martyrs in their name, causes that are worth dying for.

The precise content of the ideologies is of secondary importance if they are absolutist and exclusionary in nature. Fundamentalists of Christian, Jewish, and Islamic faiths are equally susceptible to the illusion that they have a monopoly on truth. Monotheism, in fact, tends to lead in that direction, as Barrington Moore Jr. (2000) neatly demonstrated in a study of the Old Testament. Polytheistic and animistic spiritual interpretations are less likely to accommodate zealotry, for, by their nature, they engender a great deal of tolerance for diverse versions of the social and nether world. Free-trade American capitalists are as likely to become dogmatists in defence of their beliefs as are communists in defence of theirs. Many of the twilight wars throughout the world over the course of the twentieth century were connected to the Cold War ideologies of the period, just as the religious wars of an earlier time in England and France were connected to the ideologies in their period. In the twenty-first century we seem to be returning to religious conflicts as the basis for terrorism both within and between countries. Differing ideologies emerge in all societies, and in all large populations there are extremists with monopolies on truth. But in societies where reigns of terror are launched, the ideologies have either polarized the society or divided it into "us and them," where "them" is a minority, and generally a visible minority. Ideologies have interrupted other concerns and have made it difficult for citizens to ignore the strife and get on with their lives. Activists take sides or go into exile.

For any one individual, an ideology might take the form of received wisdom: we inherit religious beliefs, for example, and their inculcation at an early age generally influences us throughout our lives, even if we abandon the practices of religion in which they are embedded. We also adopt ideologies, often without intent, by listening to others or reading their work, when what they say informs us about the nature of our own lives or the puzzles about our society. We become aware of the gap between the wealthy and the poor, and perhaps either Christianity or Marxism provides the explanation that satisfies us: "Ah," we say of an epiphany, "this is why things are the way they are." Much rarer is the adoption of beliefs that fall far outside our everyday experience. Few Westerners can get beyond an outsider's aesthetic appreciation for

Hindu beliefs and icons because they do not answer the kind of questions that arise within their secular experiences in vastly different cultures from those (there are more than one) of India. Experience, then, is both cultural and individual: we see the world through our culturally conditioned eyes, but also through the personal experiences of our own lives. For this reason, rapid social change and political paralysis tend to generate virile ideologies which use the prejudices and preconceptions of the past together with shared recognition of the meaning of the passing parade. In a society with a long history of antipathy and discrimination towards minority ethnic or religious groups, an ideological rationale for going further than discrimination, going to the limit and killing these groups, becomes tenable, given other predisposing conditions. The same people would not consider, and probably could not be induced to consider, killing members of their own ethnic group because nothing in their culture provides the basis for that behaviour.

Ideology is the bridge for the movement from centralization of power to elimination of potential or actual opponents.

In cases that have been simmering for a long period, the ideology of the victors is generally well consolidated already; in other cases it may crystallize after the coup. The formulation of an ideology is an essential act preceding governance under any circumstances; the governing parties require a binding agent for conduct of their behaviour, and if the behaviour includes murder or even extremely harsh and oppressive acts, then an ideological rationale is all the more essential. Further, not only do the governors require a justification but, even more, do the troops. If abductions, concentration camps, torture chambers, and murder are going to become features of the regime, those who will actually carry out the orders have to be persuaded that these orders are necessary, that the end justifies the means. Armies socialize soldiers to obey commanders regardless of their personal beliefs or comfort levels; they may need less of a justifying ideology than others. Soldiers in war will use torture when they are convinced that the enemy is evil and the cause for which they fight is good. The thousands of young men slaughtered in the First and Second World wars in the twentieth century were induced to believe in the justness of the cause on both sides of the struggle. Presumably the American soldiers who dropped bombs from B-52 planes in Vietnam, unable to see the victims, or hear their screams, also believed in the justness of the cause against communism.

In the numerous Latin American cases of state terrorism in the 1970s, it was anti-communism that motivated the troops.

But large-scale terror is going to involve many civilians as well, and ideological rationales are essential. When a dominant majority holds an exclusive ideology that justifies torture and killing large numbers of people, followers are induced to accept the legitimacy of the belief partly because they are persuaded they share in the exclusivity of the saved by destroying the infidels. Cultural predispositions are crucial to compliance. In the case of Allied troops in the European wars, the culture had long included an idealized version of democracy, and it was democracy that was touted as the value to be defended at all costs in these wars. In Germany the culture was authoritarian, and it was the "Fatherland" and "the German Reich" that had to be defended. In both cases, and in the American case in Vietnam, the ideology used to motivate the troops rested on these long-standing values and sentiments embedded in the culture. This history would suggest that such values, sentiments, and beliefs, which may have lain untested for a long time, can be whipped into active duty by the full formulation of ideology when leaders perceive, or are eager to persuade a population of followers to perceive, that a threat exists.

Sentiments held by large segments of a population may be deliberately activated by governments under stress and can form the basis for a larger exclusionary ideology.

Some of these sentiments may be racist. If the government proposes to target a segment of the population as a way to alter its paralytic condition, it is easier if the prejudice already exists.

The propensity to target specific victims when governments are under stress and to use terror to alleviate the condition is greater when the proposed victims have characteristics about which long-term prejudices already exist in the culture.

We should now adjust the phrase "a majority of the dominant population" holding beliefs that provide the gateway for acceptance of genocide: this majority may not be one in numbers but by virtue of its latent (if not active) power. In some cases, such as South Africa under apartheid, the culture may be bifurcated, so that a large part of the population neither consents nor dissents from the ideological rationale for oppression. It is simply so marginalized that its opinions are never solicited, and it may be impossible for it to organize resistance if its opinions are negative. Consent comes rather from the dominant (i.e., participating) majority. In the Argentine case, as another example, opinions were polarized within the active population (military, church leaders, union leaders, students), but a large part of the middle class watched and waited from the sidelines and tacitly accepted the brutal repression imposed on trade unionists and students by the military. Ideologically, they explained their inaction in such terms as "it was impossible to act," or "they (the disappeared) must have done something or the army would not have disappeared them." (The active verb is used in Latin America.) Pushed, they said that "the guerrillas and the army were two devils killing each other." The last rationale ignores the enormous difference in military capacities for the two devils, but it provides an ideological rationale for non-interference and, essentially, for complicity.

In the Rwandan case, an ideology of differences, created by colonial powers, lay dormant for many years before it was fanned into wild hostility. In Cambodia we see another aspect of the cultural problem. There, the urban population and the rural population were scarcely in the same century, let alone country. The values and habits of urbanites led them to ignore the welfare of the country people; the country people developed their own versions of urbanity and modernization, and were culturally ready for opposition to urbanites when the peasant army came to call for recruits.

Though ideological rationales are essential components of these events, they are not a sufficient explanation unless we are prepared to believe that we humans are guided, willy-nilly, irrationally or otherwise, by what goes on in our heads. In fact, most people are not prepared to engage in massacres or torture unless they have strong ideological beliefs for doing so, but the beliefs have to be attached to actual conditions at some stage. The ideologies are rooted in experiences and social structure, and the position people occupy within the social structure. The ideologies become believable precisely because they appear to explain those experiences, structures, and positions. To say that reigns of terror are caused by ideologies is insufficient at best; ideology is an important component, but it remains, always, a bridge between material or structural positions and actions in defence of those positions.

Are some religious or political cults more predisposed than others to kill those who disagree with them? Suppose they have long inhabited authoritarian cultures and might be easily persuaded to believe that the intended victims are subhuman (vermin, beastly) or superhuman (satanic, absolutely evil). Norman Cohn (1967, 1970) suggested that messianic cults were especially prone to extreme behaviour. The perpetrators, caught up in messianic fantasies where the destruction of selected others is an act of salvation for the world or the society, a deliverance from evil, are convinced that they perform a noble and self-sacrificing task. These fantasies are derived from cultural versions of an apocalypse about to destroy humanity (or their section of it) unless action is taken to stop the evil embodied in some other group or groups who are either beneath human consideration or else diabolically undermining good people. Cohn's argument is helpful in identifying the mindset of some perpetrators of gross and sustained violence against targeted groups. But one question remains: Why would some cultures give rise to such apocalyptic visions, or why would some societies so loosen the reins on people that they would kill under the banner of their myths? Collective fantasies may be widespread, but not every society, not every culture, unleashes sustained violence on the scale of genocide or politicide. In the medieval societies described by Cohn the pervasive condition is extreme inequality between members. Where those with power can use the state as an instrument to contain potential revolutionaries, those without power may use the strength of collectivities and the ideology of salvation to destroy their oppressors.

Groups that take over government by coup or who use state force to destroy potential subversives invariably see themselves as saviours. They may phrase it as saviours of the nation (as military juntas tend to do), as saviours of the true religion (crusaders), as saviours of the working class (communists), or, in the case of Cambodia, as saviours of the peasantry. Hitler saw himself as saviour of the Aryan race. Africaaners saw themselves as saviours of the white population in South Africa. And once people view themselves as saviours, they also view those from whom the nation, religion, class, or race is being saved as infidels – impure, beastly, dirty, ugly, mean, beneath contempt, not fully human, and, finally, evil. They are not merely wrong, not merely holding a different viewpoint, but evil. Such terminology is regularly used, even in secular struggles. The use of such terms indicates just how ideologically charged these events are: in order to go about killing others, people need to be fortified with a belief in evil and in their own courage to destroy it. Our fairytale childhoods have properly conditioned us to suppose that "good" and "evil" are actual conditions. We reify them and attach them to "us" and "them" whenever "them" becomes an irritant.

When a group of citizens challenges the prevailing organization of a society and its distribution of power, opportunities, and resources, the ruling powers might conclude that these actions pose a threat of such magnitude that it justifies massive retaliation. In fact, virtually every genocide and politicide is preceded by a claim that there is a threat too great to be handled by negotiation or other peaceful means. Of course rulers may see threats where none exist, and that, too, occurs fairly frequently. Hitler claimed to perceive a threat to German purity from Jews, Gypsies, Poles, and homosexuals, among others. Yet absolutely nothing in all the vast literature on the Holocaust suggests that any of these groups actually posed a genuine threat to Germany or even to Hitler himself and his party. If it was an overwhelming concern for Aryan purity (rather than anti-Semitism or xenophobia) that fuelled the Holocaust, the most these groups could possibly do against German purity was promote occasional matings between Germans and others – and such matings were not applauded by any of the groups at that time. In short, the real threat was minimal; the response to perceived threat was monumental.

Part of the explanation lies in the manipulation of ideological themes, the deliberate invocation of folklore and tales of origins to inculcate fear and loathing of "the other," and the use of genocide as a means of mobilizing the German population against a manufactured common enemy. Threat is a perception at least as much as a reality: some real threats are never perceived; some perceived threats are all in the mind of the observer. For this reason, when it comes to threats, we are obliged to concern ourselves more with perceptions than with apparently objective conditions. Is the perception of threat an essential component of the process towards committing crimes against citizens? It seems likely that those who have already moved towards centralization of power, and who have created an ideology that justifies their power, necessarily anticipate threats to their absolute control; thus, perception of threat may be merely the pervasive paranoia typical of those who control others. Their capacity to turn their perpetual fear of being toppled into a specific threat against the population they control is one of their major tools to maintain control. If, through ideological appeals, they can persuade their subjects that some power beyond them all is threatening them, diluting their strength, they can mobilize the population to oppose the supposed source of threat rather than the author of it.

ARMENIA

Turkish estimates of the Armenian population before the killings and
deportations were some 500,000 lower than most external estimates,
and their estimates of the number who did not survive this period were
substantially lower. They have argued that the deportations were a wartime measure required because of Armenian disloyalty to the Turkish
"nation." From their perspective, Armenian connivance with enemies of
Turkey could have provided the means for European dismemberment of
the Ottoman Empire. Further, they have argued that although Armenians died of famine, disease, and other conditions of war, so, too, did
some 2 million Muslims (Kuper, 1981: 113–14; Hovannisian, 1986b:
34–7). These self-explanations are discounted by virtually all observer
accounts at the time, and by later scholars, but they are important to an
understanding of Turkish behaviour. The self-explanation is summed up
in a statement by Deputy Hasan Fehmi (Atac) during the 17 October
1920 secret sitting of the Kemalist Parliament in Ankara. After acknowledging that the Christian world would revile Turks for their actions, he said, "We acted thusly simply to ensure the future of our
fatherland that we consider to be dearer and more sacred to us than our
own lives" (cited in Dadrian, 1999). Stephan Astourian (1998: 23) sums
up these arguments well: "The Turkish nationalist ideologies that
emerged in the Ottoman Empire at the turn of the twentieth century en-
tailed two concomitant and interrelated processes: the exclusion of non-
Muslims from the nation, by various degrees of violence combined with
both legal and informal discrimination, and the construction of a modern Turkish identity." He continues with the argument that while the
exclusion was rooted in long-standing prejudices, prejudice became racist nationalist theories when the Ottoman Empire encountered "European imperialism, territorial losses, financial bankruptcy, and significant
socioeconomic transformations."

Nearly a century later, the Turkish interpretation has not changed. In
2002 filmmaker Atom Egoyan produced *Ararat*, a film portraying the
events from the Armenian perspective. Turkish newspaper reviews of the
showing at the Cannes Festival condemned the film as a biased and altogether wrong-headed interpretation: "Obviously, to please the Armenian
lobby, Egoyan has made major concessions from his original project"
(*Cumhuriyet*, translated and cited in *Turkish Daily News*, 21 May,
2002). "This will be very harmful to the future of Turkish-Armenian relations. Speaking of peace on one hand and pouring fuel into the fire on

the other hand ... This film cannot be shown in Turkey" (*Hrant Dink*, Turkish journalist claimed to be of Armenian descent, translated and cited in *Turkish Daily News*, 22 May, 2002). One commentator, however, had a different point of view, demonstrating the way in which any group can justify a genocide. Said Gündüz Aktan:

The Armenian incidents do not amount to genocide because the Armenians constituted a "political group," which is not covered by the Genocide Convention. Like the Balkan Christians, the Armenians frequently rebelled for autonomy first, then for independence, and to that end collaborated with the Russian Army, which invaded the eastern part of the country during World War 1. All groups that rebelled in the Balkans eventually gained their independence from the Ottoman Empire. The Armenians lost the opportunity because they were far away from Europe; they constituted a small minority of 17 percent in eastern Anatolia; Russia withdrew from war because of the communist revolution, and the Turks waged the War of Independence which tore up the Sévres Treaty.

There was of course a civilian segment of the Armenian population that consisted of women, children and elderly who did not get involved in the politico/military struggle. On the other hand some of them wanted to live together with the Turks. Consequently one may claim that they were not part of the "political group." Nevertheless all political groups have such a mixed structure. Unfortunately it was impossible to discern and exclude from the relocation a segment of the Armenian population in a life and death war. The United States has pointed out in much safer conditions that it was acting within the framework of the "presumption of disloyalty" when relocating 110,000 Japanese from Pacific shores to inner regions. Let us not forget that the Turks were more violently uprooted and expelled from the Balkans on the grounds that they would create a problem of security for the newly established Balkan nation-states. (*Turkish Daily News*, 21 May 2002)

The first argument is that the events did not constitute a genocide as defined in the Genocide Convention. People were killed not because they were Armenians and Christians, but because they acted politically against the interests of Turkey. The second argument is that though civilians may have been harmed, this misfortune was inevitable in a state of all-out war, and, with Armenians being disloyal, Turkey was engaged in just such a war. Finally, the third argument stated that Turks also had been harmed elsewhere, so why should Turkey be especially blamed for its role in killing its Armenian population?

EASTERN UKRAINE

As James Mace (1990) observes, state-sponsored mass violence requires the state to define the enemy, and in Soviet ideology the definition had to be in terms of class. When enemies expressed nationalist sentiments, it was because they were infected with "bourgeois nationalism," or class sentiments. When peasants expressed nationalist sentiments, they were sabotaging the industrial proletariat of the motherland. In Stalin's version, the peasantry was divided into kulaks and others, the kulaks being richer than the rest, or, if not actually richer, then holding political opinions and attitudes supportive of bourgeois kulaks.

The communist ideology was important, but if, as we have argued, ideology is a bridge between what the state proposes and the understanding of those proposals by the population, then an explanation lies not in the ideology but in the structure that underlies the actions of the state. Peasants exist in Marx's writing primarily as a class that was being phased out, or at least transformed into a working class. There is a good reason for this attitude: Marx was analyzing capitalism, not feudalism. He surely did not anticipate that one of the most backward empires of the twentieth century would be the one to take up the challenge of socialism. His own writings would have suggested that this order of events was not wise: he anticipated, instead, the full development of capitalism before the sweeping socialist revolution in all the capitalist states. Capitalism was a necessary stage in development, and since the Russian Empire had not yet undergone that stage, it was not a prime candidate for jumping over capitalism to socialism. Yet to the revolutionaries of the Russian Empire, the realities were less salient than the dream of transforming a backward, feudal string of territories into an industrial, socialist state. Peasants were simply a class to be transformed into a proletariat; they were not a permanent or important component of the dream.

Egalitarianism in Soviet ideology was important. In reality, what the term meant was the extermination of those with wealth, the destruction of personal property, and the creation of conditions whereby all workers would have equal material conditions. Starving those who resisted was a rational extension of the ideological argument. Linking the resistance to the kulaks, even when all wealth had been eradicated, was an ideological bridge.

THE NAZI CASE

Most writers who experienced Nazi Germany describe it as an authoritarian culture. Leaders in authoritarian societies are the appropriate decision-makers on behalf of the constituent parts; obedience to the leaders is essential for the functioning of the organic whole. In this sense, the Prussian state that preceded Naziism, and the entire bureaucratic and military institutions established by Bismarck and his followers, were authoritarian. The structure existed to serve those at the top, not those at the bottom. Those who wanted to survive or succeed in these and attendant institutions were invariably obedient servants.

Democracy was a foreign concept, not to be considered as an alternative to the status quo before the disaster of the First World War. Nazi Germany, recently broken by war and still suffering massive unemployment, poverty, dislocation, and widespread alienation, repudiated the Weimar Republic as a foreign imposition by alien powers. As William Shirer (1961: 185) said "No class or group or party in Germany could escape its share of responsibility for the abandonment of the democratic Republic and the advent of Adolf Hitler. The cardinal error of the Germans who opposed Nazism was their failure to unite against it." And again: "During the Second Reich, the university professors, like the Protestant clergy, had given blind support to the conservative government and its expansionist aims, and the lecture halls had been breeding grounds of virulent nationalism and anti-Semitism. The Weimar Republic had insisted on complete academic freedom, and one result had been that the vast majority of university teachers, antiliberal, antidemocratic, anti-Semitic as they were, had helped to undermine the democratic regime" (251). And finally: "In the days of the Republic, most judges, like the majority of the Protestant clergy and the university professors, had cordially disliked the Weimar regime and in their decisions, as many thought, had written the blackest page in the life of the German Republic, thus contributing to its fall" (268).

Albert Speer (1970: 47), Hiter's architect and then minister of procurements, charged with war crimes and incarcerated, wrote a disarmingly honest autobiography that is revealing about Nazi Germany. He observed that his mother, who had grown up as the daughter of a rich merchant of liberal tendencies and had married a prosperous, similarly liberal architect, happened to see an SA parade in the streets of Heidelberg. "The sight of discipline in a time of chaos, the impression of energy in an atmosphere of universal hopelessness, seems to have won her over also. At any rate, without ever having heard a speech or read a pamphlet, she joined the party." Her son had already done the same, though out of deference for the liberal tradition of his parental family he had never spoken of it to her. Again and again, Speer remarks on his own perception that new energy had been injected into Berlin. He felt that his society had been in deep crisis, nearly moribund, and was now emerging triumphantly and proudly from its torpid state. Hitler, Goebbels, Goering, and others energized the young Speer and gave him a sense of his own importance in a significant undertaking.

Speer described the willingness of eminent generals, judges, and businessmen to line up behind Hitler: "These men were free of radical antisemitism of the sort Hitler advocated. They in fact despised that eruption of plebeian hatreds. Their conservatism had nothing in common with racist delusions" (43). In his view, their support for the Nazis was based on their shrewd observation that the Nazis, their name not withstanding, were no socialists. Hitler's putsch of the left wing of the party in 1934 had convinced them that he would protect their property rights.

Another feature of Hitler's makeup was a certain puritanism, selective to be sure, since he was dependent on a motley crew of drunkards and thugs during his rise to power, but persistent even so. He decried the immorality of cities, claiming that they damaged "the biological substance of the people." In contrast, he proclaimed the virtues of the healthy peasantry. But Speer offers another explanation for such statements: "Hitler was able to sense these and other currents which were in the air of the times, though many of them were still diffuse and intangible. He was able to articulate them and to exploit them for his own ends" (47). Another example of Hitler's intuitive talent for meeting his audience on its own terms was the occasion when Speer himself, as a student, was completely taken in by the demeanour of the man, more than the content of his speech. Hitler was a demagogue of remarkable talent, but he knew when to speak quietly, when to wear a bourgeois suit, which buttons to push for each kind of audience. He won over many students, Speer only one of them. He had also won over the left-wing workers of the original German Workers' Party by promising a socialist utopia; then, in 1934, he killed many of his former comrades because he knew he could succeed only with the support of the bourgeoisie. In short, for Hitler himself, the ideology was linked to opportunism, and opportunism to absolute power to control the life of Germany and, ultimately, of Europe.

Speer's insights enable us to understand something of the mind-set of Germans during this period and the towering genius who so mesmerized them. But ideology alone is not a sufficient explanation for the Holocaust. Italy also had a dictator at this time, and Benito Mussolini was powerful in his country before Hitler achieved power in Germany. His corporatist state could also be ruthless, and enemies of the leader were on treacherous grounds. Yet Italy did not engage in genocide or a reign of terror. These ideologies and perceptions explain why masses of people followed Hitler, not why they allowed him to establish a reign of terror against Jews and other minorities. To explain that, we have to recall that the German state was far from democratic at any previous time; that inequalities were extreme and persistent; that the Junkers and the conservative bourgeoisie were prepared to back any scheme that ensured their survival within a different, but still unequal state; and that the vast majority of the people demanded some kind of victory after their ignominious defeat.

Arendt, in her 1969 essay *On Violence*, observes that the minority cannot overrrule the majority, nor can a tyrant exercise power, unless the majority consents (as by refusal to resist) (42). There is evidence that German society of that period more or less adopted Naziism and consented to its conduct, at least in the initial stages. A structural explanation is that the people were humbled, impoverished, and many unemployed: Hitler promised them nirvana. A cultural explanation for their complicity might be the authoritarianism of all the institutions of that society. But in Arendt's opinion, the explanation is the atomization or massification of the society. She argues: "The effectiveness of terror depends on the degree of social atomization. Every kind of organized opposition must disappear before the full force of terror can be let loose" (55). This atomization is the essence of mass society, with each person, or each little group, uninformed and unaware of the ideas and actions of others, subject only to the leader. All institutional options for mobilizing dissent are absent. Speer's observations suggest that this was the case in Nazi Germany. If individuals, couched in bureaucracies, become desensitized to cruelty and suffering because they are so encased in their particular specialized niches, so unaware of the end results of the total operation, and so engaged in the technicalities of their craft that they are not interested in larger questions, they are, as Speer suggests, insulated against reality. Arendt argued that a "mass society," in which the individual is caught up in social movements rather than specific institutions such as political parties, replaced a society of citizens in Germany. When much of the institutional framework is either missing or being recreated as mass culture, individuals have no comprehension of the real conditions in their social environment. (As Arendt notes, if this insight is valid, the youth culture of North America during the 1960s and 1970s, and the similar movements in France and Latin America, where a theory of participatory democracy with no intervening parties or structural discipline were popular, would have likewise created what she calls mass society.) Her argument here, however, is somewhat inconsistent with her argument on the extreme bureaucratization and rationality of the Nazi state.

The case study of Nazi Germany shows how a quiescent, if not actively complicit, population may permit the demise of democracy and the rise of racism and the euthanasia movement. Hitler was able to tap into long-standing prejudices and sentiments of a large part of the German population and turn them into his own ideological rationale for genocide – with popular support. This interpretation is also suggested by much of what Speer wrote. But it is a jump to equate these developments with mass society – an undifferentiated mass, each person without individuality. Individuality may, in fact, be enhanced by such insulation. The problem may not be atomization, lack of individuality, or mass society (which remains undefined and problematic for any comparative study), but the combination of a cultural history that allowed for treating persons as "outside the universe of mutual obligation," to use Helen Fein's wording, and a structural condition that included the breakdown of government, near anarchy, impoverishment, and, finally, a leader with energy and an optimistic vision.

ARGENTINA

To the military forces and the high priests of the Catholic Church, there is one overriding explanation for what occurred: the "Marxist threat." They were persuaded that if they did not act, if they failed to kill the enemy once and for all, the country would fall to the communists and become a satellite of the USSR or of Cuba. Their explanation is that the subversive forces posed a genuine threat to society and that this defence was a full-scale war. The army defended the national interest, they claimed, and some among them have expressed these views in books and press releases (Díaz Bessone, 1988; Etchecolatz, 1983). One officer in the Marchak (1999: 272) study explained:

This government wanted to fight legally against the guerrillas through the existing justice system, but it was impossible to undertake investigations and procure sentences, because of fear, of terror. Why is that? It is very simple. A judge investigates a terrorist act – an assassination, a bomb. The only thing the terrorist has to do is phone the judge or his wife saying, for example, "You have a daughter of such-and-such age and she goes to such-and-such school and makes such-and-such journey each day – well, be careful ..." So, since the regular justice system had no success in investigating and sentencing the guerrillas, the government had to create a special organ, a special federal system, with judges who, for different reasons, were ready to put their lives at stake, their tranquillity, to investigate, judge, and sentence the guerrillas. In this way they managed to imprison many people ... So terribly harsh procedures were used for several reasons, and a main reason was that the legal processes, the justice system, and the politicians, were not up to their responsibilities.

A very different point of view is that of a priest sympathetic to the "third world priests movement" that was established in 1967 shortly before the Medellin Conference of the Latin American Episcopate. Following the teachings of Popes John XXIII and Paul VI, many Latin American priests and a few bishops came to the conclusion that socialism was consistent with Christianity; that the profit motive, inequality, racism, and much else that they found in capitalism were contrary to the teachings of Jesus. These views ran afoul of the teaching of the Argentine church hierarchy and were anathema to the military forces. This priest told (Marchak):

In 1976 I had the feeling that we were going over the precipice and were not able to stop. Just before this happened, I thought that the politicians, those who had power, the church, none of them reacted. The violence was terrible, violence in the streets. Yet they did nothing. It would have been possible to judge the president and to put a civilian in as interim president, call elections, do something, rather than have a military coup ... faced with the violence that existed before the military coup, some people welcomed the coup. Many people thought it was a solution. And the military thought they were the saviours ... In this parish we always had a great concern for reality and we were criticized because of that. The authorities claimed that we were always involved in politics. We had cared for Chilean refugees, and that was regarded as a serious crime ... I believe that the military were made to believe, made to believe – they were convinced that they were the moral reserve of the country against communism, which was seen as the destruction of the nation. And above all – another sin of our western and Christian culture – communism is against our style of life as Christians, you see? So they took the flag of the country and of religion. (262–3)

Marxism was clearly the announced enemy. But one theorist, David Pion-Berlin (1983, 1989) argues that it was monetarism that actually motivated the military to conduct its war against perceived subversives. In his view, this economic theory was capable of motivating the military, and the oligarchs behind them, to kill anyone in the way of achieving the ideological objectives: downsizing of the labour force, destruction of the unions, decrease in wages, removal of tariffs and protections for domestic capital, and reduction of the state's role in domestic affairs. Certainly, the economic ministers under both Isabel Perón and the military junta tried to impose monetarist solutions on the economy, but the military itself did not go along with many of the nostrums of neo-liberalism. For example, it never agreed to privatize many of the industries owned by the military itself. In the Marchak study, no evidence was found to support the claim; indeed, the military personnel and the priests and others who supported them were not (at least not obviously or in terms of their formal training) schooled in economic theory, so if they had a preference for neo-liberalism, it was not founded on a knowledgable basis. However, it must be noted that many of the former guerrillas and human rights advocates thought that neo-liberalism had motivated the military.

There is a tendency in left-wing ideology to suppose that military forces are puppets of an economic class above them. But in Argentina the military, having ruled the country through most years since 1930, had considerable independence. Military forces owned factories that accounted for 5 per cent of the gross national product. They had numerous sources of independent wealth. The agro-industrial elite had meanwhile lost much of its clout and did not rule the country by the 1970s. Foreign-owned companies were gradually withdrawing because the relatively small Argentine market wasn't all that profitable and the conditions of operation were not agreeable. In short, the military forces were operating on their own, though they were deferential to the various economic elites. The elites, in turn, were not homogeneous, and their needs were by no means similar. Even the domestic bourgeoisie was not homogeneous, and the various economic measures introduced by the military both during this period and at earlier times were not protective of the interests of any one sector of the elite. There is no hard evidence of any international sources that might have propped up the military. Argentina was as small a market as Canada, but farther away from other world markets to which it might have sold its products. The population at that stage was not more than 30 million, and a substantial proportion would not be in the market for their cars or other products. Argentina enjoyed no tariff preference; it had some oil, but not such a quantity that it was unique or especially valuable to the United States. It had a corrupt union bureaucracy, though this in itself was not a major disincentive for foreign investment, since the unions were deeply influenced by foreign automobile companies. Argentina had corrupt governments – but so did many other countries. That in itself is no reason to suppose that either the United States or other countries were behind the state terrorism of the 1970s, either because they favoured monetarism (neo-liberalism as it was later dubbed) or because of other reasons. In any event, monetarism failed in Argentina.

CHILE

Politics had become the overwhelming preoccupation of much of the population in Chile because the state had so much control over their lives. Chileans found themselves obliged to take sides, left or right, in a society that had no non-state institutional capacity to deal with the ideological polarization. In the view of analyst Arturo Fontaine Talavera (nd), "the key decisions of the parties from the forties on cannot be understood except as responses and reactions to what was often called 'the Marxist threat.'" Yet neither the left nor the non-military right provided a unified or organized opposition to military control. When the coup occurred, there was virtually no open opposition, and the first signs of popular opposition did not occur until 1983.

Only the Catholic Church maintained open opposition to the junta. Talavera, surveying this history, argues that the society at the time of the coup and continuing through the 1980s was divided into opposing blocks, and the military governed with the support of one of these groups. He also argues that the neo-liberal agenda emerged long before Pinochet's reign, in the Catholic University, business schools, and other public and private institutions (6). It was subsequently adopted by Pinochet, though not before the coup.

Javier Martinez and Alvaro Diaz (1996: 2–7) agree that the economic transformation was not the deliberate policy of the military junta at the time it staged the coup. They identify four fallacies in many explanations of what happened in Chile: that economic change was due to the dictatorial nature of the Pinochet regime; that the return to democracy was the result of successful economic transformation; that the process of nationalization and state intervention was an important obstacle to realization and success of the neo-liberal model; and that the Chilean experience is an example of capitalism through means of a civic rebellion against the state, limiting its sphere of action and extending individual liberties. In their estimation, the military dictatorship emerged as a reaction to the unmanageable situation in Chile during the Allende period: "The junta's claim to legitimacy was based on the restoration of political order, not economic transformation." Thus, as we will see in the case study, the radical economic program was an add-on, not a cause for the military coup. Martinez and Diaz go on to argue that it was "not so much the regime's use of force, but rather its autonomy from the immediate interests of the social groups that had brought it to power and that permitted the Pinochet government to carry out a complete restructuring of Chilean capitalism." Finally, they argue, contrary to much contemporary thinking on this subject, one of the biggest threats to the success of the Chilean economic transformation between 1978 and 1983 was the rigidity of the decision-making process, connected to the dictatorial nature of the regime.

Human rights activists and spokespersons for the several right-wing think tanks provide insights in interviews from the ideological left and right on the events in Chile (Marchak and Marchak, interview notes, unpublished, 1997 and 1998, identities protected):

Human rights activist
In the United States they created the "ideologia de la Seguridad Nacional" (national security doctrine), and this became the ideology of the militaries in Latin America. The principal issue is that the enemy is not outside, but inside, and is Marxism, and you have to eliminate this enemy: this is the ideology. So when the military in Chile took power, they believed they were to save the life of the nation, so any person that had this idea (Marxism) had to be killed. This is the terrible thing because you see, in my country 90 per cent of the people were simple people, peasants, workers, students, and they don't have arms in their hands. They were taken in the houses, in the works, in the universities.

And they took them as prisoners and treated them like an enemy, with torture. We in Chile were in chaos in 1973 because of the intervention of the United States. The intervention was with money to the right wing people in our country. For Allende it was very difficult. He tried to go with socialism by the legal institutions, because the parliament, it was still there. The society was very polarized between the left and the right. The CIA created the chaos ... Then Pinochet took the power and the international organizations gave money to the junta – the World Bank, the United States.

Spokesperson for a right-wing institute:

Communists were all the time skeptical about Allende, because communists are quite rational, are quite clear, and even Castro said "Allende, you are bad, you are a lot of socialists, they are junk people, they are quite hysterical." Do you remember the statement of Lenin about the left-wing people? He used to say that they were the child illness of communism ... all of the different political parties at that time – the Christian Democrats, the National Party, the Radicals, etc., – all of them were trying to say that the military should intervene to overthow the Allende government ... And by the way, those people who were killed were not killed because they were doing nothing ... [violence] started not in 1973 but it started before that. Think about this, in the Congress, in the socialist Congress of Chiyan [city south of Santiago], they called for a revolution at that time ... the question is, what were you doing at that time, you are calling for a civil war, you are calling for a revolution. And this is the real point.

The left and the right here were equally convinced that the society was on the precipice. Looking back on it, one commentator who had supported the policies of the Allende government acknowledged that they were too ambitious, too threatening to the middle and upper classes, rash and presumptuous. But at the time, in a highly polarized climate, with what seemed like the opportunity of a lifetime to make a real difference to the society, the young zealots of the socialist left thought history was on their side. The right-wing speaker defended the excesses of the counter-revolution with reference to the subversives who openly called for revolution, and the left-wing speaker blamed the United States and neo-liberalism for the same excesses.

*

The politicides in Cambodia, Argentina, and Chile were all embedded in the Cold War ideological context. These, and many other, societies were deeply affected by American actions taken in defence of the United States and explained in terms of threats to the well-being of Third World societies. It would be a mistake to take the American influence as the root cause of the politicides, yet equally imperceptive to ignore that context and American influence. The United States defended its economic interests and its dominant position within what it called "the free world," a term meaning the world in which American capital could flow freely over borders. The core states of empires and imperial states have always defended their territorial and their economic interests: the United States is no different from its predecessors.

5

Who Are the Ordinary Men?

Two diametrically opposed versions permeate our thinking about the people who perpetrate state crimes. One is that these events are the work of monsters and are irrational outbursts of hatred arising out of long-standing prejudices. They engage followers because people are like sheep, obeying orders. The other is that these crimes are rational outcomes of overly organized bureaucrats armed with a plan for a future society and a trained incapacity to empathize with their victims. Neither approach is convincing: genocide, much like every other huge venture undertaken by human communities, is both rational and irrational, the more so because the actors are generally steeped in a justifying ideology that erases from their memory and understanding why they are acting this way. Whether organized into detailed operational units as in the Holocaust or loosely joined together and given short-term militia training as in Rwanda, the deed is done in the name of gods, nation, tribe, or faith so that one group will dominate another. The methods may be as rational as modern science purports to be, but the intentions often take the form of killing in the belief that it will purify society. Morality is not suspended in these episodes; it is merely reinterpreted.

RATIONALITY AND IRRATIONALITY

If rationality is defined as selecting the most efficient and effective route to a known goal, with no concern about the morality or even good sense of the goal itself, then killing enemies is not necessarily irrational. In the case of the USSR's genocidal behaviour towards Ukrainians, we observed that an instrumentalist interpretation could apply:

the dominant power needed a resource, the subordinate group failed to provide it, and their failure could become contagious, so the dominant power eliminated the resisters. If instrumentalist reasoning is used, many of the genocides described here could be seen as rational means to achieve known objectives. Having determined that certain minorities polluted the space and consumed the food needed by "pure Aryans" in Europe, the use of gas ovens was a rational choice for Nazis as a means of killing the polluters.

However, if we define rationality in terms of assumptions about the world and the goals such assumptions lead to – whether they "make sense" for the society – we find ourselves in the morass of cultural judgments where what would make sense to an insider appears totally irrational to the observer. The killing of Jews in Germany appears irrational in the context of conducting a major war with external powers; only people immersed in fundamentally irrational racist ideologies could believe that such action made sense. The killing of resident Tutsis by Hutus in Rwanda appears irrational unless we shared the belief of the Hutus that invading Tutsis would kill them if they did not pre-empt their own slaughter. Pol Pot's apparently crazed determination to purify Kampuchea is beyond rational understanding for most outsiders, yet they have not experienced, as so many of his followers had, the starvation and humiliation that were the lot of peasants in pre-revolutionary Cambodia. From the perspective of many murderous regimes, the choice between killing enemies or subversives and incarcerating or otherwise persecuting them is also a rational decision: dead enemies, provided they are not able to become martyred in the process, tell no tales. Indeed, as we have noted elsewhere, genocidaires not infrequently deny at the time, and even more so generations later (as in Turkey), that any genocide occurred. Proof of annihilation is often hard to establish.

Though the term *rational* is problematic, we often hear commentary that implies that genocidal states are by their nature irrational. Autobiographical and biographical accounts of some leaders – Napoleon, Stalin, Hitler, and Pol Pot – depict power-hungry and extraordinarily egocentric characters. They are also charismatic, capable of attracting and retaining loyal followers who will go to their death in defence of their leaders. On the orders of such leaders, ordinary people, so the argument runs, act like automatons, apparently incapable of independent assessment of what is proposed and what they are doing. And what they are doing appears to be fundamentally irrational. It is possible that a disproportionate number of psychopaths are attracted to the job of torturer, and a disproportionate number of egotistical and power-hungry people are attracted to the jobs at the head of the troops (whether the troops are in armies, corporate hierarchies, universities, or political parties may not matter). Napoleon was probably a proto-type of the personality type attracted to jobs that involve high risk, huge power, ego-inflation and cultist status, and capacity to endanger or kill others with impunity (Johnson, 2002). Nasty as these leaders may have been, however, neither they nor their followers were neces-sarily irrational. When scholars examine their assumptions and objec-tives, they conclude that their methods were as rational as human methods generally are (which may not say much, but such recognition removes them from the realm of the exceptional). Indeed, some schol-ars, especially those dealing with Holocaust studies, have concluded that rationality itself is the problem.

A 1980 study of the German perpetrators of genocide concluded that not more than 10 per cent of the ss could be classified as "abnormal," as measured by conventional clinical criteria (Kren and Rapoport, 1980: 70). This percentage is consistent with the study reported by Christopher Browning (1998): the perpetrators were, for the most part, "ordinary men." They were doing their job. The question remains: How is it possible for ordinary people to inflict torture, mass murder, and other atrocities on unarmed civilians? The possible answers pro-posed in the literature include the human tendency to obey authority; praise; group support; conformity to group norms; distancing and de-humanization; and modernity.

Authority and Obedience

To begin with, there is the issue of authority and obedience. In every case that we examine in this book, and every other case for which we have adequate information, we find popular support for leaders who propose to solve otherwise intractable problems by killing off those whom they perceive to be responsible. Sometimes there are apparently good reasons to hold the victims responsible; often there is only the most tangential or circumstantial evidence. In either case, the popula-tion is willing to be persuaded of the necessity and, frequently, ordinary people not only cheer from the sidelines but actively engage in the slaughter. This response would suggest that people are conditioned to obey authority figures.

A well-known experiment conducted by Stanley Milgram (1974) on unsuspecting volunteers may be cited in support of that hypothesis. The volunteers were given the task of pressing a buzzer which, they were told, would impose electrical pain on subjects whom they understood to be other volunteers. The buzzer was to be pushed whenever the subject gave an incorrect response to a question. The electrical pain was supposed to increase with each incorrect response. The majority of volunteers did as they were told; furthermore, they did so more readily when they could not see the subject or hear the screams. Only later were the volunteers informed that the subjects were in collusion with the researcher and that they experienced no real pain. We do not know whether the pain of discovering their own culpability in this experiment permanently harmed the psyches of the volunteers. Milgram himself had doubts about its ethics. But he did demonstrate that when people are told to do grizzly things by someone they are inclined to accept as a legitimate authority figure, they do what they are told. He also found that the willingness to give the strongest electrical impulse dropped off significantly when the authority figure was not physically present, and that many of the recruits refused to comply when the orders were given by people who were not regarded as authority figures. The larger argument applicable to our study is, of course, that troops told to kill people do so because they obey authority; moreover, even untrained civilians tend to follow authority too far along the terrorist path.

Our respect for authority is linked to the more general processes involved in "legitimation." If we regard the authority as legitimate (in the experimental case, the authority figure represented science and professional education), we are predisposed to believe its pronouncements and accept its assurances. Professional soldiers would be expected to regard their superiors as the legitimate arm of the state irrespective of their personal relationships with those individuals. Obedience is a normal condition within any line hierarchy that has legitimacy. It would not be surprising for soldiers to accept as truth that a specified group is the enemy and to kill on command. Obedience would be even more assured if the soldiers had been subjected to persistent propaganda about the enemy and their own superiority to it, as was the case in Nazi Germany. Or if they were involved in a brutalizing war experience where failure to obey could result in being killed by the enemy. Another potential influence would be career objectives: armies and police forces have a hierarchy of authority, and individuals who stand up to tough conditions early on are more likely to become superior officers afterwards.

Where we accept authority as legitimate, we are more likely to follow its orders.

Earlier we noted that authoritarian cultures are more likely to spawn deadly regimes than are more democratic or permissive cultures. This observation is consistent with the argument that where we accept authority as legitimate, we are more likely to follow its orders. The legitimacy of the orders are more likely to be debated in democratic societies where political parties vie for public attention and votes and divergent opinions are encouraged within the social fabric. Of the cases examined here, Chile was the only functioning democracy before the coup that ushered in the Pinochet military regime. But even there, the culture, apart from the political machinery of elections, leaned towards authoritarian rather than liberal forms. A strong Catholic Church, a rural oligarchy, a highly centralized state, and a central place in the history and fabric of the society for hierarchically organized military forces were all vital components of the authoritarian culture. Indeed, the military came to power to re-establish traditional authority where, in the urban centres and mining towns, it was being eroded by demands for greater participation in democratic governance by the formerly marginalized populations and unionized workers. Rwanda and Burundi were endowed with the electoral machinery of democracy, but the forms did not result in the attitudes and ancillary organizations of a functioning democracy. Argentina, likewise, had the electoral machinery from time to time, and the government thrown out by the military coup of 1976 had been elected, but the history of the country from 1930 onwards included many military governments. Moreover, the state was highly centralized, just as in Chile, and the patriarchal, ultramontanist Catholic Church was the dominant non-state institution. As in Chile, the military junta's agenda was to re-establish a traditional authoritarian society against the "unpatriotic" and "communist" demands of "unruly" students and "greedy" unions. In all these cases, then, the social fabric engendered authoritarian attitudes that facilitated dictatorial governance and obedience to rulers who declared war on their own citizens.

Ersatz Power An authoritarian culture is not an explanation in another laboratory experiment, this one conducted by Philip Zimbardo in

1973 (cited in Bauman, 1991: 166–67). American male students were randomly divided into two groups labelled prisoners and guards; prisoners were given prison garb, and guards were provided with uniforms and dark glasses. They were instructed to have no personal relationships and to obey a series of regulations that were essentially humiliating for the prisoners. After that, the authority figures (the experimenters) left it up to the students to devise their interactions. Within a few days the guards had become arrogant, demanding, and inhumane in their treatment of the prisoners; the prisoners, in turn, had become submissive and accepting of their own humiliation. The experimenters concluded that when people have absolute power over others, they lose moral inhibitions against committing cruel acts. This finding is disturbing because it suggests that not only do humans tend to obey authority figures but that, when they gain some power over others, they become bullies; moreover, those without power become servile. Absolute power, as Lord John Acton observed long ago, corrupts absolutely. In less extreme examples from daily life we have all observed a similar phenomenon when some "petty bureaucrat," as we are inclined to phrase this observation, "thinks that because he has a uniform he has the right to be a bully."

All is not bleak on this score. In this and other experiments there are always a few people who resist the temptation to use force against others. No one has found an adequate explanation for these individuals, who seem to have no common characteristics other than their refusal to go along with acts they regard as repugnant, if not immoral. This finding provides evidence against an argument about genetic predispositions and suggests, instead, that socialization is the more important variable. Those who grow up in environments where they are expected to make moral decisions and take responsibility for them, and where they are encouraged to respect others as equals, are probably less likely than those raised in authoritarian environments to refuse to engage in bullying tactics. This conclusion is supposition, however, because we have insufficient knowledge about the differences between those who become bullies with a little power, or who become servile when bullied, and those who refuse to fall into either behavioural pattern.

Praise and Group Support

George Browder's (1996: 28–23) examination of the process by which the SS took over the police forces throughout Germany emphasizes the psychological dimensions involved in this transformation. Policemen were praised and their opinions solicited; they were assured, cynically, that when the Nazis took over they would "stand above politics and become truly the police of the entire people." They were authorized to act in dangerous ways and supported by group reinforcement methods that smothered cognitive and moral dissonance. Of the sD and Sipo security forces (see chapter 9 on Nazi Germany), Browder observes that many of the individuals who were recruited had in common "idealistic self-images and goals, and a need to protect their organizations from disreputable elements" (232). He continues: "Their positive human characteristics were admirable, and their weaknesses were in no way extraordinary. Yet they succumbed to sanctioned violence as extremely and thoroughly as psychopaths, while their involvement was far more deadly for the victims. They contributed their significant talents to the escalation of Nazi tendencies from mere rhetorical outbursts and random violence to previously unimaginable levels of execution."

The explanation, Browder argues, actually lies in their more admirable qualities. They were intent on creating organizations, meeting goals, competing with other organizations, and proving themselves as groups and individuals. "If those men had been born in the Allied countries," he says, "they might have been heroes in that war." He does not excuse them from the obligation to exercise moral judgment but argues that they had grown up in the despair of the Weimar Republic, had emerged into adulthood while the Nazis were developing a new ideological context, and were subject to the authority structure of the Nazi police state: all these conditions tended to deprive them of their capacity to understand what they were doing or to contravene group norms as well as orders.

Conformity to Group Norms

Christopher R. Browning (1998) examined judicial interrogations conducted in the 1960s of some 125 members of a reserve police battalion that had been obliged to round up Jews in Poland in 1942. The men were middle-aged, working-class Germans from Hamburg, too old for army duty. Most had no previous experience of the German occupation methods in Eastern Europe. Their task, involuntarily undertaken, was to round up working-age men for a work camp and to shoot women, children, and the elderly on the spot. Their commander informed them that the Jews endangered the welfare of Germans. He also told them that any who could not handle the task were permitted to avoid its more unpleasant requirements. Most of the recruits did as they were authorized; only a few refused.

While agreeing that such conditions as wartime brutalization, racism, careerism, deference to authority, ideological indoctrination, and bureaucratic segmentation or routinization of tasks had some impact in other theatres of war, Browning points out that these recruits did not act "out of frenzy, bitterness, and frustration but with calculation" (161). They had not suffered wartime brutalization through previous combat; rather, they became increasingly brutalized after they began to kill. He attributes this progression to a psychological phenomenon known as "distancing," by which "the other," as the objectified enemy, is dehumanized. Bureaucratic procedures may be a means of depersonalizing others, but these men were not in bureaucratic positions. They were "quite literally saturated in the blood of victims shot at point-blank range" (162). They had no special attributes, being similar to any other Germans in demographic and other respects. There seem to have been no self-selection or careerism factors that might have explained why most of the men complied with orders to kill Jews, or why a few refused to do so. Fear of reprisals was a possible explanation, the most common explanation given by many indicted Germans during the Nüremburg trials, but Browning points out that in the entire forty-five years during which postwar trials were carried on, there was not a single documented case in which refusal to obey an order to kill unarmed civilians resulted in the death of the soldier or policeman. He acknowledges that "putative duress" may have been involved, whereby the men believed that refusal to obey would result in dire consequences. But in the particular case of this battalion, he points out that this excuse would not have held water because a few of the men consistently refused to obey and were not punished by the officers.

In fact, he concludes, they were more likely to be punished by their peers, and in the end it was really peer pressure much more than any other condition that pushed most of them to obey the orders. Conformity, not authority, is his explanation. The conformity was not of the kind where a person is afraid of his peers' responses to his failures; more likely, he believes he will let them down or force them to do more than their share of the dirty work if he fails. It is, in short, an admirable empathetic response to the situation.

Conformity to group norms may be a superior explanation for obedi-
ence to authority under extreme conditions than merely the tendency to
obey authority.

Again, there is no simple explanation for the few – between 10 and
20 per cent in Browning's estimation – who refused to kill. Most of the
men who did not kill cited "sheer physical revulsion" rather than ethical or political principles for their refusal. The repugnance was initially
shared by the men who conformed, though later, with some changes in
procedures, they accepted further killing assignments. A very few men
expressed reservations on political grounds ("I'm against the Nazis" or
"I'm a communist") or on grounds of explicit moral principles. They
were enabled to withdraw from the action because their own commander in this particular war scene was opposed to the killings and
sympathized with those who were unwilling to proceed.

On reflection, the deduction that conformity may be more important
than authority is not a surprising revelation about human life. We are
extremely social creatures. We are utterly dependent on others for the
first several years of our lives, and most of us remain at least interde-
pendent with others for the remainder of our times on earth. We learn
to speak in languages of others around us, we conceptualize the world
in the same terms, we share the prejudices and assumptions of our time
and place, and we are embedded in cultures. Yes, we have independent
wills, but distinct limits are established by our language and culture to
how much independence we are capable of exercising. And, in fact,
very few individuals in any culture are capable of making entirely independent choices, especially choices that would be unpopular or would
bring upon them the opprobrium of their confrères. In many of the
cases we encounter in this book, even the leaders, the torturers, and
those who apprehend victims knowing what their fate will be are simply ordinary people doing what they understand to be their jobs or
their patriotic duty. Convinced that if they do not destroy the group
they have defined as enemies, the society as a whole, or their religion,
or even the whole of civilization will be jeopardized, they give and obey
orders. When the daily task is done, they go home to a loving family;
and on Sunday they go to church, secure in the knowledge that they are
doing their part for the salvation of the good people. Often these mur-
derers are idealists, or at least strongly attached to their nation or to
particular concepts of god and civilization. Army officers interviewed
in Argentina were adamant that they had contributed to the saving of

not only the nation but also the whole of Western civilization and Christianity (Marchak, 1999). If we assume, as they had been trained to do, that their society was endangered by subversive Marxist ideas, and if we acknowledge that their professional duty was to save the society, the slaughter of teenagers labelled Marxists was a rational act of national defence.

Distancing and Dehumanization of Victims

Browning suggested that the "ordinary men" in the battalion had developed a capacity to distance themselves from the victims. At its extreme, distancing involves dehumanization, not recognizing the victims as human beings with emotions and intellects similar to those of the perpetrators. It mirrors Helen Fein's concept of victims as outside the realm of mutual obligation. What is the process by which distancing occurs? Racism that has long resided in a society, and racist ideologies deliberately propagated during wartime, are among possible explanations. Bureaucratic procedures are another explanation, often combined with racist propaganda.

Individuals, when pressured or obliged to kill other human beings, may create a psychological distance between themselves and the victims so they are not able to feel human empathy for their victims. Underlying racism, ideologies, and bureaucratic procedures may enable the process of distancing.

Modern warfare is conducted on an understanding of the distancing phenomenon. American soldiers in Vietnam, in Iraq during the Gulf War, and in Afghanistan in 2001 bombarded areas they were told were held by the enemy while they flew far above their targets in warplanes equipped with every possible mass killing device. They could not see or hear their victims and, like Milgram's experimental subjects, could not empathize at such a distance. In their case, the distance was literal. In other examples it is more symbolic and depends even more on the perpetrators' capacity to believe that those whom they torture and kill are truly enemies and well outside the realm of human obligation.

The persuasion is not straightforward. In the Nazi case, there is considerable evidence that non-Jewish German citizens were not easily turned into rabid anti-Semites. Pointing out that there was a "discontinuity" between the "traditional, pre-modern Jew-hatred and the modern exterminatory design" of the Holocaust, Bauman (1989: 185–7) says: "As far as the function of popular feelings is concerned, the ever-growing volume of historical evidence proves beyond reasonable doubt an almost negative correlation between the ordinary and traditional 'neighbourly,' competition-based anti-Jewish sentiment and the willingness to embrace the Nazi vision of total destruction and to partake of its implementation." Contrary to the supposition that the German state killed Jews as part of the long history of anti-Semitism, the argument propounded in the immediate aftermath of the war and most recently by Goldhagen (1996), Bauman says there is "a growing consensus among historians of the Nazi era that *the perpetration of the Holocaust required the neutralization of ordinary German attitudes toward the Jews, not their mobilization*" (emphasis in original).

The vast majority of non-Jewish German citizens had "deep-seated inhibitions against inflicting pain and physical suffering, and ... stubborn human loyalty to their neighbours, to people whom one knows and has chartered into one's map of the world as persons, rather than anonymous specimens of a type." Indeed, Heinrich Himmler complained about the inability of even devoted party members to recognize that their beloved neighbour, a Jew, was fit for extermination. His problem, and that of Julius Streicher, editor of the anti-Semitic newspaper, *Der Sturmer*, was to convince their own followers, as well as the citizens more generally, that all Jews fit their stereotypes as criminals and competitors for essential resources.

The dehumanization of Jews was accomplished, in the view of Raul Hilberg (1985: 999; Bauman, 1989: 190–2), through a process of rationalization and bureaucratization beginning with an identification of them as enemies; then the expropriation of their business properties and dismissals from employment; then their rounding-up and ghettoization so they ceased to be neighbours and friends of non-Jews; then their exploitation as labour; then the reduction of their food supplies so they not only faced starvation but also looked unlike well-fed citizens; and, finally, their annihilation and the confiscation of their personal effects. Yet this process is not the same as that followed in all the mass murders encountered in the past century. All have humiliated, distanced, and dehumanized the victims, but not all have been as methodically planned and performed as the Nazi processing of Jews. The bureaucratization of mass murder under Hitler was neither unique nor commonplace: it was one, not the only one, of the ways that such horror shows have been conducted. Nonetheless, the mental process that is enhanced via bureaucratic rationalism, even if not invented by it, has in common with other rationalizations for genocide or politicide a stubborn argument: that these others are a threat to our survival.

Modernity, Bureaucracy, and Technology

Though authority, obedience, and conformity are fundamental aspects of human relationships, they are not everywhere harnessed to the service of corporate organization of the kind that developed in Western societies over the past few centuries. Corporate organizations are rational bureaucracies where individual careers are established along particular and predictable lines, human relationships are based on impersonal criteria, work is planned not by any one individual but by groups with specific goals in mind, and time is allotted to projects in a socially organized pattern. It is these eminently rational bureaucracies, together with deductive science and advanced technology, – in combination often called "modernity" – that some writers sell as the cause of genocide.

R. Hrair Dekmejian (1986: 86–93) argues that in both the Armenian deportation and the Nazi Holocaust there are five "distinctive features" that are "the necessary conditions for killing on a mass scale," including "organizational specificity; planning, programming, and timing; bureaucratic efficiency and comprehensiveness; technological capability; and the ideological imperative." He proposes that "these attributes are the consequences of the modernization of the state machinery." Hannah Arendt (1969) and Zygmunt Bauman (1989), both in reference to Nazi Germany, go so far as to argue that modernity, with its rational bureaucracy, is the absolutely necessary ingredient for the commitment of genocide. Guillermo O'Donnell (1979), addressing the problem of state repression in Argentina, argues that large societies at the periphery of capitalism develop authoritarian bureaucracies as the means of retaining and reproducing a capitalist economy dominated by transnational corporations. These authoritarian organizations become part of the subsequent politicide.

Max Weber, whose theory of the state is cited elsewhere in this book, is also the guru to whom many theorists resort when trying to define these bureaucracies: "The decisive reason for the advance of bureaucratic organization has always been its purely technical superiority over any other form of organization. ... Precision, speed, unambiguity, knowledge of the files, continuity, discretion, unity, strict subordination, reduction of friction and of material and personal costs – these are raised to the optimum point in the strictly bureaucratic administration" (Parsons, 1966: 21). This description undoubtedly overstates the precision and subordination of contemporary bureaucracies, but his point was that such bureaucracies are, by comparison with alternative modes of organization for complex tasks, better able to maintain order and to process the work.

Weber argued that bureaucracies were fundamental to the growth of capitalism in the form of labour markets, calculations of profit, and democratic governments. In these, the state bureaucracy would be but one of several large, complex bureaucratic organizations. And the state bureaucracy itself would be complex because its manifold sections would deal with a wide variety of state concerns. While strict subordination would be in place within any one section, and the section heads would then, in turn, be subordinate to the next level of managers, no single person or group would ever be giving all the orders. The entire edifice is efficient precisely because decision-making and authority are dispersed, and the objectives of the diverse sections differ according to the expertise of the functionaries and the tasks they are expected to perform. The operation is rational in the sense that the tasks of each section are defined and the workers are expected to determine the most efficient and effective means of achieving recognized goals. There is no room in this enterprise for private emotions or vendettas. It is an idealization of the actual operation of bureaucracies, but it serves to emphasize the difference between a personal style of governance, as when a sultan or a chief determines strategies on the basis of friendships and marriage contracts, and a bureaucratic style designed to minimize personal criteria for decisions.

The importance of bureaucracies to contemporary capitalist government persuaded one theorist, Ted Gurr (1985: 46), to define government in these terms: "The essence of the state, past and present, is a bureaucratically institutionalized pattern of authority whose rulers claim to exercise sovereign (ultimate) control over the inhabitants of a territory, and who demonstrate enduring capacity to enforce that claim." Arendt (1969: 39) suggested that bureaucracy is the modern use of power where no one is ultimately accountable – it is rule by Nobody. Bauman (1989), a sociologist, further develops this line of thinking. Modernity, he argues, not just the technologies but also the impersonal bureaucracies, the scientific method, and many other developments that have dehumanized people creates the possibility to imagine, as well as execute, the plan for killing millions. He specifies as conditions for the Holocaust the existence of a rational state bureaucracy; the availability of modern science and technology; the rational, logical approach to problem-solving which, accompanying both these phenomena, permeates modern society; and the centralization of coercion in the state. He holds that modern, hierarchical bureaucracies deplete individuals down the line of moral fibre: they remove the sense of responsibility of actions taken on command. In this way the guards in concentration camps and all along the route through which the victims of the Nazis involuntarily travelled acted with extreme insensitivity towards them.

This argument is consistent with some of Albert Speer's observations. He remarked, for example, that there was an explicit requirement that each professional group maintain its separateness from others. People became highly specialized, talking only to those of similar professional standing and lacking experience of the other currents in society. Speer (1970: 65) also said that one condition of party membership was the acceptance of authority: "The ordinary party member was being taught that grand policy was much too complex for him to judge it. Consequently, one felt one was being represented, never called upon to take personal responsibility. The whole structure of the system was aimed at preventing conflicts of conscience from even arising."

Bauman (1989: 13) supports this view: "Modern civilization was not the Holocaust's *sufficient* condition; it was, however, most certainly its *necessary condition*. Without it, the Holocaust would be unthinkable. It was the rational world of modern civilization that made the Holocaust thinkable" (italics in original). In a similar vein, Browning (1998: 168) argues: "Segmented, routinized, and depersonalized, the job of the bureaucrat or specialist – whether it involved confiscating property, scheduling trains, drafting legislation, sending telegrams, or compiling lists – could be performed without confronting the reality of mass murder." Elsewhere he adds: "The Nazi mass murder of the European Jewry was not only the technological achievement of an industrial society, but also the organizational achievement of a bureaucratic society" (quoted in Bauman, 1989: 13). Leo Kuper (1981: 121) concurs: "Though engaged in mass murder on a gigantic scale, this vast bureaucratic apparatus showed concern for correct bureaucratic procedure, for the niceties of precise definition, for the minutiae of bureaucratic regulation, and the compliance with the law." Raul Hilberg (1985, 3: 994) concludes his study of the Holocaust in similar terms: "The machinery of destruction *was* the organized community in one of its special roles."

Critique of the Modernity Thesis Bauman's argument on this point is directed, as is much of the literature on the subject, to the Holocaust. But several of the genocides in the twentieth century (and many of those before it) cannot be attributed to bureaucratic rationality or modern technology. Indeed, Browning, though agreeing that bureaucracy facilitates mass murder, pointed out that this could not explain the actions of the reservists in the initial assignments where they killed Jews in cold blood. Subsequently, their tasks were more coordinated with others, and the division of labour provided them with a means of becoming desensitized to the suffering of the victims. They became more detached and could feel they were not really responsible for the action.

Although it is tempting to see bureaucracies as the means by which modern society absolves its functionaries of responsibility and obliges them to perform cruel actions on others, some writers have reservations with the explanation in historical terms even with reference to Nazi Germany. Though the literature tends to portray the German *Wehrmacht* as the ultimate war machine, absolutely rigid in its hierarchical organization and perfectionist in planning, the record reveals a less idealized picture of that bureaucracy. By the time the reservists were killing Jews in Poland, the war machine was in deep trouble, having completely failed to identify accurately the strengths of the Soviet army. The fact that it had to rely on middle-aged reservists is, in itself, indicative of the problems the careerists were running into. Much of what has been attributed to the German bureaucratic *Wehrmacht* was actually planned and orchestrated by the auxiliary forces of the ss and by special appointees. It was the ss that manned and controlled much, though not all, of the machinery for extermination of the Jews. This responsibility suggests that the Nazi hierarchy did not trust the functioning civilian and military bureaucracies to kill civilians.

With respect to advanced technology, many of the twilight wars of modern history were not fought with modern weaponry: Armenia in 1915–16, the starvation of Ukrainian peasants in 1932–33, the slayings of Tutsis by Hutus in Rwanda, 1994; the disappearances in all the Latin American cases: none of these massacres used sophisticated weapons, though radio communication was important in the case of Rwanda, and electrical prods in the case of Argentina. People were driven off their land, starved to death, killed by machetes, and tortured in primitive ways: the gas chambers were certainly more efficient, but many more primitive methods achieved the same deadly result. Apart from the mass media (the radio) and guns that are ubiquitous the world over, the argument about the necessity of modern bureaucracy as the context for crimes against humanity is thin when it comes to other cases of genocide or politicide.

The fact that the modern state has control of coercion cannot, in itself, prove that it will engage in the creation of concentration camps and the use of gas chambers. Terror is not a necessary outcome of bureaucratic control. Compartmentalization is enhanced by bureaucracy, but not invented by it. Compartmentalization under any circumstances is a means of avoiding responsibility for social actions. We do not need a bureaucratic context to rationalize our actions. Indeed, the taking of citizenship responsibility may be a novel development in human history. It arises with states and the notion of citizenship in states. It cannot apply in anarchic situations, since there is no focus for either citizenship or responsibility. And it could only arise in situations where persons designated as citizens actually have, or believe themselves to have, a genuine role in the conduct of state actions. Further, if the culture of the state has defined some members of the society as "outside the universe of obligation" or as non-citizens, neither they nor others on their behalf are likely to take responsibility for their victimization.

Another problem with the modernity thesis is its argument that genocide is a modern phenomenon. Although it is true that populations were much smaller and less concentrated in past human history, so a genocide would not kill as many people as a modern one, and although modern methods used in Nazi Germany (death trains, gas chambers) were more efficient than more primitive methods, genocide is not a specifically modern happening. The Old Testament is replete with tribal massacres – many authored by an angry god – as Barrington Moore Jr. (2000) has shown in a study of the text. The expulsion of the Jews from Spain in the fifteenth and sixteenth centuries and, later, from Portugal were forms of genocide. The wars between Huguenots and Catholics in France and Britain in the seventeenth century were genocidal in intent on both sides. In another context, Moore (1966: 417) observes that the persistence of royal absolutism or, more generally, of a pre-industrial bureaucratic process into modern times has been an obstacle for democratization of some societies. This pattern reminds us that bureaucracy is not a modern invention, though its modern forms are pervasive today. Autocratic kings spawned their own bureaucracies, which could be extremely authoritarian and anti-democratic. The vast bureaucracies of empires that finally faded into history – the Ottoman, the Austro-Hungarian, the Russian, the Chinese – were not "modern" at all.

OVER THE PRECIPICE

In several of the cases under study, we have heard people speak about a headlong rush towards destruction, of going over a precipice where they could no longer stop themselves. Browning (1998) noted that once the German reservists had killed some of the Polish Jews, they became almost addicted to it, and they became more bloodthirsty as time went on, treating their victims as depersonalized animals. He attributed this result to distancing. But going over a precipice is also the image suggested by comments given to me by Chilean socialists in retrospective accounts about the failures of the Allende government. In the view of some of the leading figures of that time, the government was so determined to change the society fundamentally that it ignored signals of trouble. The victims were somewhat culpable in their own way, though their failures do not excuse the perpetrators of the politicide who reacted with such viciousness. A similar sense of destiny, of belonging to a period of time and of having lost the compass, was expressed to me by an Argentine citizen during another interview. She had been a member of the revolutionary student movement, the Montoneros, and she had gone underground with them after Juan Perón disowned the revolution. She explained (Marchak, 1999, interview with "Dolores": 181):

I was seventeen when the military killed people in Trelew in 1972. At that time being an activist was normal. We all believed that Argentina was going through the same process as that of May, 1968, in France, and the revolution of 1959 in Cuba. The role of Che Guevara gave us a sense of belonging. For us teenagers it was very important that he was an Argentine. We felt that we were part of the revolutionary history of Argentina. There was no possibility of being young and not being an activist; it was like a destiny.

Her understanding of that time in her country's history is echoed repeatedly by others who were young in the 1970s, including students who resisted taking up membership in the guerrilla movements. The cultural climate pushed young people towards the precipice almost as though the Pied Piper were leading the throng. On either side of a revolution, guerrillas as well as conventional armies become caught up in the events of their time, committed beyond the capacity to make individual decisions about the morality or even the rationality of group actions. It is not simply ideology that persuades them; it is a combination of conformity to group norms and a sense of belonging – an identity as a member, an authority seen as legitimate. Bureaucracies might provide these conditions, but clearly other forms of organization have the same capacities. The Montoneros, for instance, were organized into cells with an overall hierarchical structure, but were certainly not akin to a normal bureaucracy.

Bureaucracies may shield members from the totality in which they are contributors. Individuals make moral decisions about their own contributions, but we are all children of our time and place. Most of us conform or obey not because we are sadists or weak, but because we are human. This insight emerged most dramatically in the Eichmann trial, as reported in Arendt's (1964: 26–7) damning indictment of "normal persons." The defendant, she noted, was indeed a normal person, insofar as he was not an "exception within the Nazi regime." But, she said, "under the conditions of the Third Reich only 'exceptions' could be expected to react 'normally.'" Like Browning's "ordinary men" in the Reserve Battalion, Eichmann was simply doing his job. He was not particularly "evil," not a monster, not even an ideological zealot.

Ordinary people commit these crimes. The problem is that ordinary people, under conditions of war, duress, group pressure to conform, fear of real or imagined enemies or consequences of failure, or even in conditions of plunder and the excitement of adventure (as in the Belgium Congo, for example), go over the precipice. When they are in positions that do not require the commission of gross crimes against other humans, they may be able to reflect later on the times (in the cases of the Chilean socialists and the Montonera described above). But when their jump beyond peaceful interaction involves killing, the sheer power of destruction, something seems to happen to them.

One of Arendt's many critics, a torture victim of the Gestapo himself, said: "There is no 'banality of evil,' and Hannah Arendt, who wrote about it in her Eichmann book, knew the enemy of mankind only from hearsay, saw him only through the glass cage" (Jean Améry, quoted in Barnett, 1999: 24). Banality – it was a powerful image of 'ordinary men,' but, at the end of the day, inadequate. Ordinary men and women hold within them capacities for hatred, fear, blame, scorn, and arrogance even when, at their best, we can also be compassionate. We cannot identify the potential killers by their use of stereotypes or even their zealotry, though both are too often associated with cruelty. Ordinary people become hardened to the poor in their midst and reason that poverty is a choice of laziness; ordinary people justify their personal wealth and power on grounds that invariably ignore differences in birth conditions; ordinary people close their eyes to a world of great inequality. Ordinary people do so day in and day out; it is not a stance invented to rationalize killing – it merely precedes the process if the inequality is jeopardized.

The Breakdown of Authority

In all our case studies except the USSR, a breakdown of authority has almost immediately preceded the outbreak of crimes against humanity. In the USSR the breakdown had occurred earlier and the ramifications of change were still unfolding. In all cases except Yugoslavia, some sort of government had either continued on the basis of coercion or new groups had taken over the state, usually also relying on coercion. In Yugoslavia the entire state organization broke down, several different elites and strongmen took over parts of the country, and the remnants of the federal army emerged as a force without civilian control. Pressures for conformity would be enhanced in an army that exists without civilian controls, and in the Serbian army we see an entire group going over the precipice. For them the social world is divided into "us" and "them," and the "us" has to "look after itself." Looking after itself means killing others who get in the way of territorial ambitions. Others are now defined as enemies, beyond the pale of mutual obligation, no longer compatriots – indeed, no longer fully human. Where Bauman argues, eloquently, that morality precedes society in the form of "primeval moral drives" by which murder of fellow beings and other anti-social behaviour are *verboten*, we are obliged to consider such examples as Yugoslavia in the early 1990s as a laboratory where primeval drives turn out to be profoundly anti-social with respect to all groups defined as "others." Bureaucracy and rationality will not explain what happened in Yugoslavia: the bureaucracy was disrupted, and rational means to achieve known goals were invented day by day and were not self-evident even to the troops. The understood goal was survival of the "us" against "them," rational in only the most primitive sense and not reducible to bureaucratic socialization.

If we cannot blame our weakness on bureaucracy (while attributing to it an enhancement of reasons for irresponsible actions), what can we blame it on? Authority may be one reason; conformity another; distancing and dehumanization intensified by propaganda and racist or other stereotypes are all part of the package. But even with these potential explanations, we must finally ask: Is there no moral underpinning that might enable us to avoid these episodes of mass murder? If we imagine morality to consist of absolute proscriptions handed down by the gods, the only explanation must be the eternal sinfulness of human beings. That interpretation doesn't improve our comprehension at all; indeed, it provides absolution to the self-confessed sinner.

If we assume that morality is a socially constructed code, variable along with culture, we might interpret it as an ever-evolving construction explicitly designed to help people live together cooperatively. Indeed, persuading ourselves that the gods have authorized the code may improve our obedience to its strictures. We may accept this approach whether we take a Hobbesian stance on the nature of humanity (brutal and in need of being tamed by a strong sovereign) or a more Durkheimian approach (social beings dependent on society, and thus in need of a code for interactive behaviour). We might suppose that human animals, much like many other mammals (and even non-mammalian creatures), are social by nature and instinctively understand that social interaction rests on an avoidance of certain behaviours such as killing other members of the same species. But there is always an exception – where other members of the species are competing for the same essential resources. And that is the bottom line. We are capable of cooperation, and we have invented moral codes to keep us, collectively, in line. But where we find ourselves competing for whatever we regard as essential resources for our survival, we create distance, we cease to see ourselves as part of the same collectivity, and, in due course, we begin to consider elimination of the other as a way of saving ourselves.

Sometimes the competition is manifest and material. In the case of the USSR versus the Eastern Ukrainians, Stalin and his bureaucratic apparatus identified it in those terms. If they did not procure the grain, they, and the urban workers whose productivity was essential to the state, would face the threat of hunger. In the case of the Cambodian peasant army, again, the threat of hunger in the rural regions was palpable: if the urban bureaucrats were permitted to go on living their dissolute lives, the peasants would starve. In Rwanda, the Hutu had reason to fear the return of the Tutsi not only because the Tutsi might regain power but, even more, because there was already insufficient land for their own population. These concerns are, in a sense, outside morality. The decisions in each case to murder millions of people are not, in the culturally circumscribed ideas of most of the industrial world in the twenty-first century, morally excusable by virtue of the material reasons for their actions. But the point is that on-lookers and later scholars, who make judgments on the basis of the moral codes in societies where there is no real or perceived competition for resources, may be judging on spurious grounds.

In other cases the connection between material conditions and the conduct of a genocide or politicide is manufactured by the state. Hitler and the ss manufactured the pan-German odyssey not to kill the Jews, but to create a huge empire under their control filled with people who were pure and Germanic. The realization of that scheme depended on evicting non-Germans, of whom Jews, Gypsies, and Poles were leading members. The killing of Armenians in the Ottoman Empire was a means of opening up territory for Muslims so that the state would be a purely Muslim territory. The elimination of subversives in Argentina and Chile ensured that a particular authoritarian structure and class system would not be undermined. The reasoning is materialistic – sometimes with a rationale that outsiders can comprehend and perhaps even sympathize with; sometimes with a rationale that "makes sense" only within the ideological and cultural confines of those who perpetrate the genocide.

Power

To this point the problem of absolute power has not been fully confronted. The experiment by Zimbardo, reported by Bauman (1991), involving American students who turned into vicious guards and frightened prisoners with scarcely any input from authorities suggested that distancing in itself was not the complete answer. The distancing occurred always in the context of power; with or without authority, a group in all the experimental cases, and a group in the real cases of genocide, held a degree of power over others which allowed them to do as they pleased. They were not accountable to anyone. The restrictions of morality – for moral codes are always restrictive, preventative measures against the unleashing of human viciousness – were loosened. Power, ultimately, is the capacity to oblige others to do one's bidding. It may be manifested in vicious behaviour that humiliates others or, more subtly, in the cultivation of others through incentives and flattery. It may encourage others to care for their fellow humans or to distance themselves from them: power in itself does not prescribe the ideological message. But as we have observed in both experimental studies and in the gruesome examples of history, absolute power leads most frequently to the defining of others as subordinate, unequal, and finally unassimilable and unworthy of continued life. And this outcome brings us back to the original argument of this study: states, where political power is exercised, are charged with the task of sustaining an unequal hierarchy where some have power over others. Genocide and politicide are ultimately the outcomes where the state cannot achieve that sleight of hand through non-violent means.

6

The Janus State and the Problem of Intervention

The state is an organization with a monopoly of the legitimate use of armed force in a given territory and with the mandate to reproduce a system that always involves relationships of dominance and subordination. States that cannot reproduce the system have a high probability of committing human rights crimes.

Janus, meaning "opening" or "gate," was a two-faced god: Rome understood that the gates of the city had to open both ways. And that is the nature of the state as well. It must always face change and either thwart or accommodate it, yet it must always reinvent what already exists. Further, while obliged to reproduce the hierarchical system of its time, and invariably subject to the expectations and demands of those at the top, it also has to nurture and sustain a population that is closer to the bottom. When it cannot perform these dual tricks, dire consequences follow.

The Roman armies marched off to war through the arches of the city, sent to claim new territories and subject new populations to that ancient empire. But the army also marched back through the gate to pacify the population when it became restive. The army could be counted on to look after the patricians, provided the patricians were able to look after the army. When they could not do so, the army pushed them aside and took over. Much has changed over the centuries, but the basics of large human settlements have not changed. Those who believe that violence would be forever stopped if only we could change the system are unaware that, though the system has changed many times, it never really changes underneath. Empires have come and gone, economic regimes have passed by, but people reinvent systemic inequalities wherever there are large populations. This disparity is not caused by genetic differences: the genetic differences between individuals in any large population are so minimal that they could not account for the vast differences in status, wealth, and opportunities. The causes have much more to do with the way people congregate, work together, place values on diverse attributes, and define themselves and others, always trying to get a little bit more for themselves, a little bit more for those they consider their own. Class is a way of describing not only the development of difference but also the inheritance of it, and it is the inheritance more than anything else that those with power expect the state to protect. The protection of differential opportunities is the means of reproducing a system.

The two-faced state may be an imperfect human creation, but large populations need some kind of central political authority. Anarchy is unable to sustain a population for any length of time, and economic activity unconstrained by political institutions is mere plunder, as in the rape of Africa by colonial powers in the nineteenth century. A state is the means by which the ruling groups keep one another in line: the state is given the right to control the only legitimate army, and the state is charged with the task of establishing and maintaining a system of rules and laws that keeps the working class in line. In protecting the powerful, the state is also protecting the powerless, for when they are beset by war or anarchy their lot is infinitely worse. Over the centuries of the state's existence (including predecessors to modern states), less-powerful populations have persistently struggled for control of the state, hoping that control of the political realm might provide them with a capacity to prevent abuses in the economic realm. In fact, as the third millennium begins, there are capitalist societies where the state collects taxes from all, educates all, and provides a range of services that enable those at the top to live well and those at the bottom to survive with dignity. States perform a great range of tasks that markets cannot perform, and for many societies they perform these tasks well enough that peace is sustained over long periods of time.

Yet for all its utility (more than its virtue), the state is essentially an organization designed to keep a population under control, if not to wage war against neighbouring states. This situation was true in the Roman Empire; it is true in the modern state born in the Peace of Westphalia in 1648 as a conclusion to the Thirty Years' War in Europe. The growth of modern states and a capitalist economy out of the ashes of empires and feudalism in Europe eventually led to the development of nation-states throughout the world. These states represent the economic and political interests of their most powerful citizens, and for that reason they always involve a degree of coercion against their less-powerful citizens, especially when those citizens demand rights or assert themselves in ways that would strike at the balance of power in place. And by the Treaty of Westphalia, states agreed they would respect one another's boundaries. They would not intervene in one another's internal affairs.

"Nation-states" is possibly a misnomer, though over time the term "nation" has come to mean any bounded territory with a state apparatus governing it. The term "nation" also refers to an ethnic group, yet most states in the transition from feudalism and before the twentieth century were inhabited by persons of diverse ethnic descent. The Ottoman empire under the Turks was one of the first to attempt to eradicate "alien" populations – groups that were less numerous than the dominant one that held political power. Nazi Germany moved in the same direction: to bring into its territory all those it regarded as *echte* German and to evict, and finally eradicate, those whom it regarded as outside its realm of obligation. Many others of the genocides of modern history began as conflicts between ancestral ethnic groups, each with its own version of "nationhood."

At the end of the twentieth century, two major states continued to base citizenship on ancestry. Ironically, they were Germany, still denying citizenship to Turks and Yugoslavs who were into their third generation as guest-workers, yet willing to accommodate Germanic peoples who had been living in Eastern Europe since the war; and Israel, where citizenship depended on being Jewish, even when the term included people from wildly different cultures possessing highly diverse attitudes towards Judaism as a religion. Other states, however, dealing with citizens whose origins are diverse, have fashioned new cultures and their own ideologies to celebrate their "nationhood." And these, too, demonstrate the ironies of human political organization when, in the name of their respective nations that are signally lacking in ethnic homogeneity, governors act against their own citizens and defend their right to do so under the banner of "national sovereignty."

The nation-state that emerged during the centuries since 1648 was a territorial organization, backed by the potential (and often actual) use of force designed to perform two major tasks: to keep its own population under control and to prevent any intervention by outsiders. While the genocides of the twentieth century occurred, the leaders of the other nation-states accepted the sovereign right of the perpetrators to conduct their internal affairs as they pleased. Knowledge of the Armenian genocide was widespread at the time, but no other state intervened. The existence of extermination camps in Nazi Germany was known, but other states were at war with Germany, and the inmates were not identified as their business. Stalin's determination to starve Ukrainians into compliance was recognized, but no other state spoke up. The Canadian general in charge of UN forces in Rwanda tried every possible means of alerting the UN and American officials to what was happening, but no other state considered Rwanda important to its own sovereign interests. Intervention was involved in the cases of Cambodia and Chile, but it was intervention that supported the army of the ruling class in both instances, leading eventually to a substantial loss of life. In Argentina the Western world was well informed about what was happening and, despite the genuine human rights concerns of Jimmy Carter, neither the US nor other states persisted in attempts to stop the carnage. All this indifference or determined negligence of humanitarian concerns has, repeatedly, been supported by the argument that each nation-state has sovereignty over its own people and policies. This stance, of course, protects other states from interference in their affairs when their leaders choose to act in similarly despicable ways.

SUMMARY OF THE ARGUMENT

The state is an organization with a monopoly of the legitimate use of armed force in a given territory.

Armed Force

When incipient revolution becomes a regular condition of existence and other conditions coalesce to disable a state's capacity to sustain the status quo, those in control of the state are likely to move towards more extreme measures against dissidents (as they would define opposition). Such measures require physical force.

When either civilian governments or armies choose to conduct themselves as agents of crimes against humanity, they have to have sufficient capacity – both in terms of internal organization and numbers – to fully control the society with or without continued coercion. Armed force is an essential, though insufficient, condition for the conduct of these crimes.

One common condition in all the societies we have examined and in all that have instigated terrorist regimes is the existence of a military force capable of exterminating a large number of people and controlling the population during and after the onslaught. In the case of a stable government, this force may be the legitimate army of the state if the government of the day can count on it to perform the tasks. Otherwise, the government might establish an additional militia force to take on the tasks that a regular force is unwilling to perform (as in the case of Nazi Germany). In the case of internal wars, there could be more than one army, in which case the army capable of taking over the country becomes the army of the state, whether it is regarded as legitimate or not. In some cases (Turkey, Cambodia, Argentina, and Chile, for examples), the army becomes the government: the two are the same entity. In other cases, an elite gains control of armed force and, through that control, holds on to government (as in the cases of the USSR and Germany). Whichever way the army comes into existence and plays its role, that role must be played, so without armed force with those capabilities, no state terrorism will occur. This explanation would account under current circumstances for such countries as Australia, New Zealand, and Canada being unable (even if other conditions were apt) to sponsor state terrorism. It would also be an explanation for their inability to defend themselves against hostile external forces in the event of external demands for resources in their territories.

All countries have armies, some of them formally capable of taking over the state if need be, but their existence does not mean that they will do so. Armed force is a necessary but insufficient condition for the conduct of state crimes against humanity. There are also cases where armies have encouraged positive change in moribund and rigid societies or have filled a vacuum when governments cracked up. These changes might be beneficial in the long run or not, or they might be both. The Young Turks, though conducting genocide against Christian minorities, eventually reduced the rigidities and some of the inequalities in the Ottoman Empire. In that and some other cases, the army was the only agency capable of introducing a new order in the country.

Legitimacy

Governments command obedience under two conditions: when the population of their territory believes them to have legitimate control of the realm, or when they can compel obedience by force. Legitimacy is an amorphous quality that populations, including armies, may grant or withhold, depending on circumstances and the actions of governments.

Armies will respond to civilian government orders when they perceive such governments to be legitimate. Legitimacy is largely a function of established rules and customs, but as we have noted in several cases when the established government breaks down, so does the consent of the governed, including the armed forces. They may choose to define the situation as the civilian government does if it is still in place, or they may define it as requiring armed force as government. Such decisions may be based on a large degree of self-interest, but where self-interest can be explained in terms of the salvation of the state, armies are ready to become saviours.

A government has control of armed force only as long as the institutions of the armed forces consider that government legitimate.

Rwanda and Burundi give us examples of states that never quite achieved legitimacy among their own people. They were unable to fully escape their colonial ties and strike an accord among competing elites – all of which were equally unable to compromise and establish a stable state in which they all might survive. The established army and the militias were organized by a civilian government, but quickly became de facto governments on their own. Cambodia represents a revolutionary state built on a failed state, so revolutionary that its army elite made no effort to replace the state. Instead, it disbanded the population and tried to do away with the state and all its functionaries. It failed, but before it was displaced it had eliminated a large part of the population. Finally, there is the tragedy of Yugoslavia, where the state disintegrated completely, leaving only a fragmented army and warring elites with mutually exclusive territorial ambitions.

Inequality and the State

Inequality among persons and among groups of persons is characteristic of large societies. Class divisions often coalesce with ethnicity and religion, such that groups at the top of the hierarchy are homogeneous in ethnicity, and other groups at the bottom are equally homogeneous in another ethnicity and religion. But even in ethnically homogeneous societies, there are important and persistent differences in opportunities, wealth, and power among classes. The rankings are generally arbitrary, but they take on cultural meanings over time as generations are born into and take on the cultural attributes of their class or ethnic status. Other inequalities are sometimes paramount, including the division between rural and urban populations, where opportunities and wealth are vastly poorer in the rural regions. These distinctions may be characterized also as the difference between a peasantry and a bureaucratic population.

The significance of inequalities for our investigation lies in their relationship to the state and to the state's capacity to deal with them. States by their nature are obliged to sustain the hierarchy of groups among their populations. Their stability rests on their ability to sustain and, over generations, to reproduce the hierarchical system, not in precise detail nor necessarily with the same families generation after generation, but in general form and nature. Thus, if one ethnic group or religion is predominant, individual members of that group might lose their priority but the group as a whole, over time, would continue to be predominant. States, via governments and state institutions, are actively involved in ensuring that continuity.

Inequalities are not stable characteristics of a society. They are contested, sometimes with passion and organization, other times passively and in a disorganized way. When classes or ethnic or other groups obliged to occupy low-ranking places rebel, or when members of an organized working class demand more rewards for their labour, or when members of a middle class organize in defence of the poor or the working class, those in control of state institutions have to determine whether these behaviours constitute a genuine threat to the stability of the state itself or merely an inconvenience. In some cases they quell dissention and rebellion without resort to massive force. Playing off minority groups against one another is one tried-and-true tactic towards this end, and other tactics are common to large states where inequalities are sources of tension. Thus, though all states harbour inequalities, not all states use genocide as a solution, and the presence of inequalities is not, in itself, an explanation. However, inequality is a necessary condition.

States have a mandate to sustain and reproduce systems of inequality among citizens.

Genocide and politicide (ultimately the same crime against civilians, distinguished from one another because of the Genocide Convention rather than because of a fundamental difference in nature) come about because states – via the governments of the period – are incapable of sustaining and reproducing, in a non-violent way, the hierarchy of power on which they rest. In the case of a revolutionary state, the government is incapable of creating and reproducing, in a non-violent way, its intended changes in the hierarchy of power.

When states cannot reproduce the system, they have a high probability of committing human rights crimes.

Even when the challenge is tangential, as when subordinate groups act in what the dominant group defines as insubordinate ways, the dominant group may perceive a threat. For example, where groups that have been defined as inferior establish some form of superiority, such as business acumen and amassing of wealth beyond the station determined for them by the dominant group, their status inconsistency may be viewed as a threat to the dominant group. This reaction seems to be particularly noticeable where the collective identity of the dominant group is weak or, for unrelated reasons, is under threat. Dominant groups frequently perceive demands by subordinate groups for equality and civil rights as threats. In class-based conflicts, demands might be borne by middle-class leaders on behalf of labour and the poor: these groups may also be perceived as threats to the security of the established order.

Insecure, more than secure, ethnic identities, as in the Ottoman Empire and Nazi Germany, are associated with the exclusion of non-members by groups that define themselves in ethnic terms.

Yet, at the individual level, the more one's identity is tied to any collectivity, the greater the propensity to experience perceived threats against the group as personal threats to oneself and family.

Ultimately, then, inequalities lead more often to human rights crimes where the dominant group is insecure in its collective identity and where members (especially leaders) perceive their personal identities as being identical to that of the group.

Social Change and Institutional Capacities

Fundamental social change is the challenge to the status quo (or, in revolutionary states, the development of a new platform) that leads to political instability or paralysis. The paralysis, a prolonged condition whereby the state cannot solve the crisis via non-violent methods, may be a precurser to state crimes. The original cause of the political instability might be a war; it might be insufficient food and resource supplies, population pressures, or environmental disasters; it might be a more gradual process of economic development or incipient revolution. Other changes might include sharp market downturns for the products the state depends on; the withdrawal of foreign investors for whatever reasons; the refusal of international banks or the International Monetary Fund to provide loans; the provision of IMF funding on terms that dramatically alter the social infrastructure of the society and bring about extreme hardship or rebellion, or both; or declining incomes and capital flight. All these changes are potentially disastrous conditions that invite state action and often presage violence as a means of controlling the population.

Established states might try various experiments, and sometimes there are frequent changes of government with differing ideologies, yet the changes are such that, in that society at that time, the state is destined to fail. This breakdown can lead to internal war, as in Yugoslavia. It can lead to a takeover by armies, as in Chile and Argentina. It can lead to the imposition of force so great that the problem is solved at the cost of a huge loss of life, as in the USSR against the Eastern Ukraine. Sometimes the killing of one population is designed to provide space or resources for another one. The Young Turks may have shown Hitler that technique, for he is said to have observed that no one remembered Armenia. Perhaps he thought that no one would remember the Jews of Germany either.

Fundamental social change that results in, or has the potential to result in, substantial alteration in the systemic inequalities of power constitutes a potential condition for the commission of state crimes against civilians.

Healthy states tend to include a range of institutional sectors between the level of the state and the family. Examples include the mass media, economic organizations of varying size, political parties, religious organization, voluntary association, and professional, union, sports, and recreational groups. Unless they are exclusionary in their recruitment and participation patterns, these organizations, together with quasi-state organizations such as universities, schools, hospitals, and other public sectors, may provide flexibility and strength to the society when the state encounters extreme challenges. Their presence enables the state to spread the risks of governing and reduce the risk of committing crimes as a means of solving state problems.

Societies with numerous institutional sectors separate from government have a greater capacity to withstand political paralysis than societies where the state is in control of major institutions or where major institutions are closely allied with the state.

In a healthy state there are alternative elites in the wings that might, depending on the immediate circumstances, contest the right of the government of the day to continue making efforts to save the situation, engineer a coup, or stage a revolution. But in many states beset by intractable problems, leadership is weak, especially where there have been few opportunities for participation in the past. The learning curve is generally steep, and the penalties for failure can be devastating. In several of the societies we examined, the alternatives had already been exhausted. The collective presidency of a federal Yugoslavian state following Tito's death fell apart, and there was no group of leaders capable of rejuvenating the federation. There were opposing elites in Burundi and Rwanda, but no avenues by which they could peacefully take on the reins of government. In Chile and Argentina, the alternatives to military control had already been exhausted. Part of the failure of the state in these circumstances is its inability to produce alternative, non-military leadership pools under either peaceful or emergency conditions. The military force that so frequently takes over does so precisely because civilian government has failed: the military then becomes the only organization capable of maintaining the state, and often only by force.

The state may be strengthened, and its propensity to commit crimes may be reduced, where there are numerous civil and non-exclusive institutions with participation from all sectors of the population.

Social change has a less dramatic impact on democracies than on autocratic systems. We accepted this argument from R.J. Rummel (1990), who produced compelling data to the point, and also because it is consistent with our argument on the importance of diffuse responsibilities through institutional capacities in democracies.

Democracies are less likely to spawn reigns of terror on their own citizens than dictatorships or other autocratic systems.

Several influences embedded in culture may increase the potential for state crimes, but are not necessary conditions.

States in societies with an authoritarian culture, societies where human rights are not established, and societies where repression is widespread and of long duration may be especially prone to use force for the solving of societal problems.

Ideology as a Bridge

Ideology is a set of assumptions, shared beliefs, values, norms, and habits of mind that provide "rule of thumb" explanations for the nature of the world and its inhabitants. The community of believers can understand one another's actions and reasoning because they start with the same assumptions. Ideologies may mask behaviour, rationalize it, or excuse it. They may be imposed on others or used to misinform or disinform others. They are especially critical to the formation of cultural identities; they provide the basic rationale for why a group (ethnic, national, religious, tribal, or, in the Chilean case, class and occupational) is superior to others and who a member is, in relation to others.

In paralyzed states, leaders have to persuade the population that the use of extreme force against a portion of the population is justified. The success of this persuasion depends in large part on the existing perceptions and prejudices current in the population. If there is a long-standing ethnic division where a dominant group (normally but not always a numerical majority) perceives a subordinate or minority group as contemptible and beyond legitimate concern or empathy, the task is relatively straightforward. If there are no ethnic divisions of consequence, or the perceived cause of problems consists of a unionized workforce or rebellious students, the state has to persuade the rest of the population that these groups are threatening its economic survival because of their demands or are endangering everyone's cultural and national survival because of their subversive actions. It would be futile to make such claims if there were nothing concrete at stake: there has to be a crisis before ideology of such scope and justification will be promoted, sustained, and believed.

Sentiments held by large segments of a population may be deliberately activated by governments under stress and can form the basis for a larger exclusionary ideology.

The propensity to target specific victims when governments are under stress and to use terror to alleviate the condition is greater when the proposed victims have characteristics about which long-term prejudices already exist in the culture.

Ideology is not, by itself, the cause of state crimes, but it is the bridge between thought and action.

Ideology is the bridge between the perception of a group as potential enemies and the determination to eradicate them.

Ideology is the bridge for the movement from centralization of power to elimination of potential or actual opponents.

Individual Responses

The troops who actually perform some of the grizzly tasks are not necessarily motivated by ideology or even by previous sentiments and beliefs. We have learned that ordinary people, obliged to take part in such events, may do so because they respect authority and regard it as legitimate, conform to and care about their colleagues and peers, regard the tasks as requirements of their careers, want to excel at whatever they are asked to do, and are capable of distancing themselves by treating the victims as outside their realm of obligation. Bureaucracies, rational processes for conducting work, including extensive division of labour and compartmentalization, modern technology, and other aspects of the highly organized society may diminish a sense of personal responsibility. The perpetrators, in short, are normal insofar as twentieth-century industrial and agricultural societies might define the normal range of characteristics and behaviours in their population. They are not monsters.

Where people accept authority as legitimate, they are more likely to follow its orders.

Conformity to group norms may be a superior explanation for obedience to authority under extreme conditions than merely the tendency to obey authority.

Individuals, when pressured or obliged to kill other human beings, may create a psychological distance between themselves and the victims such that they are unable to feel human empathy for their victims. Underlying racism, ideologies, and bureaucratic procedures may enable the process of distancing.

NECESSARY CONDITIONS IN COMBINATION

Although all the above conditions contribute to the possibility that a state might commit crimes against its own citizens, it is the combination of the more critical and essential conditions that lead to a high probability of such state actions. The combination includes

- Fundamental social change that cannot be absorbed without major changes in the hierarchical system.
- Contested inequalities that are perceived as a threat by the dominant groups.
- Armed force capable of controlling the country through a period of major state crimes against civilians.
- A politically paralyzed state. The variants on this condition are that the state, having become paralyzed, breaks down completely and competing elites fight for control; it is taken over by a revolutionary elite or by its own military forces; or it becomes prey for external powers. A broken government prepared to impose violence in attempts to find a solution, a condition of internal war, or a revolutionary government is equally likely to commit crimes against civilians.
- A weak institutional structure that is unable to reduce the impact or to distribute the risks of the politically paralyzed state.
- An ideology that blames particular components of the population for the paralysis or for any other conditions leading to the paralysis.

Any one of these conditions alone is insufficient as a prelude to state crimes, but in combination they are lethal.

Political paralysis may be brought on by confrontation with fundamental social change that results in destabilization of the hierarchical relations between members of the population and, through that, to delegitimation of the state. When combined with armed force capable of conducting a major crime against civilians and a lack of institutional flexibility by which the risk of violence could be dissipated throughout the structures of the society, these conditions are the prelude to state crimes against citizens. The reasons may be expressed in many ideological frameworks.

Motivation

The underlying reasons for the commission of human rights crimes might consist of displaced anger over the impact of social change or the ideology alone. But in all the cases we surveyed, there appeared to be more material concerns. Some were disguised, others more blatant. In the cases of the Armenians there was a strong suggestion that Turks wanted both to be superior to all other nationalities and to take over the territory occupied by the Armenians. In the case of Germany, similarly, the Nazi state proposed to settle large German populations brought in to Germany from adjoining countries, and this resettlement required that groups already occupying those lands and even urban homes be evicted. In addition, there were more venal interests in money, jewellery, and other forms of material wealth. In the case of the USSR versus the Ukraine the interest was in obtaining grain to feed an urban proletariat and to sell in exchange for industrial machinery. In the case of Rwanda and Burundi the interest was in retaining properties against the demands or anticipated demands of the other group. In Cambodia the objective was to completely overturn a system that pushed peasants into poverty and starvation. In Chile and Argentina the objective was to rid the states of those groups and ideas that would overturn the established hierarchy and redistribute its property. In Yugoslavia the motivations were even cruder: to kill others who might make a claim against property.

The unstated objectives of crimes against humanity are usually instrumental and material.

Additional, but Not Necessary, Conditions

There are other conditions that are neither necessary nor sufficient for a state to turn on its citizens, but they may add to the urgency of plights experienced by states. They include authoritarian cultures, a previous absence of human rights, and long duration of repression. Israel Charny (1992), a foremost analyst of the Holocaust, concentrates on these variables as potential causes. To concern for human life and the quality of human experience, he adds a list of cultural characteristics of states most likely to commit genocide, including a tendency to use force in the solution of conflicts, violence in the mass media, dehumanization of the target groups, perception of victims as potentially dangerous, and legitimation of victimization by leaders of the dominant group. These characteristics may well be present in most of the instances of genocide; they are also present before the onset of war; and many of them are present in the daily lives of North Americans at the beginning of the twenty-first century. The list, however, does not provide any explanation; it simply lists symptoms, and the symptoms are not exclusive to societies at risk of committing these crimes.

Another listing by Carlos Santiago Nino (1996: 44–50), in a study of the Argentine experience, suggests certain recurrent dynamics in such events, including ideological dualism, corporatism, anomie, and concentration of power. Ideological dualism is the eternal conflict between conservative traditionalists and secular liberals, intensified in the Argentine case by the failure of liberals to promote democracy. Corporatism is associated with conservative traditionalists, though, during the Peronist era, it included the unions; essentially it is a means of controlling sectors of society via the state institutions. The doctrine of national security that emerged during the Cold War and that was encouraged by France and the United States influenced the extremely conservative military establishment and its constant ally, the Catholic Church. The third dynamic in Nino's exposition is anomie, which he defines as a disregard for social norms, including the law. (This definition is somewhat of a departure from Durkheim's term, which emphasized, rather, an absence of social norms, a condition of normlessness, as presented in the classic study of suicide, published in 1887.) In Nino's view, anomie was a legacy from the colonial period. These observations, astute and apt in the Argentine case, are less easily identified in other instances. They describe a particular culture at a particular time, but they are weak as generalizations for the range of instances that we have identified in this book.

External influences may be crucial in some cases. Chile and Cambodia probably would have embarked on the road to politicide with or without American interference, but there can be little doubt that American financing for the anti-Allende forces, military support for the military coup in Chile, or bombing of rural areas by American forces in Cambodia exacerbated the problems and hastened the day of reckoning. In the case of empires, of course, there is always an external agent in the mixture. External powers could be benign pressures against the commission of crimes, but in all the cases we have examined here they have been either irrelevant (as in the Armenian and the USSR cases, where diplomatic appeals to home governments failed to produce any moral suasion or attempts to intervene) or actively supportive of the perpetrators. Even so, we need to consider the potential for intervention as a means of inhibiting or stopping the commission of human rights crimes.

PREVENTION AND INTERVENTION

Intervention might occur at three different junctures: when the crime is being contemplated or when the country appears to be at risk of committing such crimes; when the crime is in process; and when the crime is past but the perpetrators might yet be obliged to take responsibility.

Beginning with the last of these possibilities, there is growing international consensus about the need for international norms and laws against human rights crimes. The argument holds that all states must respect the human rights of citizens, and that the international community has the right to intervene if those rights are violated. The International Criminal Tribunals for Rwanda and Yugoslavia based their right to judge the leaders of criminal acts on the grounds that state sovereignty was subordinate to universal human rights. In line with this approach, and the evolving international law reflecting positive views of intervention, General Pinochet was detained in London on the ground that he was the leader of a country while armed forces committed human rights crimes. However, in these cases, the crimes had already been committed, and international opinion had already moved far ahead of the law in judging these individuals responsible.

The objective of trying leaders by international criminal courts is to establish a global legal framework that transcends national sovereignty in matters of gross human rights crimes. If effective, the law and penalties it imposes would act as deterrents to genocide and politicide. The problem the proponents face is that the hegemonic power of our time, the United States, is unwilling to submit to higher authorities. If such a court were fully established, and if the United States both signed and ratified the convention, then some of its own leaders could be susceptible to charges. Henry Kissinger, for the outstanding example, might be tried for his roles in the US activities in Vietnam, Laos, Cambodia, and Chile. Even if the eventual legislation were to forbid charges for activities before coming into force, current leaders might be tried for their actions while in office. Obviously the strongest country with the most to lose in such battles would be the most difficult to rein in. In some ways this prolonged tug-of-war is a repeat of the long history by which the rule of law was eventually established in many societies. In those historical cases, the privileged were less than eager to have their status reduced to that of the less advantaged. Cynics may claim that the privileged never really lost their case, but that is a myopic view of the struggle. The rule of law may still be contested by privileged citizens, but the idea and institutions for resolving disputes and dealing with crimes by civil and criminal courts are well established. The law sets up barriers to the demands of privilege and acts as a leveller for the population subject to it. International courts are important means of dissuading crimes as well as of punishing them, but, ultimately, prevention of the conditions that lead to such crimes would be even better.

Entering a country while the crimes are occurring is problematic. Rarely is the situation clear; rarely is the evidence all of a piece. The events in Rwanda and Yugoslavia were murky and muddled when the genocides were in full operation. In Rwanda, only observers who had resided there for many years were capable of identifying the genocidaires; others, especially reporters who based their nightly reports on stories of refugees, were inclined to suggest that it was simply a civil war with no "side" more reprehensible than the other. The verdict on what happened in Croatia remains ambiguous; on Bosnia, it is much clearer in retrospect, but was not so obvious at the time. In many of these events, even the most noble and well-intentioned outsiders rarely have sufficient background knowledge, historical insight, or linguistic skills to sort out what exactly is happening. In addition to this general ignorance and lack of adequate preparation is the undeniable fact that outside nations act primarily in their own perceived interests, not for altruistic reasons. Peacekeeping forces under the direction of the United Nations are the most altruistic actions yet devised by the international community, and sometimes they have been effective in keeping protagonists apart and in enabling them to observe cease-fire agreements or sign peace treaties. Canadians are justly proud of their contributions to peacekeeping, an idea originally promoted by Nobel Prize winner and former Canadian prime minister Lester B. Pearson. But peacekeeping forces can only be successful if the contending parties desire peace and are willing to let the outside force create a barrier to continued warfare. As UN forces in Bosnia discovered, they become targets themselves if the warriors are determined to carry on the hostilities. And as General Roméo Dallaire discovered in Rwanda, external forces are not available for UN duty when the leaders of their countries have no material interest in the outcome.

Intervention

Given this record, are there any other ways of intervening before the onset of human rights crimes? In the Chilean case, would it have been possible to pre-empt a bloodbath by intervention when it was clear that Salvadore Allende had lost control of the army? Pre-emptive intervention has no grounding in law, is highly suspect (with good reason), and could cause more problems than it solves. Even so, if the most that intervention after the fact can achieve is punishment for a few perpetrators, there is not much hope that the genocides and politicides of history will be fewer in the future. It is too late to intervene when the genocide occurs. The perpetrators are already "over the precipice." Peacekeepers whose task is to keep the parties separated are generally too few, too late – even when they come.

But could the international community intervene at a much earlier stage – say, at the stage where social change is destabilizing the country and its government is moving inexorably towards political paralysis? If the theory presented here is valid, we should be able to predict – imperfectly, of course, but with more than pure guesswork – which states are moving in the direction of criminal acts against their own people. Before entering into a discussion in favour of such intervention, we should be warned of the many good reasons to be wary.

To begin with, external interventions tend to be motivated by material interests, just as the crimes themselves are motivated by such interests. Soviet intervention in Afghanistan in the 1970s, to cite one example among many, sprang from the probably mistaken notion that a puppet government there would serve Soviet interests. American intervention in Chile emerged from a probably mistaken notion that if Chile were governed by a Marxist, American interests both there and elsewhere on the continent would be jeopardized. There is no doubt that ideology informed the state decision-makers in both of these examples, but it was their national interests as they perceived them that motivated them to take the actions they did. In the Rwandan case, except for mild interests of former colonial powers, external powers were not interested, in the sense that they had no material interest to advance or defend: the poor country was too poor even to elicit the greed of its neighbours.

The real power of nation-states has gradually diminished over the second half of the twentieth century. The process we call globalization, not new but now affecting virtually all regions of the world, sometimes

beneficially, often disastrously, has undermined the autonomy of nation-states. Economic intervention is widespread; only the most powerful nations are able to avoid it. What is signally lacking is a political
and legal world order to curb economic and political exploitation. But
weak states on the verge of committing genocide are unlikely to accept
international intervention, and in the year 2003 the United States, the
strongest state, is unwilling to submit to international conventions and
laws that would turn intervention into a decision of the United Nations
rather than a unilateral one. Again and again the United States has refused to sign United Nations conventions or to allow the United Nations to overrule its own sovereign authority. It will not permit its
soldiers in peacekeeping missions to be subject to international laws
that affect all others; it will not support the International Criminal
Court. Until the strongest nation is prepared to accept multilateral conventions and law, intervention is problematic.

Intervention that is unilateral and undertaken for self-interested
reasons is not the kind of intervention most likely to prevent countries
from committing crimes against their own citizens. The "pre-emptive
strike" against Iraq by the United States in 2003, is a prime example of
the genre. In this case, the United States, by far the military power of
the era, bombed Iraq on the ground that it presented a "clear and
present danger" in the form of weapons of mass destruction which the
US administration claimed Iraq had, in common with, for examples,
the United States, India, Pakistan, China, Israel, and Russia. The unilateral war had been temporarily avoided in September 2002 by an
agreement struck by the United Nations with Iraq to allow weapons in-
spectors to enter its territory, but by the following March the United
States insisted on war. A unilateral pre-emptive strike presents a disturbing precedent. Any country, following the US lead, is now enabled
to undertake a pre-emptive strike against its enemy. Intervention, especially by a powerful country against a much weaker one, opens up a
Pandora's box that could destabilize the world for a long time to come
and return it to the political and military tableaux before the Second
World War (Valaskakis, 2002). Does this mean that politically motivated intervention is always worse than no intervention? This conclusion seems to follow from a proposal for unilateral, self-interested
intervention.

There is another reason to be sceptical of intervention: the post-war
history of good intentions gone sour. In theory, the IMF was designed
to help countries in economic trouble. But, instead, its policies tended

to exacerbate the inequalities within the impoverished states, hurry along domestic capital flight, encourage corruption, and ensure that the poorer states would continue to be indebted. Joseph Stiglitz, the Nobel Prize-winning economist, former chair of the US Council of Economic Advisers, and, from 1997 to 2000, the chief economist of the World Bank, is one of the more prominent commentators on the failure of this institution to deal successfully with the kind of economic problems that so frequently precede outbursts of genocide and politicide. In his book (2002) he considers whether the blockages lie primarily in the developing countries' social and political infrastructure, in corrupt or stupid governments, in their culture, or in the global marketplace and conditions for borrowing money they encounter. While he recognizes indigenous problems, he places most of the blame for underdevelopment in many developing countries in the post-war period on the IMF. He argues that the recipients of IMF loans did not have adequate information about markets, that markets themselves were manipulated by rich countries, and that the already deficient infrastructure of the recipient countries was made even less operable by virtue of the oppressive conditions for the loans imposed by IMF officials. Here, intervention has done harm rather than good, and Stiglitz argues that the bottom line is ideology: the ideology of the free market adopted uncritically by IMF officials that obstructs their understanding of what is actually happening in these poor societies. Their officials, trained in finance rather than educated more fully, imposed one solution on all societies irrespective of their infrastructure, culture, or level of economic knowledge. Zygmunt Bauman, were he to address the same topic, might argue that the basic problem was bureaucracy: the inability of bureaucratic functionaries, with their technocratic training, to grasp the whole picture. Whether ideology or bureaucratic incompetence is at fault, the failures of the IMF have become legendary.

Stiglitz advances a second argument in his arsenal against the IMF: that it has systematically acted on behalf of the financial institutions and wealthy investors rather than on behalf of the countries it was supposedly designed to help. The creditors get their financial rewards when the IMF ensures that defaulting countries have enough to pay off loans, even when their own people are starving. In his words (Friedman, 2002: 52):

Stabilization is on the agenda; job creation is off. Taxation, and its adverse effects, are on the agenda; land reform is off. There is money to bail out banks but not to pay for improved education and health services, let alone to bail out workers who are thrown out of their jobs as a result of the IMF's macroeconomic mismanagement.

The lack of concern about the poor was not just a matter of views of markets and government, views that said that markets would take care of everything and government would only make maters worse; it was also a matter of values ... While misguidedly working to preserve what it saw as the sanctity of the credit contract, the IMF was willing to tear apart the even more important social contract.

Putting Stiglitz's argument into the framework of the concerns in this book, we might recognize in the history of the IMF the same premise as we have advanced for genocide by states. The IMF is designed to sustain and reproduce the inequalities of the world of nations, not necessarily in clone-like fashion but in overall systemic patterns. Stiglitz is not arguing a simple or cynical case against the IMF; no Machiavellian overlord designed it purposefully to harm the poor and ensure that they remain that way. Rather, the organization operates on the same principles as states, where power and wealth inevitably determine outcomes, and they determine them in such a way that their interests are advanced. Like two sides of a coin, where those interests are advanced the interests of the poor are most often defeated. Further, we see in the reaction of powerful and wealthy states to the demands of poor states within the forum of the United Nations that poor states, if they were taken seriously and developed some moral clout, would be perceived as threats by strong states. Indeed, the United States has already seen them as threats, since it refuses to pay part of its dues until "imbalances" are redressed. The United Nations replicates the experience of member states, attempting to placate its wealthy and powerful members (without whom it cannot survive and would have no power at all), yet simultaneously trying to sustain its poorer member states.

Alternative Perspectives

If institutions like the IMF end up enriching the already wealthy and impoverishing the already poor, we might be tempted to throw up our hands and abandon ideals. But, in fact, there are counter-examples. Stiglitz argues that the world, now dealing with a globalized economy, is beginning to discover that its diverse national societies need, even deserve, more socially beneficial economic strategies. George Soros (2002a and 2002b), one of the world's most successful financiers, has proposed concrete ways of improving the lot of poor nations. He has created a network of what he calls "Open Society" foundations in Eastern Europe to set up post-communist institutions such as universities. He supported an international movement of concerned activists who succeeded in getting debt relief for some of the poorest countries. He and others who share his liberal views have criticized the way financial markets have operated and the way that industrial countries have created hurdles to entry for commodities produced in poor countries. He has steadfastly criticized many of the policies of international institutions, rich country governments, banks, aid programs, and investors where they have exploited the poor and their territorial resources. He, and Stiglitz, have propounded the view that, ultimately, it would be in the interests of rich countries to enable poor countries to improve the conditions of life for their people. Indeed, since September 11, 2001, this view has quietly slipped into more discussions as people consider the possibility that poverty, unemployment, lack of education, and despair in poor countries engender the kind of terrorism launched against the United States.

Poverty and despair are also in evidence in African countries where state terror has occurred – indeed, are almost endemic. Elsewhere it is not widespread poverty itself, but the great gap between those with power and wealth and those without, and the oppression inflicted on the latter by the former. True, every situation has subtleties and curious turns; true, the threat to the state often comes from the unionized rather than the more impoverished workers, or from the middle-class than from the very poor. True, that when revolutionaries on behalf of the peasants or the poor take over the state, they are at least as vicious as their former oppressors. Viciousness breeds viciousness. But it is also true that where the gap between the rich and the poor is smaller and the poor have some opportunities for upward mobility, or where workers are included in the political process that fashions the governments for a state, the frequency of state crimes decreases. Institutional capabilities for dealing with tough conditions improve. Something closer to democracy begins to take root where dictatorships have hitherto dominated.

Global institutions could act in a way that states do not reach the point where they go over the precipice. In hindsight, the world has generally acknowledged that Hitler would never have come to power had the Versailles Treaty dealt a different hand to Germany in 1918. Harry

Truman's government recognized this possibility and created the magnanimous Marshall Plan to reconstruct the economies of the Axis powers after 1945. This plan was self-interested, in that it prevented the expansion of Soviet power in Western Europe and created markets for American products, but it was a self-interested plan that also prevented a repetition of the Nazi phenomenon. Had the Entente powers earlier in the century followed through on their own demands, Armenia would have become a separate nation beyond the control of the Ottoman Empire, but those powers were too preoccupied with their own preparations for war, and Armenia was not high on their agenda. It is possible that Stalinism could have been avoided in the former Russian Empire had the Western powers of the time been generous in enabling the revolutionary state to obtain industrial machinery and become industrialized. But the West at that time, besides having its own issues to deal with, believed that it was best to starve communism than to prove to its adherents that different economic ideologies might coexist. The genocides in Rwanda and Burundi could have been avoided had former colonial powers taken more responsibility for enabling the new states to develop on the basis of full participation by all factions or by facilitating migration to the colonial countries. Instead of intervening on behalf of powerful military forces in Latin America, external powers might have opened up commodity markets for produce from the poorer regions and provided aid and funding for elected governments, even when these were not of the preferred ideological stripe.

We have to acknowledge that aid packages, direct investment by transnational corporations (TNCs), bank loans, and many other approaches touted at the time as ways of helping poor countries were, in fact, disastrous failures or contributors in the process that led to genocidal states. One pattern does not fit all, and intervention, if it is to be genuinely helpful to the recipient countries, has to take into account the structure of the state, the range of civil institutions, the culture, the demographics, the history, and the willingness of the state to be intervened. But intervention need not appear as intervention at all. If the world community actually cares about its whole population, countries at risk could be enabled to work out peaceable strategies for their dilemmas without anyone calling it intervention, without anyone complaining about assaults on national sovereignty. The solutions lie not in the moment of criminal activity or even in penalties for perpetrators, but in economic and political justice created and nurtured long in advance of reaching the stage of desperation.

CONDITIONS FOR PARALYSIS

We return now to our starting point. Conditions for political paralysis are events or processes that make it impossible for states to sustain and reproduce the system in which they are located and which inevitably include populations that are dominant and other populations that are subservient. Inequality is built into state systems, but, in states at risk, those with power are unwilling to share either the power or the wealth that goes with it. They have military forces capable of controlling the country. They do not have institutional capacities to cope peacefully with conditions of social change. They subscribe to ideologies that encourage inequalities, stereotyping of ethnic and religious groups, and labelling and dehumanization of "others." Their material objectives, beneath the ideological rationales, target certain groups as potential enemies and potential victims.

By contrast, states that are not at risk of committing crimes against their citizens at the beginning of the twenty-first century have addressed the conditions that lead to vulnerability. Scandinavian states, led by the same bourgeois elites as other states, have established taxation rules that reduce the gulf between the rich and the poor, and social and legal rules that reduce the gulf between the powerful and the less powerful. These are small-scale human experiments that demonstrate the possibility of relatively egalitarian states that show no signs of political paralysis. They have accommodated substantial social change over the post-war period. Their demographic profiles have changed as they absorbed immigrant populations. They have adapted to the world economy by ensuring that their population is at least bilingual (with English) and, in many cases, multilingual. They have reorganized their economies to reduce environmental damage. In short, these are societies that demonstrate the possibility of states coping intelligently with the challenges of a changing world.

Western European states, for the most part, have also created mechanisms and institutions for spreading risks, reducing inequalities, and coping with dramatic changes. They have agreed to redistribute wealth via welfare states that include health insurance, social and occupational security measures, and other social measures that require high taxation. They have steadily dismantled large armies and reduced expenditures on military equipment. They have deliberately created new institutions that already dilute the separate national capacities of individual states. And lest anyone claim they are lacking in economic power as a consequence, several European economies actually had higher productivity ratios in 2001 than the United States (*Financial Times*, 20 Feb. 2002; Judt, 2002). The dramatic transformation in Europe is in substantial part because Europeans recognized that their competing national economies and the political ideologies that fuelled them in the past were simply too dangerous. They chose to pre-empt a repeat performance in modern garb of the conditions that led to the two European wars. These European states, then, are not at risk of committing gross human rights crimes against their own citizens.

But outside Europe – in Africa, the Middle East, in parts of Asia, and in some Latin American countries – states are at high risk of continued violations of human rights. They have not travelled the same excruciating path of violence as European states, they have not developed what might be called "social inoculation" against the conditions that precede human rights crimes. In many cases, they themselves have been victimized by the violent interventions of European nations at an earlier stage of history. As seems to be eternally true, people repeat the crimes that victimized them but that they did not cause. The cycle continues until protagonists, like contemporary Europeans, identify themselves as the potential enemies, irrespective of who abused them in the past. Like Walt Kelly's comic strip character Pogo, they say, "We have seen the enemy and the enemy is us."

The world that is not now at risk has a stake in what happens elsewhere. We are more than ever part of the same global population, global polity, and global economy. To continue with the ideologies of national sovereignty and national defence when our neighbours are clearly in deep trouble is no longer a rational strategy, if ever it was. Military intervention is not a solution; even peacekeeping has limited capacities. An International Monetary Fund that continues with the soul-destroying tactics that were dictated by the greed of First World investors is worse than nothing at all. But we know this fact and we are capable of moving on to a new level of humane and reasonable interaction. We can recreate institutions at the global level that rein in the greed of First World banks and provide enabling strategies for domestic capital where transnational corporate capital has become established. We could begin to live up to the notion of "free markets" in our own national states so that commodity producers elsewhere are able to compete on reasonable terms. We could give economic preferences to countries that develop social welfare systems for their poor: a revolutionary idea contrary to everything the IMF has stood for. We could stop producing and marketing armaments that fuel the genocidal episodes in many states. We could preferentially provide aid to countries that are willing to decrease their investment in military forces and armaments. We could anticipate the impact of changes that we know are destabilizing countries and offer help that would encourage governments to reduce the gap between their powerful and powerless citizens rather than rigidly enforce it through coercion. Guiding all these pre-emptive actions would be an ethic – an ideology, yes, admit it – that assumes we live in one world, we are all children of the same ancestors, and what we do today will determine the fates of our progeny in the future.

PART TWO

Case Studies

7

Ottoman Empire, 1915–16

The Armenian massacre of 1915 was the first internationally recognized and condemned genocide of the twentieth century. The international literature, written by Europeans, Russians, and Americans, attributes to the Ottoman government under Turkish control a death toll of at least 800,000, over a third of the Armenians then resident in the Ottoman Empire. Men of fighting age were incarcerated and executed, while the women, children, and elderly were deported. Many died while struggling along without food, shelter, or aid. They were robbed, raped, and mutilated by bandits and armed men, and many who survived were burned alive or otherwise killed when they reached refugee camps in Syria or Mesopotamia. A quarter of the deportees survived (Dadrian, 1995: 225). Any items survivors had with them were taken; their land and other possessions were appropriated by the state. The genocide of 1915 followed three decades of increasing violence and discrimination, and there were continuing attacks on surviving Armenians for several years after the mass deportation.

Though the Turkish parliament of that time, and major newspapers and statesmen, admitted that a terrible event had occurred, and though the leading governors who had authorized it were castigated and eventually charged (in absentia) with war crimes, the Entente powers who called for the creation of a separate Republic of Armenia failed to follow through, and a new Turkish government continued with the same policies. Within a few years the government denied that any genocide had occurred, and that has remained the position of Turkish governments ever since. Historians, even so, have compiled extensive and detailed accounts of the genocide (see, in particular, Dadrian, 1999; Hovannisian, 1986a and 1998; Kirakossian, 1992; and U.S. Official

Documents, 1995), Turkish writers have countered with their version of the events. They argue that "the Armenian Question was in reality a Turkish struggle for independence or self-determination against a campaign of invasion supported also by foreign powers" (Öke, 1988: 127).

Virtually all scholars who have dealt with the subject treat the episode as the outcome of long-standing and intense ethnic and religious conflict. However, there is also the context of a disintegrating empire, several defeats in war, external powers slavering in their eagerness to carve up the corpse, and the rise of Turkish nationalism. The Ottoman army was involved in the execution of the planned extermination, though it used Kurdish tribesmen and criminals to do some of the dirtier work. That there was ethnic and religious conflict is not in doubt. The question remains: Would that conflict have led to genocide in another context, or is the context itself the propelling factor?

HISTORICAL CONTEXT

Ottoman rule over sprawling territories in both Europe and Asia was gradually disintegrating by the mid-nineteenth century. The "sick man of Europe," as the empire was rudely called, was a backward, brutal, and corrupt conglomoration of national units under the Islamic Sultanate. Its origins went back to the early fourteenth century, and its control of Constantinople, taken from the Byzantine theocracy, had begun in 1453. Britain, Russia, Germany, and France were all meddling in the affairs of the Ottoman Empire, keen to participate in the spoils once the old body collapsed. Economic concessions in the empire had been doled out in such generous proportions, by way of staving off the inevitable conclusion, that one author argues "the Sultan's empire lacked true independence, and it became a partial economic colony of European interest" (Kirakossian, 1992: 2). Ottoman army leaders and other Turks were also conspiring to hasten the demise so they could reinvent the empire as a modern Turkish state.

National liberation movements in the Balkans and among Armenians in the empire had also taken form, threatening Turkish control. The Russian-Turkish war (1877–88) was fought, in part, over the demands of Slavs in the Balkans. Britain provided extensive military and financial aid to Turkey as its safeguard of British interests against Russia's claims, but Russia won the war. According to the terms of the San Stefano treaty, several regions were to become independent, but the most that was promised to the Armenians was a guarantee of their security from the Kurds and Circassians (Kirakossian, 1992: 7, citing Article 16 of the treaty).

Under earlier Ottoman rule, Christian Armenians had achieved substantial autonomy in religious and political matters. However, rising nationalist sentiment among the Armenians, combined with their divergent religious orientation, came into conflict with Turkish sentiment by the seventeenth and eighteenth centuries, when the Ottoman government imposed discriminatory heavy taxes on minority Christians, including Armenians, and increasingly harsh restrictions on movement and economic options. Although many Christians emigrated, others, accommodating to restrictions in the military and civil service, became adept at trade and commerce. These enterprising individuals became a prosperous middle class by the mid-nineteenth century. They controlled much of the commerce in the interior region of the country and represented a substantial proportion of the professions and trades in Constantinople, Izmir, and other cities. They invested in urban enterprises, rather than in the rural regions where most Armenians lived. Their success attracted negative attention by Turkish authorities, who encouraged persecutions of Armenian businessmen (Kirakossian, 1992: 3). Leo Kuper (1981: 117) suggests that the status inconsistency between the low position of Armenian Christians and the high position of wealthy business people was a possible cause of Turkish hostility. This argument is also put forward by Vahakn N. Dadrian (1999). However, the vast majority of Armenians still lived in rural regions and were dependent on farming. They were poor, as were Muslims in their districts.

Demography is of some importance to this history. A Russian writer of Armenian descent, John S. Kirakossian (1992: 19), observes that Turks constituted only a quarter of the total population of the Ottoman Empire of 28 million at the end of the nineteenth century. At the onset of the genocide, there were some 2 million Armenians in the Ottoman Empire. Another 1.5 million lived in Russia, 80,000 in Iran, and 100,000 elsewhere (89). Of those in the Ottoman regions, 1.4 million were in Western Armenia, 440,000 in other parts of Asiatic Turkey, and 183,000 in Constantinople and European Turkey (tables 1 and 2: 261–2). Kirakossian argues that in several districts Armenians regarded as their homeland, they accounted for nearly 40 per cent of the population, Turks about 25 per cent, and Kurds just over 16 per cent. The same data is interpreted by the defender of Turkey's actions at that time, Mim Kemâl Öke (1988: 78–9), in a very different way: "Ottoman and Western sources are agreed that Armenians never constituted a majority in [the provinces] which Armenians regard as their original homeland." He argues that Armenians were outnumbered by Muslims forty-five to one in these regions, and any argument about homelands and self-determination is, in his opinion, unfounded. Diverse ethnic groups were Muslim in religious orientation.

The proportions of Armenians in these regions at the turn of the century may not be indicative of the settlement patterns at earlier times. The Ottoman government had, throughout the nineteenth century, encouraged Muslim ethnic minorities who resided in the eastern provinces, Russia, and other nearby states to resettle in traditional Armenian territory to create a persistent competition for land. In subsequent forays against the Armenians, the Turks used the rivalries to obtain cooperation from these minorities. Borders in Armenian territories were redrawn to accommodate such demographic changes.

Though many Armenians had fought with Turkey in the Russo-Turkish war of 1877–78, discrimination and oppression persisted. Leaders frequently appealed for resolution of minority complaints and establishment of civil rights. Eventually, young Armenian revolutionaries joined roving squads to commit violent acts against Kurdish immigrants and Turks. The various revolutionary organizations were not united, some arguing in favour of socialism, others wanting only independence in their homeland, and not all favoured armed tactics. However, revolutionary atrocities became the explicit reason for escalation of Turkish assaults on Armenians. In the late 1880s an uprising by Armenians in the mountainous province of Zeitoun concluded with the defeat of a Turkish counter-revolutionary force, signalling to the Turks that the Armenians, in regions where demographic and geographic conditions favoured them, were capable of mounting successful resistance.

A clandestine organization, the Committee of Union and Progress (known in the West as the Young Turks), led a revolution in the empire in 1908 and, in 1913, finally seized power through a coup. They proclaimed plans to modernize their country. The Young Turks recognized that it would be impossible to rule over the Muslim majority without finding an acceptable replacement for the fictitious religious power of the sultan (Kirakossian, 1992: 75, citing Young Turks' publications): they had to bring on side the Islamic clergy. This collaboration meant that religious, civil, and many state activities continued to be determined by interpretations of the Koran. Pan-Islamism was included in the agenda. In fact, there were few changes after the new government took office; in the absence of regular salaries, officials continued to live off bribes and corruption continued, unabated by a fine-sounding constitution. After a few skirmishes, a triumvirate of Ismail Enver Pasha, Mehmed Talaat, and Talaat Pasha controlled the government during the period of the war and its immediate aftermath.

While decisions about the continued relationship with minorities were being made (in a contradictory manner because of differences between public and secret plans), the Balkan War of 1912–13 interrupted the process. Sustained oppression and atrocities allegedly committed by Turks against Macedonian Bulgars and others had led to the formation of the Balkan League. Armenians were divided in this war, some fighting with the Macedonians, others with the Turks. The Turks lost the war. The peace agreement signed in February 1914 by Turkish and Russian officials required that Turkey undertake reforms governing Christian minorities and, specifically, the Armenians. The Turks recognized that the reforms would eventually involve autonomy, with Russian support. Turks claimed that Armenians had sought intervention from other European powers against Turkey and did not undertake the reforms (Dadrian, 1999: 125–6).

In all their pronouncements and legislation, the Young Turks made it clear they assumed that Turks had the right to control the Ottoman Empire, and that all regions formerly controlled by the sultan were reasonably included in their heritage. In 1910 a prolonged general meeting of their governing council (the Ittihad) declared that "Turkey [was] for the Turks." They resolved at a 1911 conference that Turkey should be an exclusively Islamic country, that all citizens should be Ottomans and Muslims. The term "Ottoman" was used synonymously with Turkish, but with allowances for other Islamic peoples. Their intransigence on this position suggests that more was at stake than their conflict with Christian Armenians. The leaders of the Young Turks came to the fore during a period of extreme deterioration in the empire. The sultan's armies had lost several wars, and the armies of the New Turks were also suffering defeats. They were threatened by the diverse minorities in their own territories, including Arabs and Kurds, and they were threatened by persistent European designs on their lands. Pan-Turkism was their response to these many threats, a policy that defined who Turks were and why they had the right to all the Ottoman lands and, as well, the Transcaucasian territory over the Russian border.

In that context, they were quick to find evidence that Armenian Christians were collaborating with external powers and to view any evidence as proof of subversion and fuel for the argument to eradicate

Armenians. Indeed, Armenian pleas for civil rights and self-determination were proof of subversion. Their attitudes towards Christian Armenians were in accord with popular sentiment. Arnold Toynbee (1915: 30), who wrote extensively about the events in an attempt to get the British government to act, quotes a Turkish gendarme: "First we will kill the Armenians, then the Greeks, then the Kurds." Though the Armenians came first, all minorities would eventually be eradicated if the Turks who supported this policy were successful.

Turkish defenders of the genocide argue that Armenians, and particularly the Armenian Catholic Church, were going outside the country to gain support for their cause and to appeal for aid in fighting against Turks in the empire. Öke (1988: 90–1) argues that England, determined to prevent Russia from gaining territory there, was planning to set up an Armenian state under its protectorate, while Russia, equally wily, was trying to annex Eastern Anatolia. Germany, likewise, had interests in the empire. On the eve of the First World War the great powers were in the process of partitioning the empire, only to be interrupted by the assassination of Archduke Ferdinand of Austria and the intensification of armed hostilities.

The Turks allied themselves with Imperial Germany during the war. German military schools trained Turks both in Germany and in the Ottoman territories. Armenians were conscripted into the Turkish army, but they were disarmed and isolated into what were called labour battalions. Historian Vahakn Dadrian (1999: 118–20) concludes that the intention to murder the conscripted Armenians was already in place. Several prominent supporters and members of the Young Turks aimed to rid Turkey of the Armenian minority on the ground that it was a danger to Turkey's existence. The advent of war added urgency to the Turkish plans, based on the belief that Armenians were collaborating with enemies.

Collaboration with enemies is a frequently cited explanation for genocides. In this case, the claim goes far back to the previous century when the Armenian Christian reform movement concentrated on attempts to gain civil rights, the rule of law, and, through these mechanisms, an end to discrimination. This movement was strongly supported by Armenians. A more revolutionary movement emerged when it became clear that Muslims were not willing to extend civil rights and were strongly opposed to social or legal equality. The Armenian revolutionary movement, beginning around 1860, was not unified in its ideology or tactics. The original group called for socialist reforms and advocated insurrections. A breakaway faction spurned socialism completely. A federation of revolutionary groups at the turn of the century called for democracy and freedom, equality of all nationalities and creeds before the law, and freedom of speech, press, and assembly. It called for armed insurrection to achieve these goals. This federation was still calling for revolution when the war broke out (Nalbandian, 1967).

POLITICIDE/GENOCIDE

In 1915 the government proclaimed its intention to order the deportation of Armenians, though it was disguised as a relocation policy. The Ottoman parliament accepted the decisions of the cabinet, the Ministry of the Interior had overall responsibility for the action, and local authorities carried out the particulars. Other ministries were involved in various aspects of the plan. Young Turk Party members forced reluctant local officials to comply. A secret extra-legal body organized the massacres in and near relocation camps. A special commission procured and disposed of Armenian possessions, and some properties were used as rewards for complicit action. Young girls were auctioned off and young boys taken as slaves by both Kurdish tribesmen, who were given licence to raid convoys of deportees, and members of the secret organization.

The initial deportation included all the provinces within Western Armenia and continued through 1915 and 1916. This phase of the onslaught has since been recognized as "the Armenian genocide." In fact, however, the slaughter continued within the Russian territories of Transcaucasia. In 1918 Enver Pasha ordered the Ministry of War to exterminate Armenians across the border while the Transcaucasian government was incapable of defending them. Russian troops had been withdrawn after the revolution in Russia.

Witness Accounts

Among the external observers to the eradication of the Armenians was an American consul, Leslie A. Davis, who was stationed at Mamouret-ul-Aziz (Harput) in the heart of Western Armenia. He wrote lengthy and detailed reports to the embassy in Constantinople and to the secretary of state in Washington. Though he made it clear that he had no affection for Armenians as a national group, he reported what happened to them and made heroic efforts to save those few he was able to help. The following quotations are excerpted from his dispatches (which have now been published as United States Official Documents, 1994, 1995):

It is difficult to reconcile the apparent kindness of heart of many Turks with the cruelties which they perpetuate in the name of their religion or by orders of their government." (1995, III: 46)

During the month of June the reign of terror that had existed in May became even worse. Many of the men who had been arrested and released were now re-arrested, together with hundreds of others ... Almost all of them were brutally tortured ... On the night of June 23, 1915, several hundred of the most promi-nent Armenians were sent away in ox carts from the local prison to an un-known destination ... Not one of these men escaped and for a long time nothing definite was known about their fate ... It was afterwards learned that nearly all these men were massacred. (1995, III: 54–6)

On Saturday afternoon, June 26th, we were all startled by the announcement that the Turkish Government had ordered the deportation of every Armenian, man, woman, and child (there were not many men left) ... The alleged destina-tion of the Armenians was Ourfa, which was about a week's journey from Har-put by wagon ... Much of the way was over the desert where little food or water could be obtained. It was summer and there is no protection from the sun on the hot Mesopotamian plain. For these women and children to make the journey on foot, as most of them would have to do, would require a month, and they could not carry food enough with them for more than a few days and would often have to go for several days without finding water, it was certain that most of them would perish on the way. (1995, III: 56)

The scenes of that week were heartrending. The people were preparing to leave their homes and to abandon their houses, their lands, their property of all kinds. They were selling their possessions for whatever they could get. The streets were full of Turkish women, as well as men, who were seeking bargains on this occasion, buying organs, sewing machines, furniture, rugs, and other articles of value for almost nothing ... The scene reminded me of vultures swooping down on their prey. It was a veritable Turkish holiday and all the Turks went out in their gala attire to feast and to make merry over the misfor-tunes of others. (1995, III: 58)

There were perhaps 3,000 who left Mamouret-ul-Aziz on that hot July day. A few had ox-carts, a few had mules or donkeys, some carried their scanty effects on cows, but the most of the people had to leave on foot carrying their baggage on their backs and their children in their arms on that terrible journey over the burning sands of the desert. The return soon afterwards of the donkeys and mules which the Government had provided indicated all too well the fate of those who had left. (1995, III: 63)

There were parties of exiles arriving from time to time throughout the summer of 1915, some of them numbering several thousand. The first one, who arrived in July, camped in a large open field on the outskirts of the town, where they were exposed to the burning sun. All of them were in rags and many of them were almost naked. They were emaciated, sick, diseased, filthy, covered with dirt and vermin, resembling animals far more than human beings. They had been driven along for many weeks like herds of cattle, with little to eat, and most of them had nothing except the rags on their backs. When the scant rations which the Government furnished were brought for distribution the guards were obliged to beat them back with clubs, so ravenous were they. There were few men among them, most of the men having been killed by the Kurds before their arrival at Harput. Many of the women and children also had been killed and very many others had died on the way from sickness and exhaustion. Of those who had started, only a small portion were still alive and they were rapidly dying. (1995, III: 79)

Reports by other American observers have also been compiled and published in several volumes of documents. They provide similar descriptions of the deportation and murders. The American consul general sent a memorandum to the secretary of state in Washington in November 1915 in which he states:

The old men and women and children are driven in hordes sometimes consisting of many thousands, without food or shelter or water, until they die. There seems to be no fixed place to which they are driven and no ultimate place of rest ... from 800,000 to 1,000,000 human beings are now going through this process of slow and hideous torture, and the movement instead of waning is increasing in ferocity, so that before it is finally over, in the neighborhood of 2,000,000 people will be affected, a very large proportion of whom will certainly perish as they are driven along for weeks and months without food or shelter and without the means of procuring these. (1994, II: 118–19)

These observations may be contrasted with the version provided by Öke (1988, 129–331). He argues that Armenian revolutionary committees were sabotaging Turkish war efforts, collaborating with the enemy, and staging rebellious demonstrations. They were warned that if they persisted, strong action would be taken against them. He continues, "after having shown patience for nine months following mobilization," the Ministry of the Interior ordered the closure of Armenian revolutionary organizations and the arrest of "harmful Armenians." He claims that all persons who were arrested were properly processed through the courts and that, in some cases, the death sentences were not carried out. Öke says that, in spite of all their attempts to placate the revolutionaries, the agitation continued, and finally the army insisted on the passing of the relocation law:

The Ottomans took the necessary measures to carry out the decision to relocate the Armenians in an orderly manner and under safe conditions: Armenians who came to their new places of settlement were to be accommodated either in houses to be built in existing villages and towns, or in new villages to be established in locations selected by the government. The lives and goods of relocated Armenians would be protected; they were allowed to take with them all their movables, and arrangements would be made for feeding them and for ensuring their rest. The goods which the Armenians would not be able to take with them, and their immovable possessions were going to be sold by public auction and the payments would be made by the government. (1988, 133–4)

The evidence is on the side of those who claim that a genocide took place. Apart from eyewitness accounts, there are numerous official telegrams and orders from the central government to provincial governors and army officers which were obtained after Allied troops took Aleppo on 26 October 1918. One, dated 18 November 1915, informs local authorities to beware of foreigners witnessing events: "From the point of view of present policy it is necessary for foreigners in such localities to be convinced that the transfer is solely for the purpose of relocation" (Kirakossian, 1992: 115, quoting telegram sent by Minister of the Interior Talaat). Another telegram states: "It has come to our attention that foreign officers are photographing corpses of known persons [Armenians] piled up along the roads. We strongly urge you to dispose of these corpses by burying them immediately" (115, citing telegram dated 18 September 1915). A collection of telegrams from Talaat to Enver on the subject was published in London in 1920; other information obtained from diverse sources within the government was published in a Russian-language newspaper issued in Baku in 1919. Henry Morgenthau, the United States ambassador to Constantinople, wrote of the events: "None of the fearful horrors perpetrated in the various zones of the war can be compared with the tragic lot of the Armenians" (117, quoting an article written by Morgenthau in 1918). Other documents, which were preserved in the aftermath of the war and which are reported to be in Turkish archives, have never been made public.

EXTERNAL INFLUENCES

By the middle of the nineteenth century, external powers were already expressing concern about Turkish treatment of minorities, as evidenced by the guarantees for internal reforms in the Ottoman Empire written into the Treaty of Paris in 1856. Again in the Treaty of San Stefano (1878), following the Russian-Turkish War, the Ottoman Empire was obliged to "guarantee [Armenian] security against the Kurds and Circassians" who were occupying Armenian territory. As noted above, these and further interventions were ineffective: reforms were not carried out, and Christian minorities in general, Armenians in particular, continued to be victims of discrimination. Indeed, one major writer on the period, Richard Hovannisian (1986b: 28), contends that the reaction to European intervention was intensified repression, including the massacres of 1895–96.

Though yet another set of reforms was imposed on the Ottoman government in 1909, Germany and its allies were not inclined to concern themselves with Turkey's internal affairs while Turkey joined their cause. They did have knowledge of the deportation: a German missionary who had published an account of the earlier massacres witnessed the events of 1915 and returned to Germany to inform the government. Similarly, documentation was available in England, consisting of neutral eyewitness accounts in a published form edited by the eminent British historian Arnold Toynbee (1915, 1916). In May 1915 Britain, France, and Russia spoke out against the massacres, and the American ambassador in Constantinople sent out messages about the deportation, including accounts such as those cited above. Informed public opinion in these countries was outraged, but under the cover of war Turks maintained their position. With the end of the war, the European powers were preoccupied first with peace negotiations and then with preparations for yet another war. External interventions on behalf of the Armenians had little punch, since no country was actually prepared to take further action. Although the Treaty of Sèvres (1920) recognized

Armenia as a free and independent state and obliged the Turks to desist from committing genocide, and although there were trials of some leaders of the massacres, these sanctions were not effective: the trials were of small significance, and the treaty provisions were easily ignored while other international events pushed Turkey out of the limelight. In due course, Turkey denied that the genocide had ever occurred.

Many eyewitness accounts and some European interventions were motivated primarily by revulsion against genocide, but European actions were predicated on a history of self-interested attempts to gain Ottoman territory. Such predatory concerns were chief among the reasons for the Young Turk's policies against the Armenians. In the wake of earlier disastrous wars, Turkish leaders were anxious to preserve their land intact. This concern became, in turn, the Turkish explanation for the genocide.

EPILOGUE

In the immediate aftermath of the war and for a short period thereafter, the Turkish press and parliament frankly discussed the Armenian genocide. Many voices were raised in shock and anger that these events had been ordered and executed by Turks. A military tribunal was established to investigate the crimes, and, later, the Entente powers set up another investigation. The Ottoman Empire ceased to exist by decree of the Entente powers in January 1919. The Turkish nationalist movement, now under Mustafa Kemal, took over the government in 1920, but persecutions and extermination of surviving Armenians, and also of Greeks in Western Armenia and in other parts of Turkey, continued into the 1920s. Kemal expressed his government's intention to prevent his nation from being "split and sacrificed to the intentions of the Greeks and Armenians" and demanded that Turkey's "indisputable" right over Western Armenia and Cilicia be recognized by the Entente powers (Kirakossian, 1992: 189, quoting a telegram from Kemal to the sultan).* The Allies finally extended recognition to the Republic of Armenia in August 1920 and, via the Treaty of Sèvres, imposed its decision on Turkey. None of the Allies, however, was prepared to monitor Turkish rehabilitation efforts, and by the beginning of 1921 it was clear that the agreement had been violated and that refugees were still being created and exterminated.

---

* The sultan continued as the titular head of state, though he did not have much power. In 1919 he had ordered the arrest of Kemal, but his command was not carried out.

8

The USSR, 1932–33

In virtually every case where large-scale massacres have occurred, the individuals and groups charged by international opinion with perpetrating the event have denied it. Yet there are survivor and witness accounts that are impossible both to verify and to ignore. Unfortunately, world politics are generally involved in these events. Neighbouring states may undermine governments that are incompatible with their interests or may ignore bloody events when their national interests are better served by silence. In the aftermath of war, Western powers chose not to risk confrontation with the revolutionary communist state created in the ashes of Russia in 1917. The record was bloody, but we may never be sure how much of what we think happened actually occurred, and how much was either invented or embroidered by the subsequent events of the twentieth century.

Some scepticism, for example, might well greet R.J. Rummel's (1990) estimations of deaths caused by the government of the Union of Soviet Socialist Republics (USSR) between 1917 and 1987: nearly 62 million people, of whom nearly 55 million were citizens. Other estimates range from 20 to 80 million, though none with as explicit an accounting system as Rummel's. Mass murders in the development of the USSR under Vladimir Lenin, and, even more, under the more mature state presided over by Joseph Stalin, certainly occurred – there is too much evidence for this charge to be a fabrication. The question, rather, is whether the higher numbers are accurate and whether such mass murders became commonplace. What is known for sure is that the deaths took many forms, including deportation to concentration camps where slavery, starvation, exhaustion, and frigid temperatures ended millions of lives. Other deaths were attributable to outright slaughter and the forced starvation of national groups.

Here we will outline only one event, the forced starvation of between 5 and 8 million Ukrainian farmers and their families (generally
referred to as peasants)* in the Eastern Ukraine during 1932–33,
with a brief aside on Kazakhstan to situate the genocidal event. Ethnic Ukrainian peasants also starved to death, for the same reasons, in
the Kuban or River Don region of the North Caucasus. We have relied for this account on eyewitness and survivor descriptions that are
largely sympathetic to the Ukrainians and on scholarly, diplomatic,
commissioned, and journalistic studies conducted by Europeans and
Americans. Although these are all credible sources, and the second
group provides substantial evidence to back up its interpretations,
there are naysayers who claim that the accounts of man-made famine
in the Eastern Ukraine were fabricated by "fascists from Hitler to
Harvard" (Tottle, 1987). I accept the historians' version and cite the
eyewitness accounts because, after reading extensively on the subject,
I am convinced that a terrible and deliberate policy of starvation was
imposed on the Eastern Ukrainian farming community in the early
1930s. The reader, however, has been warned that there are other
views and will recognize that the capitalist world of the past century
has been steeped in virile anti-communism.

Of the 140 million people in the whole of the USSR in 1921, an estimated 30 million were Ukrainians and 75 million were Russians. In
1926 the estimated population of the Eastern Ukraine was 26,189,000
(Maksudov, 1986: table 1, 38). The subsequent censuses are suspect
because they were altered to fit political interests. Robert Conquest
(1986: 239) estimated that 5 to 7 million people in the Eastern Ukraine
died because of the famine. James Mace (1984, 1986) estimated that
7.5 million died. A Ukrainian scholar, S.V. Kul'chyts'kyi, estimated
that the deaths due to the famine were between 4.5 and 5 million (cited
by Liber, 1992: 237 n23). Even the lowest of these estimates would
represent 15 per cent of the Ukrainian population. The inability of observers to state the number of deaths accurately is due to Soviet refusal
to acknowledge the forced famine, untrustworthy censuses in 1937 and
1939, and the paucity of Ukrainian scholars who survived. Even the
untrustworthy censuses indicated a death rate in the millions, for
which the officials in charge of the 1937 census were arrested, many of

---

* Though the term "peasants" is widely used for all people engaged in farming, it is not
  strictly correct. Since the abolition of serfdom, the population engaged in farming had
  consisted primarily of independent farmers. On larger farms, there were also employed
  (often seasonal) workers.

them shot, and their work suppressed because they failed to hide the deaths. The 1939 census reflects awareness of these penalties for truth (US Commission, 1988: viii–ix) and is regarded as unreliable. Current sources, from the 1980s to the turn of the century, cite the figure of 7 million. M. Maksudov (1986), in an excruciatingly cautious demographic analysis, deliberately took the lowest possible figures of losses that were not due to natural deaths from the censuses between 1927 and 1938. He concluded that nearly 4.4 million had died within the Ukraine, and at least 600,000 had "migrated" (a euphemism for expulsion). In proportional terms for the decade from 1927 to 1938, he concluded that some 40.2 per cent of the population deaths could not be attributed to normal mortality rates (table 2, 39).

Genocide in Nazi Germany, Armenia, Burundi, and Rwanda was committed by governments against citizens who were defined in biological or at least ethnological terms. In the case of the Eastern Ukraine, Stalin's government focused on the failure of the peasantry to develop successful collective farms, not on the fact that the peasantry under attack was Ukrainian and many of its members were Ukrainian nationalists. The reasoning for the war was couched in terms of the failure of the peasantry to do something that the government wanted done – in this case, become "modern" workers on collective (factory) farms and abandon their claims to independent status as farmers. That defence by the Russian-dominated USSR of the time has been challenged by many Ukrainians and others who argue that this episode was a genocide, as defined in the Genocide Convention: it was rooted in the determination of the Russians to eliminate the Ukrainian population (see, for discussions, Oleskiw, 1983; Hryshko, 1983; Conquest et al., 1984; Dolot, 1985; Serbyn and Krawchenko, 1986; Conquest, 1990; Liber, 1992). Though nationalism and ethnicity are widely cited as the basic causes for the event, the Russian explanations and Stalin's determination to industrialize the USSR rapidly and at all costs cannot be ignored.

HISTORICAL CONTEXT

Russia had long been an empire, similar in many ways to the Ottoman and Austro-Hungarian empires. It had, like them, spread out from its core into lands occupied by various ethnic groups. Its armies fought territorial wars with neighbouring empire-states, enlarging or losing territories over several centuries. By the twentieth century it was running out of steam. Like the Ottoman Empire, it had a form of government that could not enable it to shift into industrial capitalism to compete successfully with the capitalist states of Europe and North America. Its technology was backward and it was still an agrarian-based society with a semi-feudal land policy. Though serfdom had been eliminated, rich landlords continued to own much of the land while the peasantry eked out miserable livings on small plots or remained indebted to landlords. Education was not generally available or affordable. Peasants were often labelled by urban dwellers, and later by Soviet leaders as much as by landlords, as stupid, backward, and loutish, yet cunning. This prevailing stereotype had some bearing on Soviet policies aimed at dispossessing peasants of their land and the profit from their labour. To the extent that Soviet policies drew from Marxist texts (though Marx certainly did not anticipate that so backward a country would become the bearer of his ideas), they were informed that the peasantry was conservative and backward, even reactionary (Marx and Engels [1888], 1970: 75).

The Russian Empire sustained enormous losses during the First World War. Historian Paul Robert Magocsi (1996: 468) provided these data: 1.6 million killed, 3.8 million wounded, 2.4 million imprisoned, and great losses of civilians, property, and livestock. The economic structure and the transportation network had broken down, and there were severe food shortages throughout the country, especially in the urban centres. In March 1917 imperial troops, called on to stop demonstrations in Petrograd, instead joined the workers.

Revolutions broke out in many centres, including the Ukraine where nationalists attempted to create an independent state. They failed, owing to internal battles for control of the nationalist movement and charges by revolutionaries in Russia that the Ukrainians were betraying them. When the Bolsheviks took power in Russia in November 1917, their regional counterparts gained power throughout Dnieper Ukraine. The 1918 peace negotiations between the Union of Soviet Socialist Republics and Germany and Austria-Hungary concluded with the Treaty of Brest-Litovsk, whereby some territory on the western frontier of the Ukraine and Ukrainian territory in eastern Galicia were scheduled for "delimitation," contrary to the wishes of the Ukrainian delegates, but these treaties recognized Ukraine as a sovereign state. Soviet Russia agreed to conclude a peace with the Ukrainian National Republic and to remove pro-Soviet troops" (Magocsi, 1996: 485). An agreement with the Central Powers included the exchange of a million tons of grain by the Ukraine within a few weeks for the return of Ukrainian prisoners of war. But on the day the initial signing of the treaty took place, Bolshevik soldiers drove out the government in Kiev and occupied other Ukrainian territories. The displaced government fought back, but it could not count on the loyalty of – let alone the surrender of grain by – the peasantry. Recognizing the weakness of the Ukrainian government, the German Army moved in. This German "client-state" lasted until the November 1918 conclusion of the war.

The American historian Richard Pipes (1964: 137) called 1919 "a period of complete anarchy" in the Ukraine. Magocsi argues that the same was true of most of 1920 (1996: 494). Peasant uprisings erupted when the farmers thought the land might be turned back to large landowners under the Germans, then again when they saw that the Soviets were planning to force confiscations of grain for the Red Army. Magocsi spares no one when he notes that "murders of Bolshevik officials, pogroms against Jews, Germans, and other well-to-do elements (1,136 pogroms were recorded in 1918–1919), and attacks on towns became the order of the day. Anarchy pure and simple reigned throughout the Ukrainian countryside" (499). The civil wars came to an end through exhaustion in late 1920, with the Bolsheviks in control of the Eastern Ukraine, and Poland in control of the Western territories.

Meanwhile, Bolshevik control of most of the former Russian Empire was becoming consolidated – not, however, without conflict on many fronts. Nationalism was debated, but only the nationalism of the proletariat was accepted as legitimate. Moreover, there was a steady undercurrent of Russianization for the entire USSR. In the Ukraine, now under the Soviet Ukrainian government backed by the Red Army, both politicians and citizens debated how much autonomy would be admissable. But these debates took place within a cauldron of class and nationalist small wars staged by unsympathetic citizens ranging from peasants to urban workers and professionals throughout the whole country. An opposition army (known as Whites in contradistinction from the Reds) formed, some of its groups anti-communist, some nationalist or in favour of the monarchy, and a few calling for constitutional democracy. Peasant rebellions were never fully subdued. In response, arbitrary murders, mass shootings, and torture became a regular part of covert Soviet policy. An armed insurrection in 1921 pitted peasants of Tambov province – who had rebelled against government expropriation of grain, together with organized supporters from army units – against government forces. Both the Whites and the rebels were contained, but containment involved force and terrorism on an escalating scale. A mutiny by the Kronstadt naval base sailors in 1921, in sympathy with peasants who rebelled against continuing expropriation of grain and confiscation of farm animals, intensified the incipient civil war. Lenin stepped back from this war and introduced the New Economic Policy (NEP). It promised a cessation to requisitions from the peasants and reintroduced market forces for their produce. However, he simultaneously increased deportations to forced labour camps, introduced a criminal code that made it legal to send people to such camps for political crimes, and authorized the killing of "enemies of the people." This interlude under the NEP lasted until 1928, when Lenin died, and Stalin became the leader of the USSR.

The Stalinist period began during a worldwide economic depression. His initial challenge was to provide food for urban, industrial workers and the Red Army and to obtain industrial machinery in the West for the development of further industry. He proposed to do so by turning the rural agricultural sector into a series of modern, efficient factory farms in the form of "collectives," capable of supplying the nation's food. In parts of the countryside, there was a tradition of village communes in which farmers retained control of their own land but worked together, purchasing their provisions jointly and sharing in the produce. Although these communes were not the collectives proposed by Soviet planners, government leaders believed they were a possible beginning for the collectivization process. During the NEP they survived through adaptation to Soviet plans, but in 1929 the Communist Party and the Soviet government decreed the collectivization of all farmers. By 1932 all communal farm property was said to be state property, and extreme penalties were imposed against anyone "confiscating" state property.

An Aside on Kazakhstan

Before concentrating on the genocide in the Eastern Ukraine, we should note that the collectivization movement and seizure of produce by the Soviet government had deleterious effects on farmers and peasants throughout the USSR. Starvation was not widespread, but in addition to the Ukraine and the Don region of the North Caucasus, hunger was severe in Kazakhstan and in the Volga Basin. In the Kazakhstan case, forced collectivization of agriculture against the Kazakh herders was met by a rebellion in 1930. The herders killed their cattle to avoid their seizure for collective farms. The number of sheep and cattle in the region declined by nearly 80 per cent from 1928 to 1932, with the number increasing after the initial kill because of inadequate alternative food supplies (Olcutt, 1981: 122–23). Over the next year, starvation took many lives. An estimated 1.5 million Kazakhs (21 per cent of the population) either died or escaped the region. Food was finally sent to Kazakhastan in 1932. The US Commission of Inquiry (1988: 136) concludes that the Kazakhstan episode "seems to have been more the result of official neglect than of deliberate policy," but that "starvation ended resistance." The Volga-Ural region, ethnically heterogeneous, also suffered starvation, but the original cause appears to have been a natural drought. However, the Volga German Republic was hit much more severely than other parts of the Volga region, and there is some debate as to whether this outcome reflected Soviet procurement policies as well as the weather. Robert Conquest (1986: 306) estimates that a million Germans died. Aid was sent to the worst-hit regions in 1932, in the form of grain seized from the North Caucasus, though that region was already suffering mass starvation.

GENOCIDE/POLITICIDE IN THE EASTERN UKRAINE

In 1929 and 1930 villages in the Ukraine and elsewhere were pulled into the five-year plan that featured collectivization by the "Twenty-Five Thousanders," party activists who were mobilized to organize the rural areas. The Thousanders were urban people who had no experience of rural existence and who, according to the memoir of one Ukrainian survivor, were initially laughed at by the villagers (Dolot, 1985: ch. 1). The laughter died down when, first, all village leaders disappeared without explanation, and then their families were forced onto trains taking them to unknown northern destinations. Those who disappeared were labelled "kulaks," meaning rich farmers, though the meaning was more political than economic. Many dissidents were killed or deported on the grounds of being kulaks if they had resisted collectivization or otherwise failed to show enthusiasm for the plan. Then, one move following another, the farmers were forced to accept collectivization, and any who objected either disappeared or were summarily shot.* Intellectuals and other potential leaders of the Ukrainian

---

* The word *kurkul* in Ukrainian, or *kulak* in Russian, was defined by the USSR as a usurer or rich farmer, but it became a political term for anyone who opposed collectivization.

agrarian population were likewise liquidated in advance of the forced famine. By 1932 the government had exterminated everyone who could possibly be classified as a kulak. It had likewise extinguished the lives of real or perceived nationalists, priests, intellectuals, human rights activists, and any others who might have provided ideological leadership to Ukrainian farmers.

In mid-1932 Stalin demanded shipments of grain from the Ukraine that could not possibly be met. In 1930 the region had produced more grain than it had since the revolution, and the central state had procured more than it had ever done before. In 1931 and 1932 the harvests were somewhat smaller, though not so small as to have caused a famine. By that time soldiers were guarding the graneries, and a substantial part of the harvest was taken by the state. In some regions of the Ukraine the procurements were so heavy that nothing was left for workers. James Mace (1986: 10) argues that, "although Ukraine produced only 27 per cent of all grain harvested in the USSR, it was forced to supply 38 per cent of all grain procured." Further, the quota in 1931, despite a decline in the sown area (related to the collectivization in process), was the same as for 1930. When the hunger that had set in during 1931 resulted in few labourers for the spring sowing in 1932, the local Ukrainian officials were blamed. Contrary to claims by apologists for the Stalinist period, there was no drought in the Eastern Ukraine in 1932. Even Soviet historical meteorologists found no evidence of a drought (US Commission, 1988: x).

State property was declared off-limits for the local population, so anyone caught taking the smallest of vegetables was executed or sentenced as an enemy of the people. A decree in December 1932 alleged sabotage of the grain procurement campaign in six Ukrainian villages and subsequently extended the allegation to much of the region. This charge resulted in the closing of stores and the removal of all goods from the villages, a ban on all trade, a purge of local institutions and "foreign elements," and various other measures that could only have been designed for – and, indeed, resulted in – mass starvation. Though Stalin had been informed by several people about the starvation in the Ukraine, he not only denied its existence, but intensified the pressure through 1933. The Soviet authorities, claiming that the peasants were not providing enough, ordered soldiers and activists to search through barns and pantries of the Ukrainian agrarian population. They stole grain and seeds, even baked bread, everything that could be used by the peasants for food or for barter and sale. Domestic animals and wild animals were hunted and killed so the peasants could not get at them. The peasants were left to starve and the borders were sealed. New impossible quotas were imposed, and officials renewed efforts to ensure that there were absolutely no edible foodstuffs available to the peasants.

In view of these data, the US Commission (1988: xv) bluntly charged that "the Ukrainian Famine of 1932–1933 was caused by the extraction of agricultural produce from the rural population." It argued, further, that such a famine would not otherwise have occurred, as demonstrated by Soviet crop statistics for the period.

As in the case of Young Turks against Armenians, and German Nazis against Jews and Gypsies, this politicide and genocide was carefully planned and organized so that many units of government, police, army, and local authorities participated. The Twenty-Five Thousanders included a battery of propagandists, selected from the ranks of the Communist Party or the Young Communist League. These urban officials reorganized the administration of villages once the natural leaders had been removed. They divided each village population into "Hundreds," and the "Hundreds" into "Tens" and then "Fives," with each unit obliged to have an assigned individual in charge. To refuse an assignment was to invite severe penalties and possible death. Propagandists, who disseminated communist ideology, and "agitators," who were supposed to mobilize people in support of policies, were attached to each of the Hundreds (Dolot: 8–10). In addition, there were special units, such as "Bread Procurement Commissions," whose task was to ensure that no one was hoarding food.

Stalin clearly intended that millions of Ukrainian farmers would die. It was his policy, and though he received reports about the starvation from army and police in the region, he chose not to take any counter action. Several army commanders and well-placed officials broached the possibility of sending food to the region. To one and all, Stalin replied that no food would be sent. He made it clear, moreover, that if relief was sent, the government would have to admit there was a famine and it would no longer be possible to blame it on the kulaks (Conquest, 1986: 325).

The highest officers of the USSR were aware of the famine, whether or not they were complicit in its planning and execution. Brigades of activists were organized to seek grain and beat up people. The brigades consisted of various officials, someone labelled as an expert in grains, and a local teacher (often involuntarily attached to the brigades). These people, along with state and party officials, were given food rations; in some districts there were restaurants for party officials, in the midst of the famine region or at the borders. Officials were often brutal in their treatment of dying peasants and sometimes threw the dying as well as the dead into mass burial pits. Officials who could not tolerate the brutality, who expressed pity for the children with the distended bellies of starvation, or who began to disbelieve that this treatment was necessary for the great communist revolution were soon sent to concentration camps – or their own death. Dolot (1985) recalls that when the brutality began, as far back as 1929, the reason given by the Thousanders was that collectivization was necessary to drive out the kurkuls (kulaks). In 1932, when starving farm families tried to escape to regional towns in the hope of gaining work or food, they came up against a new passport law that prevented them from getting employment or food rations. "The passportization was supposedly directed against the kurkuls, as Soviet propaganda proclaimed: 'Passportization is a mortal blow against the kurkuls!' All villagers had been collectivized by this time. There was not a single independent farmer left in our village by the end of 1932. Could the members of a collective farm be kurkuls" (175)?

PERSONAL ACCOUNTS

There are numerous harrowing accounts of whole villages dying, children with bloated bellies, parents turned into skeletons, madness caused by hunger, cannibalism, desperate attempts to swim across rivers to reach food on the forbidden other side, corpses lining the railway tracks throughout the entire Ukraine, and corpses loaded onto trains. Even Nikita Krushchev, in unofficial memories smuggled out and published in the West, told about a conversation he had with the first secretary of the Kiev Regional Committee. Comrade Demchenko told him about "a train ... loaded with corpses of people who had starved to death. It picked up corpses all the way from Poltava to Kiev" (as reported in Mace, 1986). But there are more graphic stories, such as the one written by a native Ukrainian functionary of the party, Victor Kravchenko, in 1946 (as reproduced in the Widener Library account, 1986: 48–9):

We arrived at the large village of Petrovo towards evening. An unearthly silence prevailed. "All the dogs have been eaten, that's why it's so quiet," the peasant who led us to the Political Department said. "People don't do much walking, they haven't the strength," he added ... we were conducted to a peasant hut for the night ... Our hostess was a young peasant woman. All feeling, even sadness and fear, seemed to have been drained from her starved features. They were a mask of living death. In a corner, on a narrow bed, two children lay so quietly they seemed lifeless. Only their eyes were alive. I winced when they met mine.' [The visitors shared their provisions with the family and the woman spoke.] "I will not tell you about the dead," she said. "I'm sure you know. The half-dead, the nearly dead are even worse. There are hundreds of people in Petrovo bloaded with hunger. I don't know how many die every day. Many are so weak that they no longer come out of their houses. A wagon goes around now and then to pick up the corpses. We've eaten everything we could lay our hands on – cats, dogs, field mice, birds. When it's light tomorrow you will see the trees have been stripped of their bark, for that too has been eaten. And the horse manure has been eaten.

Art, literature, and music were banned if they failed to glorify the great Russian experiment. The Russian composer Dmitri Shostokovich wrote about Stalin's massacre of Ukraine's blind peasant folksingers. Minstrels in the region were, by tradition, blind men who travelled from village to village and maintained, in musical form, the oral history of the people. Stalin organized a gathering of them, what Shostokovich called "a living museum, the country's living history. All its songs, all its music and poetry." He concludes, "And they were almost all shot, almost all those pathetic blind men killed" (from Shostakovich, 1979, reprinted in the Widerner Library collection, 1986: 53–4).

The victims of this tragedy were not all alike in their ideological perspectives. Outstanding among them, no doubt, were the staunch defenders of the Ukrainian Greek Orthodox Church and of Ukrainian nationalism, and the reformers who had consistently called for democracy and guarantees of human rights. Those who were willing to have cooperatives but not collective farms, and others who were unwilling to have any sharing of farm operations on their properties, were, in their actions, demonstrating their conviction that collectivization was ideologically unacceptable or, at least, impractical. Stalin fully recognized that these people, the rural leaders and the intelligentsia, were the most dangerous opponents of his policies, and they were the first to be assaulted. By 1933 the surviving Ukrainians were mainly farm people, peasants in the terminology of the USSR. Although, according to Stalin, the "nationalist problem is, in its very essence, a problem of the peasantry" (Conquest, 1986: 219), the peasants were by this time primarily focused on survival. Their nationalism was muted as they tried to cope with the pressures to collectivize and to produce far in excess of the capacities of the land. That they cooperated with senseless demands up to the point where there were no more crops and no food left suggests that they were not embedded in a strong or militant opposition movement.

EXTERNAL INFLUENCES

Borders closed, media controlled, government by stealth and terror: there was little room in this scenario for either external supporters or observers. But some foreign journalists did get into the Ukraine in 1933, when the forced starvation was far advanced. Some European and American communists were living in the USSR and learned of the event. There were also soldiers whose trains passed through the Ukraine. Conquest (1986: 252, 308–16) argues that adequate reports were published in many of Europe's and America's major newspapers, though journalists were subjected to censorship and expelled if they reported the facts too clearly. A few writers chose to eulogise the Soviet Union. Foremost among them was the Moscow correspondent of the *New York Times*, Walter Duranty, who, in dispatches and books, dismissed rumours of starvation in the Ukraine, North Caucasus, and Lower Volga (Widener Library, 1986: 38–9). Despite his dispatches in the American press, Duranty informed British consular officials in Moscow in 1933 that the population in the Ukraine had decreased in the previous year by some 4 to 5 million, and for the North Caucasus and Lower Volga by some 3 million. Eugene Lyons, the United Press correspondent in Moscow from 1928 to 1934, ruefully admitted in 1937: "The whole shabby episode of our failure to report honestly the gruesome Russian famine of 1932–33 ... reflects little glory on world journalism ... Not a single American newspaper or press agency protested publicly against the astonishing and almost unprecedented confinement of its correspondent in the Soviet capital or troubled to probe for the causes of this extraordinary measure" (quoted in Widener Library, 1986: 38–9). An exception to this generalization was the Moscow correspondent of the *Christian Science Monitor*, William Henry Chamberlin, who subsequently published a full-length book report of the famine (his article in the *Monitor*, 29 May 1934, was photographed and shown in the Widener Library, 1986: 41). Another correspondent, Malcolm Muggeridge, writing in the *Manchester Guardian*, visited the

Ukraine, wrote honestly about it, and, like Chamberlin, subsequently wrote several articles and two books about the experience.

British diplomats were informed of the events by numerous observers in Russia. Michael Marrus, who has written about the Jewish Holocaust, refers to the published British documents, in contrast to the "callous diplomatic officers in London who feared that the damning descriptions of Soviet reality would upset their courtship of Moscow or impede the hoped-for Soviet accession to the League of Nations" (Carynnyk et al., 1988: foreword). In fact, Britain was a major importer of wheat from the USSR. Wheat was selling at an all-time low during the worldwide Depression of the early 1930s. The poor market price, compared to the high price of industrial machinery, was a severe problem for the USSR while it was trying to industrialize its cities. The wheat was being purchased by Britain against loans that financed industrialization. Indeed, the cycle was even more complicated: according to Carynny et al., Britain lent between £30 million and £40 million to Germany and the Germans passed on credits to the Soviet Union, which used them to purchase heavy machinery in Germany. "Britain was thus financing Germany's export trade with the Soviet Union," say the authors. A public campaign to send food to the Ukraine would have reduced Soviet grain exports, "and that would have upset the international banking system, in which London had such a great stake" (xlviii).

Yet for most of the world, this event remained shrouded in secrecy long after Stalin's reign. Stalin persuaded Western inquirers who had not actually seen the starving peasants that no famine occurred. He adopted a method of deception – the "big lie" as it was later called in reference to Nazi propaganda – that apparently subdued criticism. Even after Krushchev began to assess the past of the USSR critically, many years passed before outsiders were able to access archives and speak to people who had experienced the famine and other mass killings. At the conclusion of the century, while most people knew something about the Nazi Holocaust, knowledge of the plight of Ukrainians remained scant. The US Congress investigation of 1988 and the publication of the British Foreign Office documents in 1986 were the beginnings of more widespread dissemination of information.

At this same time – the mid-1980s – both eyewitness accounts, such as the one by Dolot, and trenchant denials that a politically designed famine had occurred came into the Western literature. Douglas Tottle (1987), one of the denunciators, blamed the Hearst Press and Harvard

University for their persistent anti-communist research, "often in collaboration with U.S. military and intelligence agencies" (57), together
with Nazi propagandists. He points out that anti-communist propaganda had been widespread from the 1917 revolution forward and that
the Soviet government had attempted the mighty task of transforming
"a backward land plagued by poverty and illiteracy into an industrialized country with a modern agricultural sector." In his opinion, the opposition of the peasants to collectivization, approaching a civil war in
scale, was the chief cause of food shortages, and drought was a compli-
cating factor, together with "widespread sabotage, amateurish Soviet
planning, Stalinist excesses and mistakes" (2).

It's true that the external, capitalist world was anti-communist and
that American sources might have overstated Stalinist excesses and
mistakes, particularly before the collapse of the USSR. The problem
with that defence, however, is that there were credible eyewitnesses and
that, since the fall of the "Iron Curtain" many others who do not share
the "American agenda" have come forward with personal testimonies.

9

Nazi Germany, 1933–45

The most widely known occurrence of state terror in the twentieth century is the Nazi Holocaust. Whole libraries are now devoted to its description and explanation, and for many writers this event is unique, so comparative studies are not welcomed. Obviously, I do not share this belief: the Holocaust was a terrible event, and there were other terrible events during the same century, all of which demand that we try to understand why and how they occurred. To ignore their similarities is to place impediments to the process of comprehension. Further, to insist that there are similarities between this and other genocidal episodes is not tantamount to denying the particular history or the particular horror of the Holocaust.

The larger part of the literature concerns the attempted eradication of Jews. An estimated 5 to 6 million Jews were deported to concentration camps or otherwise killed. So, too, before the enunciation of the "final solution," some 80,000 Germans, deemed by the Nazis to be physically or mentally deficient, were subjected to involuntary euthanasia. Homosexuals and persons labelled as antisocial were also murdered. Thousands of Poles, particularly the intelligentsia and other leaders, were shot. About a million Roma and Sinti (Gypsies) were killed, many in concentration camps established years before the camps for Jews. At the Russian front, an estimated 2 million prisoners of war were killed and, as the war progressed, many more Poles, Slavs, and other civilians were killed. Jews were undoubtedly the largest single ethnic group subjected to mass murder, but in trying to understand this terrible event we need to recognize that whatever it was that motivated killing on this scale, it cannot be explained with reference only to anti-Semitism. As well, though it was Germans who organized the concentration camps, the

Polish, Hungarian, Vichy French, and other European governments allied with or under German occupation collaborated in rounding up Jews
in their territories and deporting them to the camps.

Because this event has attracted more attention than other genocidal
attacks, there is a richer analytical literature than for others; indeed,
for some writers who have focused on this event, their generalizations
from it to other attacks lead to unsupportable conclusions. The focus
on the extermination of Jews from Europe obscured the more general
policy to eradicate a range of persons whom the Nazi leadership considered "life unworthy of life," or "impure," and prevented understanding that the systematic killing of hospital patients and then of
Gypsies was not an incidental forerunner to the killing of Jews but fully
related to the larger project of eliminating "lower" forms of life as
Nazis defined them. The long-standing anti-Semitism in Europe was
crucial to the Nazis' determining Jews to be primary among the
"lower" forms of life, but to understand the Nazi project we have to
move away from the much too narrow version of mass extermination
under the Genocide Convention.

HISTORICAL CONTEXT

Germany was a slow starter on the road to industrial capitalism compared to Britain and France. Beset by extreme religious cleavages and
clashes between princelings with fiefdoms, neither modern capitalism
nor democracy took hold in Germany as they did in other Western
European countries during the eighteenth century. Indeed, following the
disastrous thirty Years War and the Peace of Westphalia in 1648, much
of the country lapsed into feudalism. It remained in that state for the
next two centuries. Junkers (a class of estate owners in Prussia) emerged
as a dominant force through persistent warfare with neighbouring
groups and extreme exploitation of serfs. Otto von Bismarck, one such
Junker, became the chief architect of a united Germany in the late 1860s.
Under his guidance, the Prussian army was strengthened, and Germany
under Prussian control fought several wars to become the dominant
power of northern Europe. Austria was excluded from the German
union, and King Wilhelm 1 of Prussia was proclaimed emperor of Germany in 1871. Bismarck is also credited with creating a remarkable bureaucratic framework for affairs of the state and with nurturing the
development of industry. Though he fashioned a nation, the sense of national identity was slow to develop; when it did, it hinged on a patriar-

chal notion of "the fatherland." After Bismarck's period, industry continued to develop, and Germany began to embark on imperial ventures that brought it into conflict with Britain, France, Belgium, and other European countries for control of colonies in Africa and Asia. Conflicts led in due course to the First World War in 1914–18.

Following defeat in that war, Germans suffered through a period of extreme hardship: unemployment was widespread, and people were impoverished as well as humbled by the terms of a harsh peace treaty. Added to hardships subsequent to a failed war were the repercussions of a worldwide depression from the early 1920s through the 1930s. The Weimar Republic government defaulted on its reparations payments in 1922, and French forces occupied the Ruhr the following year. General strikes, a steady decline in the value of the Deutschmark, and rapidly rising inflation further eroded the living conditions of the working class. The belief that the Versailles Treaty was grossly unfair was widespread, as was the rationale that Germans were being punished for a war that was in large part caused by their enemies.

The National Socialist German Workers' Party (NAZI) was established in 1920 (its progenitor, the German Workers' Party, was formed a year earlier) on a platform of nationalism and working-class interests. An eloquent demagogue, Adolf Hitler, became the party's chief in 1921. The party blamed minorities, especially Jews, as well as the victorious powers for the economic depression. Hitler appealed to patriotism and manipulated the frustration, fear, and rage of his countrymen towards hatred of the victorious powers together with Germany's "internal enemies," who had "stabbed them in the back." These potent phrases were well received in Germany, where many believed that the war would have been won, or at least that the treaty would have been less harsh, but for "sellouts" of German interests by the Jews and other non-Aryans. The imagined enemies were frequently called "November criminals," a phrase that Hitler repeatedly used in his speeches. These beliefs, widespread poverty, and unemployed soldiers, together with the anti-democracy rhetoric of a substantial segment of the population – monarchists, many owners of large companies, and army officers, teachers, university professors, medical doctors, and other professionals – contributed to the failure of the Weimar Republic.

The Nazi Party began, covertly, to train a militia force, later known as the SA (Sturmabteilung) or "Brownshirts," whose explicit mission was to advance the cause of the party through violence and to foster the establishment of a socialist state. Simultaneously, the Nazis moved

ahead as a democratic political party, which had its first success at the
polls in 1930 and a majority in the Reichstag in 1932. It received funding for a time from industrial magnates, but this support dried up after
months of endless conflicts in the Reichstag. The Nazis undertook covert and minimally legal manoeuvres in an attempt to get full control of
the Reichstag and to make Hitler the chancellor. They were not alone
in scheming: German politics in the early 1930s was rife with intrigues,
or as historian William Shirer (1961: 175) phrased it, "cabals within
cabals." The Reichstag had become unmanageable. Near the end of
1933 the chancellor, General Kurt von Schleicher, attempted to win
over the trade unions through legislative action against the interests of
industrialists and big landowners. When called to account by the president, Paul von Hindenburg, Schleicher pointed to a scandal involving
major Junker landholders, Hindenburg among them.

Despite further intrigues and virtual blackmail, the Schleicher government fell in January 1933 and Hitler was appointed chancellor.
Amid rumours of an army plot to establish a military dictatorship, the
SA was put on alert, and the army was ordered to support the new government under Hitler. The cabinet was an incompatible combination of
conservatives representing the Junkers with their allies and the Nazis.
But it represented the country, which, in Shirer's words (1961: 175)
"bordered on paralysis of existing institutions – the Army, the
churches, the trade unions, the political parties." Shirer adds that the
"vast non-Nazi middle class and the highly organized proletariat" were
part of the paralysis and weakness of Germany at the beginning of
1933. Another part, in his opinion, consisted of the wealthy landowners and big businesses that tacitly undermined the Weimar Republic by
failure to defend it or pay adequate taxes to maintain democracy.

Hitler called for a new election once he had the power of the chancellor. His ally Paul Joseph Goebbels began preparations for what he
called "a masterpiece of propaganda," with the full resources of the
state, including radio and press capacities. In short order, the Nazi government had banned Communist and Social Democratic Party meetings
and suspended their newspapers. The leader of the Catholic Trade
Unions was beaten by Brownshirts, other opponents of the Nazis were
assassinated, and numerous bureaucratic offices were removed from re-
publicans and turned over to SA officers. Finally, in a brutal attempt to
persuade a sceptical population to believe that communists were
plotting to take over the state, Nazis set the Reichstag afire and blamed

the conflagration on communists. Though the communist leaders were subsequently found innocent by a court, Hitler, long before the court could deliberate on the crimes, had persuaded President Hindenburg to sign a decree that effectively suspended the constitution and civil liberties. This decree was the final blow to the fourteen-year-old Weimar Republic: its fall was all quite legal and remarkably well orchestrated. Supporters ranged all the way from monarchists and landed aristocracy to trade unionists.

Only the Social Democrats objected to the demise of the republic, and they were en route to oblivion. By the end of 1933 Hitler persuaded the German people that they had the right to rearm, contrary to the prohibitions of the Versailles Treaty. Shirer (1961: 212) notes: "There was no doubt that in defying the outside world as he had done, he had the overwhelming support of the German people." Within weeks, the Nazis removed political power from state governments and centralized it in their own regime; they occupied union headquarters and effectively destroyed independent trade unions; the central bank president was replaced by a Nazi economist; and other political parties were vigorously suppressed, their leaders terrified if not jailed. Hitler provided the means for Heinrich Himmler to turn a former wing of the SA, the SS (Schutzstaffel) or "Blackshirts," into the Prussian Gestapo, which became a secret police empire. Hermann Goering also created a personal police force near Berlin. Violence was epidemic.

Hitler obstructed attempts by his own socialist followers, including the Brownshirts, to mount a "second revolution" against big business, the aristocracy, the Junkers, and the Prussian generals, who still controlled the army. He needed the institutions and backing of the upper classes, and he risked the alienation of his troops by preventing attacks on the establishment. In this and many other calculated risks, Hitler triumphed. In June 1934 the left-wing workers in the party, including many who provided the manpower for the Brownshirts, were murdered by Blackshirts on Hitler's orders. Whether there was a genuine threat of a second revolution is not known, but this public purge showed the bourgeoisie and the army that Hitler was prepared to work with, not against, them. Over the next three years Hitler achieved an agreement with the highest officers of the German army, even managing to persuade the armed forces to swear an oath of allegiance to him personally, as Führer of the German Reich and people and as supreme commander of the armed forces. He was not just the chancellor of the state but a commander above the state.

The Nazi police state was organized by Himmler, the Reichsführer of the ss and chief of all German police, and his appointed second in command, ss general Reinhard Heydrich, the head of the ss Security Service, the sd (Sicherheitsdienst). Immediately following the takeover of government by the Nazis, the police were reorganized throughout the Reich by the ss, beginning with an infusion of ss troops into the regular police forces. The resulting organization was complex, involving first two branches, the Orpo (Order Police) and the Sipo (Security Police). The Sipo, in turn, had two divisions, known as the Gestapo and the Kripo. The Gestapo was charged with the task of eliminating opposition to the Nazi regime; the Kripo was expected to control society and eliminate non-political threats. These diverse groups, with ss officers in paramount positions, were the "enforcers" of Nazi policy and were given great powers, but they were also, inevitably, in competition with one another. In a state that glorified physical strength and "hardness," the competition often took the form of proving how tough they could be.

George Browder (1996), in a detailed study of the police organization, argues that the much vaunted efficiency of the bureaucracy may have been overrated: much of the organization was ad hoc, overlapping, and confusing, and the competition among groups was not always beneficial. In addition, the definitions of traitors, subversives, and opposition tended to shift as Nazi policies evolved. Where detectives were earlier assigned to focus on communists, they soon had to concern themselves with Nationalist and Centre parties, and then with Jews and Freemasons and other religious organizations. He concludes that as late as 1937, the sd, by then holding enormous power, "had not achieved anything like its image of all-seeing eyes. It had not outgrown its amateurish origins, and it remained overwhelmed by its missions" (231). The Gestapo, he says, has become something of a myth; it was, in fact, "simultaneously the embodiment of its police-gangster image and the professional police force to which it aspired." Though shot through with contradictions and ambiguity, these police organizations had between them the task of ridding the society of dissidents – whose numbers ever increased as new definitions proliferated.

Within a short period, Germany was Nazified. Joseph Goebbels brought the arts, sciences, and communications industries under the control of his Ministry of Propaganda and encouraged students to burn "dissident" books. Many artists, writers, and scholars emigrated; others had no voice or platform. Jews were prohibited from participating in the arts and the professions, and their work, including the music of Mendelssohn and other composers, was forbidden. Education in the Third Reich became whatever the Propaganda Ministry supported. Young people were socialized to accept the dictates of the Nazi government and were rewarded for their loyalty. The justice system was undermined, and Hitler's word became the law of the land.

In 1934, while these events were unfolding, the eminent journalist-historian of the period, William Shirer (1961), was taking up residence in Germany. His observation is worthy of note: "The overwhelming majority of Germans did not seem to mind that their personal freedom had been taken away, that so much of their culture had been destroyed and replaced with a mindless barbarism, or that their life and work had become regimented to a degree never before experienced even by a people accustomed for generations to a great deal of regimentation" (231). Most explanations for this acceptance rest on the pathetic state to which the German population had been reduced, the authoritarian culture, and the rejection of democracy and the Weimar Republic. The theories that motivated Nazi policy towards minorities and others they considered "unfit for life" may have had their roots in a frustrated sense of German superiority that had emerged during the last two decades of the previous century, together with the anti-Semitism that went back as far as the reign of Constantine.

Throughout the long history of European anti-Semitism, sometimes fervently, at other times passively, European Christians discriminated against and at times persecuted Jews. When they were prohibited from owning agricultural land, Jews entered the professions, the arts, and the commercial sectors of the economy. A wealthy class of Jews emerged in tandem with the emergence of European nation-states. This group became known as "the bankers of Europe" because they were adept at procuring and organizing capital for monarchs and nascent industrialists – a fact emphasized in explanations of the Holocaust. However, the majority of Jews were neither bankers nor wealthy.

Roma and Sinti were also long-term victims of discrimination throughout Europe. Unlike Jews, Gypsies were not as a group successful in business or wealthy. They were nomadic people, possibly originating in India, who travelled throughout Europe selling small wares, performing dances, and reading fortunes for pennies. Several German states, and particularly Bavaria, established discriminatory laws against them, and persecutions were common even under the Weimar Republic.

The legacy of nineteenth-century biological sciences was a rationale for inequality. Darwin's theories were applied to human development not only in Germany but also in Britain, the United States, and other countries in the late nineteenth and early twentieth centuries. Theories abounded about correlations between brain size and intelligence, the racial inheritance of intelligence, and numerous other "scientific" formulations of popular prejudices. Criminal tendencies were attributed to "lower classes" not by virtue of environment but because they were "born for evil." The "science" of "eugenics," first established in Britain, merged with social Darwinism and was advanced in the United States under the sponsorship of leading family trusts (Carnegie, Harriman, and Rockefeller). Before the First World War German eugenics developed along the same paths as in the United States, yet with more emphasis on class than on race; divergent approaches emerged, however, with one school arguing that the Aryan races were superior to others (Friedlander, 1995: 10). Under the Weimar Republic, eugenics continued as a viable academic subject, widely supported by all political parties. Only after the Nazis gained power were the theories addressed to radical anti-Semitism. Indeed, up to that time Jewish scientists had been among those developing the discipline of eugenics and were prominent among academics dealing with the subject in leading universities.

Coming to power in 1933, the party began a systematic persecution and expulsion of minorities. Nazi racial regulations against Jews, Gypsies, and the disabled were enunciated in 1933, followed by a law allowing enforced involuntary sterilization and incarceration in concentration camps. Expulsion was advocated by a 1934 law, and in 1935 the Nuremberg racial laws classified Gypsies, Jews, and Blacks as racially distinctive minorities of "alien blood." Gypsies were catalogued as "racially inferior asocials and criminals of Asiatic ancestry." Police harassment, restrictions on freedom of movement, sterilization, and other such acts were commonplace. Before the 1936 Olympics in Berlin, a directive was sent by the chief of the Berlin police to arrest all Gypsies; they were deposited in a concentration camp next to a sewage dump and then assigned to forced labour. During this pre-war period, however, the systematic extermination of minorities was not yet Nazi policy. Jews were encouraged, even forced, to emigrate, and their properties were confiscated. But even as late as 1939, the chief directors of population policies, Himmler (chief of the German Policy and Reichsführer SS, appointed as Reich commissioner for the Consolidation of German Nationhood after the onset of war), and Heydrich (who became the special officer responsible for implementing the solution to the Jewish question, and was also in charge of the Central Immigration Office and the Central Resettlement Office) were still developing plans for Jewish reservations on Poland's eastern border and, later, in Madagascar. Heydrich justified the Madagascar project in these terms: "The Jews are considered hostile to us because of our standpoint on race. For this reason they are of no use to us in the Reich. We must eliminate them. Biological extermination, however, is undignified for the German people as a civilized nation" (Aly, 1999: 2–3).

POLITICIDE/GENOCIDE

Meanwhile, institutionalized patients who were classified as mentally ill, the term included many who had speech impediments, were mute or deaf, retarded, epileptic, or physically disabled – became the focus of attention in some of the scientific circles. A range of others was soon added, many categorized as "Asozial" – "human beings with a hereditary and irreversible mental attitude, who, due to this nature, incline toward alcoholism and immorality" (Friedlander, 1995: 17, citing German documents). Euthanasia, or assisted suicide, was recommended on the grounds that such persons were a burden to everyone and costly to the state. Under the Nazis these ideas flourished, with Hitler pledging to preserve the "purity of German blood." Before the war, the preservation meant exclusion of the impure and took the forms of institutionalization, incarceration, sterilization, and forced emigration. In 1940 the policy changed. First the institutionally disabled were targeted for enforced euthanasia, then other groups of undesirables.

Gypsies were gradually incorporated into the category of "Asozialen" and suffered the same fate as the disabled. During this time the Jews were excluded in diverse ways, forced into ghettos, where their property was confiscated, or exiled to places where they could not possibly eke out a living. They were persecuted and many died of starvation and forced labour, but they were not yet subjected to systematic eradication.

Conventional wisdom on the development of the genocidal project ties it entirely to the long-standing anti-Semitism in Germany (Goldhagen,

1996). This connection raises difficult questions, however, precisely because the anti-Semitism was so long-standing and pervasive throughout
Europe. Why did it come to a head at this particular time? Why did it co-
incide with a large-scale war launched by Germany? Indeed, why did it
emerge in Germany when, in fact, there were larger Jewish populations
in Poland and Hungary, and substantial populations as well in Romania
and France? Explanations have generally focused on Hitler's irrational
hatred of Jews, or at least on the cultural climate of the time in Germany.
There is no doubt that Hitler was rabidly anti-Semitic or that the culture
of the group he gathered around him was characterized by perverse
forms of "genetic" nationalism, Social Darwinism, racism, anti-liberal-
ism, anti-democracy, and admiration for extreme force. The determination to create a police state was already in place when the Nazis took
office, and the authoritarian approach to any potential threat erased the
distinction between actual threats to the society and perceived threats to
Nazi control. Even then, however, we lack an explanation for the formulation of the extreme "final solution" while the country was at war.

Historian Götz Aly (1999) has suggested a different explanation –
one that ties the genocide to the relocation policy which was part of the
pan-German movement initiated under the Nazis. He points out that
the men who were in charge of immigration and resettlement of the
Germans from outside Germany's formal borders were also the ones in
charge of solving the "Jewish question" and, with it, the "problem" of
other minorities. The resettlement proposals of 1939 began with occupied Poland, where Poles and Jews were to be expelled to make room
for ethnic Germans who were to be "returned" to the Reich; similar
proposals were developed for other occupied regions. The returnees –
many of whom had not chosen to be relocated or did not even see
themselves as specifically German anymore – were to be settled on land
held by Poles and Jews, and were to receive other property previously
owned by the earlier occupants. The problem, then, was what to do
with the displaced Poles and Jews who were not only numerous but impoverished by these policies. Possible havens elsewhere were closed off
when other countries refused entry to persons with no legal assets.

Various deportation schemes failed before the establishment of the
"final solution" in 1942. "Instead of 30,000 Gypsies," says Aly, "only
2800 were deported to the end of April, 1941. The ghettoization of the
Jews was achieved very inconsistently." Hitler had promised to resettle
ethnic Germans from Eastern Europe and South Tyrol, so more Jews
and others had to be deported. He had made it clear that his priority

was to "establish a Reich boundary that does justice to historical, ethnographic, and economic conditions," meaning the annexation and settlement of territories throughout Europe by ethnic Germans (speech to the Reichstag, 6 October 1939). By the Nazi-Soviet non-aggression pact concluded in August 1939, Russia and Germany agreed that the ethnic German population from the Soviet countries would be relocated in Germany or in occupied territory in Poland.

Once war was declared, deportation to "reservations" replaced the policy of forced emigration. The numbers, however, continued to grow as the German Reich expanded its reach throughout Europe. To keep these people on some kind of social subsistence while Germans were engaged in a war was out of the question, and total eradication was beginning to be hinted at late in 1941. Before plans for large-scale genocide were enunciated, however, thousands of Jews, Gypsies, Poles, Slavs, and other minorities who were not useful to the German war effort died from starvation, exposure, slave labour, lack of medical care, and other consequences of deliberate and explicit policies of the German Reich. Aly (1999: 17) quotes Himmler: "It is high time that this riff-raff be herded together in ghettos; then bring in epidemics and let them rot." Similar sentiments were freely expressed by others in the administration, including reference to the Jews as "subhumans." The authorization to murder was already stated by Hitler in 1935, with reference to mentally ill Germans. The justification was phrased in economic terms: the saving to the Reich of hospital care and food for people who were "idiots." By 1940 Roma and Sinti were being sent to concentration camps where they were killed. A year later, the German Reich, now bursting at the seams with relocated ethnic Germans, was considering plans for ridding Europe of its largest non-Aryan ethnic group.

The possibility of murdering large numbers of Jews had been proposed and discussed throughout the early years of the war, but deportation had still been the official policy except for Jews and others who were "unfit for labour." In some regions of Germany, miscellaneous killing parties had already exterminated thousands of mentally ill persons, Jews, and others in roving vans equipped with gas (Aly, 1999: 214–15). In the summer of 1941 many prisoners in the concentration camps at Mauthausen, Buchenwald, Auschwitz, and Sachsenhausen were gassed because they were judged to be incapable of useful labour. Proposals for mass sterilization were actively considered for Jews, "Mischlinge" (German-Jewish "hybrids"), Eastern ethnic groups, and others. In any discussion of these proposals, the need for food supplies for "good" Germans and the armed forces was a major consideration. As the war against the USSR dragged on, and as it became evident that the anticipated grain supplies from the Ukraine would not be available to Germany, the demand for killing off "useless" people whose food intake deprived others became more insistent. In the first four months of the Russian front, some 500,000 Soviet Jews in occupied areas were murdered (Aly, 1999: 217). By mid-August 1941 huge extermination camps were under construction throughout the eastern occupied territories.

While the earlier persecutions were public, the "final solution" that emerged throughout 1941 and was presented to selected state secretaries more formally at the Wannsee Conference in January, 1942* was more secretive. At that conference, over 11 million Jews from all of Europe, the occupied territories of the USSR, and French colonial territories in North Africa were scheduled for systematic extermination (estimates based on Wannsee Conference statistics reported by Aly, 1999: table 2, 197). By this time mass extermination had already begun, though the term "evacuation" was the euphemism for murder.

The planning and conduct of the earlier deportation schemes, the concentration camps, and the mass extermination were organized and led by ss officers and others specially appointed by Hitler or his immediate senior deputies. The guards at the first camp at Dachau, established only two months after Hitler became chancellor in 1933, were all ss men and Storm Troopers. After the liquidation of sa leaders, Himmler, as chief of police, took charge of the camps. The Waffen-ss was a special military division interjected into the Wehrmacht, where its personal loyalty to Himmler and Hitler could infect or at least confuse professional military men. As the plan for eradication progressed, the ss expanded its police battalions and drafted reservists as well as new recruits. These battalions were stationed in German-occupied central Poland, annexed Polish territories, occupied Czechoslovakia, the Netherlands, and other occupied territories. In the eastern occupied territories, special reserve units were created to round up Jews and put them on trains for the camps. They were brutal operations, often requiring the men to kill reluctant Jews in cold blood (Browning, 1998). The regular army was involved in some of the logistical tasks, but for the most part its manpower was absorbed by the war.

* The video "The Conference at Wannsee" is reportedly based on the only surviving original transcript of the meeting. The conference centre at Wannsee has been turned into a Holocaust museum.

Many institutional sectors of the state were involved in the identification, deportation, and ultimate killing of victims, including civil servants who prepared regulations, German railways personnel, and other bureaucrats who were involved but not on the front lines. The forced labour of concentration inmates was organized by sectors of industry, and certain companies were beneficiaries of the labour. Other companies manufactured the gas and the "showers" that fed the gas to victims. The killing operations were organized by the military arm of the Nazi party, the SS. In short, this massacre was organized, involved the active participation of thousands of workers in different sectors of the civil service and the economy, and must have had the support of a large part of the population to succeed. Throughout, the SS was the leading group, with the army and the police maintaining control over daily operations. Still, the efficiency of the operation may be overstated; the extraordinary miscalculation of USSR armed capacities and the length of the war on the Soviet front, as well as the potential for victory, obliged the hierarchy to reschedule and hurriedly alter plans for the deportations and extermination. Limited resources and other practical constraints had to be taken into account. Conflicts over the definition of mixed-blood Germans and what to do with them, and less philosophical conflicts over priorities for use of trains in the midst of a war, were indicative of reality intruding on the mythology of extreme rationality in the German conduct of both genocide and the war.

We cannot absolve the other sectors of society which might have stopped the Nazis at earlier stages or at least have had the courage to dissent at later ones. These groups included the Junkers and the businessmen who had hated the Weimar Republic simply because they hated democracy and wished for a return of aristocratic rule. They included the intellectuals who accepted the destruction of universities and libraries, and even colluded in these barbaric acts, because they actually agreed with the Nazis and feared being dissenters. They included members of the judiciary who quickly bowed to Nazi control of the judicial system – again, apparently, because they essentially agreed with the Nazis in the early stages of the Third Reich. They, too, had contempt for democracy. Many school teachers and artists also stayed in Germany and supported the Nazis, either afraid to speak up, or essentially in agreement.

Hitler provided Germans of all classes with rewards that no one else had dared to claim, let alone win: full employment in emerging war industries, a growing military establishment despite the prohibitions of the humiliating treaty, and a sense of their own power and importance despite their defeat in the war of 1914–18. It is generally assumed that the elimination of the Jews and Gypsies was accepted by a majority of Germans of that time as an reasonable price for these rewards: indeed, according to virtually all writers who observed this period in Germany, the killing of Jews was seen as their "deserved fate," and few in Germany publicly doubted the appropriateness of their destruction. This interpretation may be conventional wisdom established in the postwar period, however. Christopher Browning (1998) is one of the few historians to question its validity. In his opinion the virulence of anti-Semitism has been overstated, and the majority of Germans were as concerned with many other issues in the Weimar Republic and during the twelve years of Nazi rule. The persistent propaganda, group dynamics, and the declaration of war and its overtly racist overtones encouraged anti-Semitism where, earlier, it had been, at most, a quiescent racism. As well, he argues, the Jews encountered by German soldiers and police in the eastern occupied territories were not the assimilated, middle-class Jews resident in Germany. They were more easily objectified and seen to be members of different species. This argument runs directly counter to the Goldhagan (1996) thesis, and the two authors have carried on a debate on these issues.

EXTERNAL INFLUENCES

Most European states were involved to some degree in the persecution, deportation, and extinction of Jews. France under the Vichy regime was complicit. The Austrian government and many institutional sectors, both before and after annexation, participated in anti-Jewish persecutions, as did Hungary and other Eastern European states. The government and people of Poland engaged in anti-Semitic acts before the war and in murderous raids on ghettos and in deportation of Jews during the conflict. Although the Allied powers were informed and had considerable knowledge of these events, they were either unconcerned, preoccupied with preparations for and then the conduct of the war, or actively complicit in anti-Semitic and anti-Gypsy sentiments. Canada, for instance, allowed only 5,000 Jews to immigrate during the late 1930s and early 1940s.

10

Burundi and Rwanda, 1972–95

Two Central African countries – Burundi and Rwanda – were German imperial holdings in the late nineteenth century. Belgium took them over after the First World War, as protectorates under the League of Nations, and they gained independence in 1962. They were populated by the same groups: the Bahutu (also called Hutu), who formed a large majority in both countries, and the Batutsi (also called Tutsi), a minority comprising about 10 to 15 per cent of the total population, but whether these groups are properly designated as ethnic is open to debate. The Hutu were mainly engaged in agriculture; the Tutsi, in herding. The occupational divisions were not absolute. Further, there were persons of mixed heritage who might have engaged in either of the major occupations. In addition, a very small population of pygmoid people, the Batwa, continued a hunting-gathering lifestyle in both regions. Language, culture, customs, clan names, and other social conditions and symbols were shared fully by the two major groups. By the time of the genocidal events in which Tutsi killed Hutu in Burundi, and Hutu killed Tutsi in Rwanda from the early 1970s through to the mid-1990s, they were no longer legally tied to European imperial powers, but their colonial experience remained a critical part of their culture.

Before considering their respective histories – there are distinctive features worthy of independent scrutiny – we should listen to several anthropologists and historians who emphasize that the terms Tutsi and Hutu were not used as racist terms, and may not even have been used as ethnic terms, before the colonial period. Catharine Newbury (1988: 10–16), who studied Rwanda's history in depth, provides evidence that the term *tutsi* or *tuutsi* was used in reference to people with wealth to or upper-class people, people who owned cattle. The term *hutu* was unknown in the part of Rwanda where she was located and, in any event, it certainly had no political meaning. Some observers have concluded that there is no racial distinction at all between these two peoples; the racist implications were, in their opinion, entirely created by the Belgian overlords during the twentieth century. One of the major scholars of the region, Gérard Prunier (1995: 16–17), though attributing the racist meanings to the colonial powers, acknowledges that the two groups probably did have different origins at some remote period. But, like most contemporary scholars, he argues that the differences were minimal compared with the similarities. What happened, in his opinion, as in Newbury's, was that the colonial powers turned the labels into racist terms and treated the two groups differently, creating, in effect, ethnic identities where they were not previously consequential.

BURUNDI, 1972

In reference of the events in 1972, the leading ethnographer of Burundi opened his study with this statement: "Nowhere else in Africa has so much violence killed so many people on so many occasions in so small a space as in Burundi during the years following independence" (Lemarchand, 1994: xi). In that conflict, between 100,000 and 200,000 people were slaughtered in a population of about 6 million. Another 15,000 to 20,000 were killed by government forces in 1988, and yet another 3,000 in 1991. René Lemarchand strongly denies that there were long-standing animosities between the Tutsi and the Hutu of Burundi. The evidence fails to support the idea of a feudal Tutsi aristocracy "hell-bent on the dehumanization of Hutu serfs" (22). He suggests, instead, that ethnic reification created a mythical past for both groups: for the Hutu, it created a past in which they were an oppressed majority; for the Tutsi, the past was harmonious and the present was being interrupted and spoiled by manipulative politicians. These two reconstructions of the past, and by contrast the present, are "evolving perceptions of 'otherness' (xv).

According to Lemarchand, several other myths fuelled the genocide. The second myth is that ethnic conflict is a direct outcome of colonial rule. Several other scholars argue the truth of this case, but Lemarchand claims the myth was created by a group of Tutsi intellectuals. He observes that although there is evidence of divide-and-rule policies, Belgian colonial rule was primarily directed at princely factions rather than at the level of ethnic relations. "Although the colonial state did not create ethnic divisions, it did reshape them in profound ways" (25). The third myth, in Lemarchand's opinion, is that the 1972 murders were a Tutsi plot. This argument can be spun out at great length but with little credibility except – and it is an important exception – among Hutu. Finally, there is a myth that ethnic violence came about as the result of an imperialist plot by Belgian or other foreign powers. This one is favoured by Tutsi. Again, there is no evidence of a plot, though foreign powers are not entirely innocent of involvement in the affairs of former colonies.

Historical Context

Burundi was unlike Rwanda in the nature of its kingship and the distribution of power. Stated briefly, in Burundi, power was not identified specifically with Tutsis; it was seen as above either of the major groups in society. It consisted of a king and a number of princes, who might be sons of the king or sons of a previous king, all of them seeking the support of the central power, yet simultaneously attempting to increase their own range of control. As long as the monarchy remained both steady and above the fray, the two major groups (both of them further divided into clans, lineages, and regional groups) were at peace with each another. There were tensions of other kinds in the society, but the most persistent had to do with domination by the princely caste (which was neither Tutsi nor Hutu) and subservience to its chiefs and princes (collectively known as the *ganwa*). In particular, there were grievances against the various obligations, including corvée labour, compulsory crop cultivation, and taxes.

At the beginning of the twentieth century several natural calamities created extreme scarcity; children were sold to itinerant traders by desperate parents, and the lineage system gave way to control by the princes. Then, overriding this system, the colonial power could, and sometimes did, remove or install the princes according to colonial interests. This interference disrupted the entire arrangement by which some popular support was needed to legitimate the power of the various, always competing, princes. No longer requiring legitimation from the people, the chiefs became increasingly aggressive in dealing with their subjects.

The Belgian colonial powers exacerbated the problem by deciding in 1929 to reduce the number of chiefdoms. Only three out of twenty-seven Hutu chiefs survived the cuts, and by 1945 no Hutu chiefdoms remained. Tutsi chiefdoms were also cut, but ten still existed by 1945

(Lemarchand, 1994: 43). More critically, the impact of these changes affected regions inhabited predominantly by Hutu. The chiefs who remained became ever more ruthless in exploiting the labour of their subjects. Moreover, those chiefs who were most favoured by the Belgians were increasingly unpopular with the Hutu.

Under international pressure to reform its governing stance and prepare its colonies for independence, Belgium finally turned the king into a constitutional monarch. In preparation for planned elections, two political parties entered into a continuing struggle for control of the state. Paralleling this struggle was another between the Belgian authorities and the United Nations. The Belgians provided resources to one of the parties, the PDC, and impediments to the other, the Uprona, on the excuse that the less-favored party was pro-Lumumba, pro-communist, and anti-Belgian (reported by Lemarchand, 1994: 51–2, following the autobiographical account of the last vice governor general of Rwanda and Burundi). The PDC was also supported by Hutus, who saw its leader, who had a Hutu wife, as the one more sympathetic to its concerns. The United Nations Trusteeship Council contested an election in which the PDC gained a majority of seats, while the leader of the Uprona was temporarily jailed, along with hundreds of other political prisoners. Under UN resolutions, the Belgian government was obliged to dismiss the interim government and call another election in 1961. Uprona won 80 per cent of the votes cast and most of the seats in the Legislative Assembly. Less than a month later its leader, a prince and the son of a former king, was assassinated. The PDC was subsequently proved to be responsible for the crime. The population in general speculated and believed, based on some evidence, that Belgian officials had approved the assassination in advance (Lemarchand, 1994: 54–5).

A series of crises followed, each one contributing to further loss of legitimacy for the Belgian administration, the monarchy, and both the Hutu and Tutsi elites. Ethnic loyalties gathered momentum, as riots sponsored by a youth organization with an anti-Hutu orientation shook the country in 1962. The state became paralyzed in the face of seemingly intractable hostilities. The riots were strongest in the major cities, where a substantial economic gulf had emerged between Tutsi and Hutu.

The revolution in neighbouring Rwanda added to the malaise and encouraged the Hutu to look more suspiciously at their Tutsi compatriots. As thousands of Tutsi refugees from Rwanda swarmed into Burundi, both the Hutu (who identified with the Hutu majority in Rwanda by this time) and the Tutsi (who increasingly recognized that the plight of the Tutsi in Rwanda could be their plight, too, if Hutu in Burundi followed the same path) moved quickly towards polarized positions and a tense standoff. The rebellion in Zaire (1963–64) also played a small part, with Burundi being used as a strategic arms depot. In 1965 a Tutsi refugee assassinated Burundi's first prime minister, a Hutu. A second prime minister was shot by Hutu army officers. Hutu leaders were apprehended, some tried, many shot, and a continuing deadly battle took over civic life in urban centres. The government, still dependent on a king and court at its centre, disintegrated. Another king was appointed and overthrown. The army, according to Lemarchand (1994: 74), "was now part of the government" and the government was Tutsi.

But to say the government was Tutsi is only a partial truth. The government – or rather, the state, since the king had been deposed – was the prize sought by conflicting elites among the Tutsi clans. There were always two sets of conflicts in motion, the Tutsi versus the Tutsi, and the Hutu versus the Tutsi. Lemarchand (1994: 77) characterizes the situation this way: "The state, far from being a mere abstraction, emerges as a cluster of individual contestants and cliques actively involved in the struggle for control over the party, the army, the government, the civil service, and parastatal organizations. The crystallization of group identities is not a random occurrence; it is traceable to specific strategies, pursued by ethnic entrepreneurs centrally concerned with the mobilization of group loyalties on behalf of collective interests defined in terms of kinship, region, or ethnicity. Access to the state thus becomes a source of potential rewards for some groups and of deprivations for others."

Genocide/Politicide

In the wake of the attempted coup by Hutu in 1965, army leaders decided to expel or eliminate Hutu soldiers. Since most of the enlisted men were Hutu, it became a massacre. Mock trials with trumped-up evidence, arbitrary incarceration, executions, murder of witnesses, and torture became commonplace in the months before the Hutu rebellion in 1972. In April of that year a small contingent of Hutu seized armouries in two districts and killed both Tutsis and Hutus who did not join the rebels. An estimated 2,000 to 3,000 persons were killed, a majority of them Tutsi. The president (Michel Micombero) proclaimed martial law and requested military assistance from President Mobuto of Zaire. Troops from Zaire guarded the airport while government troops went on a rampage, killing an estimated 100,000 to 150,000 people, most of them Hutu civilians. Educated Hutus were targeted. Universities, secondary schools, and even primary schools became slaughter grounds. Hutu priests and pastors, school directors, and teachers were killed along with students. Any persons defined as Hutu (now treated as a biological category where at least one grandparent was enough to result in classification as a Hutu) were executed. Tutsi who called for restraint or tried to stop the carnage were also executed. The one-sided war continued from April through to August. Any male Hutu who survived did so by joining the 150,000 refugees who fled to neighbouring countries. The refugees, nurturing excruciating memories of the horrors they had experienced and witnessed, became the instruments for succeeding bloodbaths in 1988 and 1993–95 (The nature of the memories and their bearers is examined by Liisa H. Malkki, 1995).

The army was now staffed almost exclusively by Tutsi officers and soldiers. In addition, buildings were looted and people killed for their possessions, but not necessarily by army personnel or as part of the original plan. The president, who was in charge of the army and the country, represented and protected the interests of the Hima, a particular segment of the Tutsi.

External Influences

The manipulation of ethnic rivalries by Belgian administrators set the stage for much of what followed. The clash between the Belgians and the United Nations heightened tensions in the early stages of the move towards independence. Munitions were supplied by European countries. No external powers interfered while the genocide was in progress. After the 1988 massacres, the international community warned that it would enforce economic sanctions unless there were reforms to the political structure. Humanitarian aid was provided in 1988. However, the 1993 assassination of a subsequent Hutu president, Melchior Ndadaye, attributed to the army, intensified the violence. Lemarchand (2002) notes that the country had not recovered nearly a decade later; indeed, in my own experience, there were warnings to travellers against entry in 2002.

RWANDA, 1994

Rwanda differed from Burundi in its pre-colonial period. Although Lemarchand (1997b: 409–10) argues that here, as well as in Burundi, the relationships among members of the same groups were not significantly different from relationships between the two groups, a rigidly hierarchical society maintained an elite, consisting primarily of Tutsi, and a peasantry consisting primarily (but not only) of Hutu. As for Burundi, Lemarchand writes: "It was the colonial state that destroyed the countervailing mechanisms built around the different categories of chiefs and subchiefs, thus adding significantly to the oppressiveness of Tutsi rule" (410).

Other observers have argued more strongly that the actual ethnic differences between the two groups were minimal or non-existent: the divisions, in their opinion, have been socially constructed by colonial powers rather than biology. African Rights (1994: iii) for example, argues: "The war in Rwanda has often been presented as a tribal conflict. This is highly misleading. Hutus and Tutsis existed a century ago, but the two categories were defined in very different terms in those days. They were far less mutually hostile. Colonial rule and its attendant racial ideology, followed by independent governments committed to Hutu supremacy and intermittent inter-communal violence, have dramatically altered the nature of the Hutu-Tutsi problem, and made the divide between the two far sharper and more violent. In short, political manipulation of ethnicity is the main culprit for today's ethnic problem."

Historical Context

Belgian colonial policies led to a highly centralized and efficient government bureaucracy in Rwanda. They also encouraged the creation of a strong Catholic Church in control of education. Belgian rule appears to have exacerbated differences and destroyed the cushions that had made the prevailing hierarchy tolerable, when, in the 1920s, it prescribed identity cards specifying ethnicity. Yet in the census of 1934, the Belgians used ownership of cows as the criterion for determining race because the actual physical differences between Hutu and Tutsi were too variable for an accurate identification (African Rights, 1994: 8), and high intermarriage rates obscured whatever differences might have actually existed. Even so, Christian missionaries speculated about the "hamitic" origins of the Tutsi, suggesting that the Tutsi, unlike the Hutu, originated elsewhere (in Ethiopia). While the missionaries apparently approved of the imagined origins of Tutsi, their speculations became a reason for Hutu anger against the "outsiders" who oppressed them.

Belgian policy abruptly changed in the mid-1950s. After long-standing support for Tutsi rule, and in response to pressures for democratization from both Catholic missionaries and the United Nations Trusteeship Council, they increased educational opportunities to Hutu and began a process of social reform. Tutsi chiefs objected, Hutu leaders rebelled against them, and the deaths on both sides were brought to an end only by the intervention of Belgian troops. But enmities simmered as the country moved to self-rule in 1959. A Hutu-led Belgian-assisted coup in 1962 abolished the monarchy in favour of a Hutu-dominated regime. Episodes of violence against Tutsi erupted in 1963, 1966, 1973, and then repeatedly in the early 1990s. An estimated 600,000 to 700,000 Tutsi (number disputed) went into exile in neighbouring countries between 1962 and 1964 (Prunier, 1995: 61–3). Over the next thirty years these exiles, and the later waves of new exiles, established the FRP/RPF (Rwandese Patriotic Front), a revolutionary army bent on regaining control of Rwanda.

Political turmoil in Rwanda did not consist solely of Hutu-Tutsi rivalry. Within the Hutu camp, politicians from various geo-political regions vied for power. The decade of the 1960s and early 1970s was dominated by politicians from the south-central regions. A coup in 1973 gave power to northerners under Major-General Juvenal Habyarimana (also recorded as Habayalimana), who led the MRND (Mouvement Révolutionaire National pour le Développement) party. After the coup, some forty politicians from southern regions were killed in jail (Klinghoffer, 1998: 8). Soon thereafter, northern Hutu took over a majority of posts in the universities and the civil service, as well as the officer corps of the army. Indeed, the fight against the Tutsi was sometimes used as the excuse for further domination by northerners over southerners. Internal conflict between diverse Hutu factions, constituted primarily along regional lines, intensified during the late 1980s, culminating in the murder of a potential successor to Habyarimana (Colonel Stanislas Mayuya) in 1988.

The earlier events in Burundi, and further turmoil there in 1988, inflamed the imagination of Rwandans, causing great fear among Hutu of the Tutsi in their midst and in exile at their borders. When the elite of the Burundi Hutu was killed or rushed into exile in Rwanda, there was a tenuous peace while the next generation of Hutu matured, bitter and unforgiving. The ethnic divisions that were once of no particular consequence became major cleavages.

By the late 1980s in Rwanda, there were grave economic problems in an overpopulated country with an insufficient food supply. Land tenure became a burning issue, and Habyarimana encountered challenges to his dictatorship from several directions. Tutsi exiles in the RPF recognized the crises in Rwanda as providing a platform suitable for an invasion in October 1990. Facing the 2,000-strong invading force were the Forces Armées Rwandaises (FAR), an army of about 5,000 men, well equipped by the French. Gérard Prunier (1995: 99) warns: "The game was not two-sided as the later tragic events in Rwanda have tended to make onlookers believe, but in fact three-sided, between the Habyarimana regime jockeying for survival, the internal opposition struggling to achieve recognition, and the Tutsi exiles trying to make some sort of a comeback."

The government was solidly supported by France, with troops, equipment, and financial aid, as well as the moral shield of a former colonial power. Belgium also sent paratroopers and aid to the government forces. A fanatical anti-Tutsi organization, the Coalition pour la Défense de la République (CDR), demanded a stop to all negotiations with Tutsis. The RPF invasion was stalled by 1991, but low-level guerrilla warfare continued. During this same period the army was expanded to an estimated 35,000 men (African Rights, 1994: 44–5), and military officers, the gendarmerie, and political leaders began to organize civilian militias soon to be known as the *interahamwe*. A portion of the *interahamwe* was trained, armed, and uniformed by the Presidential Guard in Kigali. As a whole, however, they were organized ostensibly to protect civilians against anticipated RPF attacks along the northern borders, though the training and their numbers exceeded the needs for self-defence. Estimates of their numbers vary up to 50,000 by the eve of the 1994 massacre. They were trained in camps throughout the country, evidence that the massacres were well planned in advance (African Rights, 1994: 50–1).

Meanwhile, organized political parties intent on gaining democratic elections and opposed to Habyarimana's dictatorship made overtures to the RPF, and a cease-fire was announced. Habyarimana, battered by opponents on all sides, entered into the Arusha Peace discussions in July 1992. By February 1993 both armies had resumed their battle. The number of refugees steadily increased, as RPF forces moved further towards the capital. RPF forces retaliated against earlier massacres of Tutsis with atrocities of their own making. Caught in the spiraling cycle of violence, Habyariama signed the Arusha Accords in August 1993, providing for power-sharing between the diverse forces in the parliament, army, and civil service and the establishment of a multi-party transitional government and matching institutions.

Because the Hutu Presidential Guard refused permission for the UN Assistance Mission in Rwanda (UNAMIR) or other external observers to investigate at the crash site, it is impossible to know for sure who shot down Habyarimana's plane as he returned from a meeting in Dar es Salaam in 1994 together with the Burundian president. At that meeting, agreements had been reached about security measures to implement the Arusha Accords. The Rwandan government immediately blamed Tutsi for the killing and justified the subsequent genocide as retribution. However, the most probable assassins were Hutu extremists, using technology provided by outsiders. The RPF had nothing to gain and much to lose by this death. (Prunier, 1995: 213–29, provides extended discussion of other theories.)

Genocide/Politicide

The killing of the president was the signal for the onset of the genocide. Hutu moderates, carefully listed in advance, were the first victims. The next victims were the Tutsi leadership and rank and file of opposition parties, the prime minister, and other high-ranking officials who might have intervened or sympathized with Tutsis. After the decimation of the leaders, Tutsi civilians and thousands of Hutu who were not extremists were slaughtered. Churches and mission compounds in which Tutsis and moderate Hutus had sought refuge became killing grounds. Klinghoffer (1998: 45, originally reported by Eric Ransdell, 1994: 74–5) observes that Tutsi were hunted in their homes in the capital, Kigali, identified through coded notations placed on residences during the 1994 city census. Throughout the attacks, the government-owned radio station and a private station, Radio Mille Collines, urged the killers on. In some regions, Hutus were ordered to kill Tutsi neighbours on pain of death for their own families.

The fact that many of the murders were performed with crude machetes, leaving victims to slowly bleed to death, suggested to some observers that this massacre was a civil war in which the killers were ordinary farmers, defending themselves as best they could with farm implements. Virtually all the more serious investigations done by NGOs and scholars show, rather, that it was a well-organized genocide, despite the primitive technology. Also, while citizen militias used machetes, the army, police, professional guard, and professional *interahamwe* used modern weapons provided, in the main, by France, with supplementary supplies from Egypt and South Africa (Human Rights Watch Arms Project, 1994).

In Rwanda the central organizers were the ruling family, or, more specifically, the president's wife's family, certain close advisers who vehemently disagreed with the president's willingness to negotiate a peace with the enemy, and army officers. They included, for examples, the director of services in the Ministry of Defence, the defence minister, several military aides, a colonel in the Gendarmerie, the secretary-general of the Mouvement Révolutionnaire National pour le Développement et la Démocratie, several businessmen who had financed the *interahamwe*, and a leader of the CDR militia who, curiously, was a Tutsi (Prunier, 1995: 240–1, provides the names of these individuals). Rural organizers were recruited among government bureaucratic personnel. They provided a middle level of officials who supervised the killings in rural districts. The interahamwe, often working together with the police and the gendarmerie, were ground-level operatives, trained to kill and ideologically convinced of Tutsi evil. Physicians for Human Rights (1994: 11) estimated that this group, consisting of 1 to 2 per cent of the Hutu population, killed some 200 to 300 persons each. Burundian refugees were inducted into the death squads. Finally, there was the presidential guard, consisting of about 6,000 well-trained soldiers who were scheduled for replacement under the Arusha Accords. They were responsible for the killing of opposition Hutu and Tutsi immediately after the crash of the presidential plane in 1994 and provided much of the leadership and armed killers for the genocide. Lemarchand (1997b: 414) notes that a large number of intellectuals, professionals, and priests were accomplices in the massacre: "Journalists, medical doctors, agronomists, teachers, university lecturers, and even priests ... were identified by survivors as accomplices in the massacre of innocent civilians. Landless Hutu peasants and unemployed people also joined in the slaughter." Both the government and a private radio station whipped up hatred for months in advance of the genocide as well as during it, urging Hutu civilians to kill their Tutsi neighbours and praising the army, police, and interahamwe for their role in the slaughter.

The slaughter was not, as Western media tended to present it, an instantaneous uprising of frightened peasants. On the contrary, death-lists had been distributed before the assassination of the president, and the militias had been trained to begin the killings immediately following it. For the most part, the massacre was conducted in an organized and orderly fashion. It was preceded by mass killings in various parts of the country between 1991 and 1993, and virtually every observer argues that the genocide was predictable. The United Nations commander-in-chief, Canadian general Roméo Dallaire, pleaded with UN officials to recognize that a genocide was about to occur, but was unsuccessful in persuading them to become involved in preventing it.

Both Hutu and Tutsi demonized the other. Tutsi were seen by Hutu as Hamitic invaders from the north who maintained a feudal and despotic regime. The Hutu saw themselves as Bantu people, indigenous to Rwanda, who were tricked into allowing Tutsi into the country. These ideas may have come from Christian missionaries who provided the racist basis to the genocide, and they were disseminated via radio. The racist theme of the genocide was supplemented by internal conflict between Hutus of different regions and, by the early 1990s, embedded in different political organizations. Accompanying the racism was the recurrent theme that Tutsis were on the verge of a takeover of the country and that they would slaughter all Hutus if they won the war or had been allowed to share in power as prescribed under the Arusha Accords. The fact that Hutus were in a substantial majority in Rwanda was a pivotal part of the argument: they insisted that majority rule meant Hutu dominance. While calling this stance "democratic," Hutu ideologues called the Tutsi "feudalistic" and "anti-democratic" because they were a minority, had lost control of government in the early 1960s, and had no legitimate "right" to reclaim benefits (such as government positions) in Rwanda. The killing was viewed as a necessary act of survival.

African Rights (1994: 37–41) provides the text of some of the government radio broadcasts. Again and again these programs emphasized that the Tutsi would kill "anybody they want to kill" and subordinate Hutus if they could: "[They think] that we should bow and kneel down and let them walk over us with their boots." Some Tutsis who sought refuge in one of the churches claimed that soldiers beat them and said, "Now we will make you feel what your great grandfathers did to us." Events in Burundi supported the Hutu expectation that Tutsi, if given the opportunity, would treat Hutu badly. Among the "ten commandments" published in one extremist manifesto are warnings that any Hutu who marries, befriends, or employs a Tutsi woman will be considered a traitor; similarly, any Hutu who befriends, employs, lends or borrows money, or has any other dealings with Tutsi men is a traitor (African Rights, 1994: 39–40, citing the journal *Kangura*).

External Influences

The French government was a major external influence favouring and supporting the Hutu government while Habyarimana was in power. Belgium also participated on behalf of the Hutu, and the Catholic Church appears to have provided support as well. French armaments dealers were the major suppliers of arms to the Rwandan government and assisted in military training of the presidential guard and the *interahamwe*. France provided ground troops to assist the Rwandese army in the initial stages of the war against RPF forces. Finally, French financial institutions extended credit against the shipment of arms from Egypt in 1991 (African Rights, 1994, gives details).

French and Belgian ground troops and other nationals were evacuated once the genocide started. Prunier (1995: 102–7) addresses the question of why the French (who were not the earlier colonial power in Rwanda, though they had always had business, religious, and educational ties to the country) were so deeply involved as partisans. He argues that the French were protecting a francophone African country against "les Anglais," since the RPF forces in exile that had resided in Uganda had become anglophones. This interesting argument goes beyond our concerns in this book, though it introduces yet another ideological strand to the heady mixture.

The roles taken by Belgian and French decision-makers and soldiers is of utmost importance in this terrible event. L.R. Melvern (2000: 2–3) describes the plight of about 2,000 Tutsis huddled in a school, without "even a stick" by way of armaments, surrounded by Rwandese armed soldiers protected by ninety UN peacekeepers. At that moment Colonel Lemaire, the UN representative in that location, was informed that Belgium was removing its 400 solders from Rwanda, and that France also was recalling all its nationals. Lemaire was ordered to evacuate his troops, leaving the Tutsis to their fate. The UN forces throughout Rwanda were obliged to watch as thousands of people were murdered. Spokespersons for the United States and the European nations were unwilling to commit forces or finances towards a cessation of hostilities. Dallaire tried repeatedly to bring about a cease-fire and use UN troops to stop the genocide, but he was rebuffed by his superiors (UN Commission of Experts, 1994; *Report of Independent Inquiry*, 1999).

11

Chile, 1973–88

Chile is not the worst example of Latin American governments that turned on their own people. Guatemala claims that tragic honour. However, it is a particularly controversial case because of its experiment with "neo-liberal" economic policies and the involvement of United States military and CIA personnel. It is also notable because, like Uruguay, it suddenly slipped from a long history of democratic government to military dictatorship and terrorism. This slippage has to be explained: R.J. Rummel (1994) saw democracy and authoritarianism as polar extremes, but the Chilean and Uruguayan cases raise pertinent questions about that supposition.

In these two cases we see an unambiguous form of politicide. In neither case was there ever a suggestion that the opponents were members of a different ethnic or religious group. Yet army officers treated many victims as if they were not of the same cloth: they informed the press and relatives of the victims that these people were "not really" Chileans or Uruguayans. They meant that such people were outside the framework of mutual obligations and had ceased to be worthy citizens. Yet it was because of their political beliefs, not ethnicity or religious beliefs, that for the army they had ceased to exist as citizens.

In the Chilean case, history is significant. Two opposing political philosophies have been pitted against each other, often polarizing the population into two camps. And from its inception as a Spanish colony, the Chilean military forces have had a major institutional role in the development of the society.

HISTORICAL CONTEXT

As a Spanish colony on the narrow western edge of the South American continent from the early sixteenth to the early nineteenth century, Chile was a poor outpost. In 1810 Spain abandoned the colony, and the settlers took over the government. The constitution of 1833 created a highly centralized republic in which a powerful president was reined in by two unusual provisions: he had to seek permission of the Congress to permit armed forces to be within 50 kilometres of the capital when the legislature was in session, and he had to get permission at regular intervals to maintain a standing army and navy (Alexander, 1976: 5). The stage was set for a divided republic with a nervous relationship to the military forces.

Despite the constitution and the republican format, Chile was in fact governed by a rural-commercial oligarchy for the remainder of the century and well into the twentieth century. For much of this period the franchise was restricted by sex, literacy, and property rights, so only educated propertied men had the vote. Within those restrictions, opposing parties of Conservatives and Liberals fought over economic policy and the role of the Catholic Church. Conservatives represented a landed oligarchy and some sections of small business; Liberals represented workers and much of the urban middle class. The battle erupted so violently in 1891 that the country experienced a civil war lasting the better part of a year. The two requirements in the constitution were not met, the president and the Congress were at odds, and the army had to choose which faction to support. In the end a rebel army recruited in the north took over the state. Through all this turmoil, the rural aristocracy remained powerful, providing the political funds for those who worked on its behalf and rigging elections where necessary.

Throughout the nineteenth century the agricultural economy not only sustained the population but left sufficient produce to serve a small export trade. Before the fracas of the 1890s the army had contested Argentina's attempt to gain the southern regions of Patagonia and Tierra del Fuego and had also fought against Bolivia and Peru in the northern desert area. Chile won the latter war and was able to annex territories that had been held by these neighbours. The wars ensured that the military forces would continue to be powerful institutional units of the society, and the land acquisitions became the basis for a booming export trade in nitrates that greatly enriched Chile. But the nitrate economy was not so easily subordinated to the oligarchy. A growing working class began to demand the franchise and a greater share in the profits of the expanding economy. Government services expanded, and civil servants became another constituency with its own demands. The franchise was gradually extended and two new parties were established. After the First World War, which had stimulated the Chilean economy, the oligarchy lost control of the executive branch of government.

Simultaneously, the nitrate economy collapsed when synthetic nitrates were developed in Germany. The mining industry was developing well, but the economy experienced a severe blow from the demise of the nitrate trade. A constitutional crisis in 1924 concluded with the resignation and exile of the elected president and the takeover of government by a military junta. The president was reinstalled after a year and was able to get much of his legislative package through, including the legalization of unions and the establishment of a central bank, but the military continued to interfere in matters of state. In 1932 elections were reinstated and continued to occur at regular intervals until the coup on 11 September 1973. Successive presidents kept the military under control by carefully selecting the generals and watching always for signs of insurrection.

The Popular Unidad (Unity) Party, a coalition, first appeared in the 1938 election and, under different leaders, governed to the mid-1940s. This government encouraged the growth of unions, (including some for rural workers), reformed electoral laws (including the extension of the franchise to women), and began to develop legislation for changing taxation, land ownership, and labour and social welfare. But the party split into internal factions over the politically correct position to take during the early years of the Second World War, bringing about its temporary demise. Particularly contentious was the role of the Communist Party and Communist-controlled unions in breaking agreements with other groups.

The early 1950s were dominated by pervasive industrial strife and frequent strikes. As foreign companies in the mining and some manufacturing sectors energized the economy and began to transform the society, the contradictions became ever more apparent, with the protected agricultural sectors in one direction and the modernizing industrial sectors in another. The respective rights of landed gentry and corporate management were in contest, as well as the rights of workers and other subordinate populations vis-à-vis estate owners and corporate managements. To complicate these conditions, the balance between imports and exports was reaching an impasse, as in Argentina. No further substitution was possible within the industrial capacities of the country and the purchasing capacities of a small domestic market. The economy could no longer meet its own food requirements, let alone furnish all its other needs or wants.

In 1952 General Ibáñez, a former military dictator who appeared now as a populist in the style of Juan Domingo Perón in Argentina, replaced a coalition of moderates for a short period in government. He reduced inflation and launched a policy of housing reform for peasant workers in agricultural regions, but Chile was still an underdeveloped country in terms of nutrition, the number of children in school, and the adequacy of sanitation in homes and places of work (Alexander, 1978: 52). Electoral reform had brought many more people into the political forum, and they demanded extensive economic and social change.

Eduardo Frei and the Christian Democrats won the election of 1964 against a coalition of left-wing parties. For the remainder of that decade they introduced land redistribution policies that transferred much of the country's fertile land to peasants' cooperatives and even individual peasants, gained majority public control of large copper companies, and improved employment practices. They encouraged agricultural workers' unions, various organizations at the neighbourhood level, increased participation of workers in management, and expansion of industries in non-traditional sectors. This period was marked not only by internal changes but also by the external context of the Cold War and the extreme anti-communist ideology propounded by the United States.

By the 1960s, Chile's copper deposits, the largest in the world, were the main source of the country's income. It is not surprising, then, that the Frei government's attempts to turn the large American and Canadian copper companies into publicly owned enterprises roused hostility in the world mining community. This opposition became part of the context for Chile's modernization. The Christian Democrats ran into four main obstacles: hostility engendered by its land reform laws and nationalization bills; extreme dependency on imported foodstuffs, combined with declining income from other exports; demands from left-wing supporters for more extensive reforms than the party was prepared or able to enact; and US opinion that viewed nationalism, nationalization of resources, and social welfare policies alike as communist actions. Chile had to contend with this perception while extra-parliamentary political movements on both the left and the right proliferated during the 1960s and expressed their views in increasingly belligerent street demonstrations.

The left-wing groups again formed the Popular Unity Party – a coalition, but not a unified political party. Under Salvador Allende, the party won the election of 1970 by a very small margin and only a third of the total votes. In close contests of this kind, under Chilean law the decision rested with the former government. The assassination of General René Schneider, the commander of the army who had made it clear that the armed forces would support whichever candidate and party had been duly elected, further complicated the situation. Later information disclosed a conspiracy to kidnap Schneider, funded by the US Central Intelligence Agency, and he died in this bungled kidnap attempt (Hersh, 1983; Senate Committee, 1975a).

Marxist theories of the historical decline of the bourgeoisie and the rise of the industrial proletariat were popular in Chile, as they were in many other countries, through the 1930s and again in the 1960s and early 1970s. The prevalence of poverty and the striking inequalities in material condition between the rich and the poor were fuel for revolutionary fervour. Countering Marxism, the liberal arm of the Catholic Church in Chile was at the forefront of reform efforts to reduce inequality and overcome poverty. These two ideological movements coalesced in the Popular Unity Party. Allende and his immediate cabinet were Marxists or at least socialists. Allende chose to work within a democratic electoral system and had, in fact, contested elections since the 1930s, so he clearly did not support the violent overthrow of elected governments. Nor could he have created a communist state in Chile at that time, given its history, culture, and economic condition. His followers were not all of the same ideological stripe: many were simply poor people, landless people who wanted "in" to the system; others were "on the left" but not socialists or communists. The party ideology was less a coherent theory of class struggle than a sense of injustice and anger at being excluded from economic opportunities. It was a party of convenience for fighting a democratic election. But popular fronts are notorious for falling apart once the main goal has been achieved.

"Once Allende was elected in 1970," according to Arturo Talavera (nd: 2), the polarization of Chilean society advanced rapidly. In a few months, at all elections, even for student bodies at elementary and secondary schools, partisans and opponents of Marxist parties came to grips." Allende continued and expanded the reforms introduced by the Christian Democrats. He attempted to nationalize virtually every large production and distribution company in the mining, banking, manufacturing, and commercial sectors. These nationalized firms were added to an already large public sector that included railways, electrical power, oil exploration, transportation systems, and steel. He succeeded in nationalizing much of the mining sector, but two American companies, Anaconda and Kennecott in the copper industry, refused to accept the compensation he offered and became leaders of the opposition forces. In some sectors of industry, Allende offered no compensation, and the affected firms became staunch opponents of the regime (Alexander, 1978: 153–5). At the same time Allende, like Frei, had to cope with his own unruly followers when they staged takeovers of small farms and small businesses contrary to the government's promise that only large operations would be nationalized.

Land reform was of particular significance to the Popular Unity Party. Allende's government proposed a limit on the extent of land that a private owner could control. The terrible example of the collectivization process in the USSR half a century earlier was probably not known in the 1970s; in any event, the government was committed to collectivized agriculture. This policy incurred not only the wrath of large estate owners but the opposition of small landholders. Even the landless peasants were angry at the government because they had anticipated that they would gain personal ownership of properties. They did not expect the state to retain ownership. According to the Communist newpaper *El Siglo* in 1972, the government had expropriated 3,500 properties in a period of eighteen months (Alexander, 1978: 161). Rebellion in the countryside resulted in a drop in agricultural produce, necessitating a substantial increase in imports. The situation was not made more acceptable by providing administrative jobs on collectives to party supporters and the numerous squabbles with peasant organizations not controlled by the coalition. Although 1971 legislation designed to redistribute income had been successful and popular, and further legislation preventing price increases enabled workers to purchase more, inflation began to eat up the benefits. Investments decreased throughout the private sectors, and middle to upper income groups began to invest their money outside the country.

By the end of 1972 the opposition to Allende's government included large and small landholders, peasants and farm workers, owners of both large and small businesses, and the former owners of large mining and manufacturing companies that had been nationalized. During the following months some of the unionized workers, the mainstay of the government, engaged in strikes and demands that put the government in impossible positions vis-à-vis its own supporters. Added to Allende's woes were the policies and practices of the United States government, its aid agencies, the IMF, the World Bank, and the large American corporations such as Anaconda, Kennicott, and International Telephone and Telegraph. Eventually, Allende was challenged in the courts, where he lost an important battle when the Supreme Court and the majority of the Chilean Congress declared his administration to be "unconstitutional." This decision provided the rationale for a coalition of small and large business, truckers, and small farmers and estate owners, who actively opposed the government through capital strikes and other disruptions. The truckers' strike immediately before the 1973 coup was crucial because the trucks were essential to delivery of essential food to the population.

POLITICIDE

In September 1973 the Chilean military forces, supported by the CIA, the American military, and some of the multinational corporations, launched the coup. Known supporters of the Popular Unity Party and many others were immediately shot; others were incarcerated without charges and killed later. A large number fled the country.

General Augusto Pinochet was the leader of the coup solely by virtue of having recently been appointed by Allende to replace the assassinated René Schneider as chief of the army. He, and others of the initial junta of military forces, promised early elections and the resumption of democracy. The problem with that option was that, if the Popular Unity Party and the Christian Democrats joined forces, they would again capture power. Besides, the coup had been extremely violent, culminating in the death of Allende and the killing of several hundred protestors and unionists known to be his supporters. It would have been difficult to return to democratic procedures, and, moreover, the supporters of the coup wanted some acknowledgment of their support. Perhaps the landowners anticipated that the military junta would restore the *status quo ante* by nullifying the legislation of the previous decade, and the mining corporations expected a reversal of the nationalization acts. Possibly small businesses and small farmers anticipated changes that would benefit them, though such benefits could not have been granted even had the government intended them: land reform was too far advanced to be reversed. Much of the earlier protective legislation had prevented new investment in businesses; agriculture was backward and could not feed the population; and industrial initiatives had dried up. In short, the same dilemmas that had plagued the earlier governments were still there.

The military government promised to compensate nationalized mining corporations, and that incentive removed a major complaint of the

United States. But in the immediate aftermath of the bloody coup, the military government was treading water and there was no indication that it had a strategy, either political or economic, when it came into power. The coalition that sponsored the coup consisted of disparate groups whose sole common condition was dissatisfaction with the Allende government. Foreign-owned companies, the landed oligarchy, truckers, small farmers, small commodity producers, non-commercial groups and some groups of professionals had no common agenda beyond reaction to the legislation and actions of the extremists.

Though there was no apparent strategy in the early days of the military junta, there was a common ideological thrust to their operations. Anti-communism was strong in all the forces, and this attitude coincided with the national security interests of the CIA and the American military forces that supported the coup. For many years the American military forces had provided anti-communist, anti-guerrilla warfare training for officers in the forces of all Latin American countries, first in the Philippines and later in the United States itself. Chile's officers shared this ideology and justified the continued dominance of the army as a necessary measure to combat subversive communism. In Chile's case, unlike other countries in Latin America, Allende was a genuine, if self-declared, Marxist on whom the threat could be blamed. Pinochet provides his own explanation in an autobiography where he describes his enemy as "all those filthy people who want to ruin the country." He, Airforce General Leigh, and others who spoke to the nation after the coup emphasized their commitment to fight communism. It was, they said, their patriotic duty to save the country.

It was this ideological rationale that motivated the continuing terror following the coup. The new rulers dissolved the National Congress, declared the Popular Unity coalition illegal, outlawed the Central Union of Workers, destroyed the electoral register, and proclaimed a state of siege. Pinochet effectively suspended the civil judiciary and civil liberties. The junta declared that decisions of military tribunals, which were established by decree, could not be appealed to the Supreme Court.*

Within a few months of the coup, two army generals retired, two other coup leaders died in a helicopter accident, and power was increasingly concentrated in the hands of the supreme commander of the

---

* The more significant of these laws are noted in the bibliography as Chile, 1973; Chile, 1975; Chile, 1980; Chile, Ministerio del Interior, 1975; and Chile, Ministerio de Defensa, 1978.

army. Within a year he had established the National Intelligence Directive (DINA) responsible directly to himself, and in December 1974 he
had himself named "president of the republic."

Throughout the first year, émigrés talked about thousands of murders
and detentions, while the junta persistently denied that any human
rights violations had occurred. Uncertainty and ambiguity about who
might be next on the list of targets created a reign of terror. There were
also assassinations outside the country. In the early period the most famous was that of a former chief of staff under Allende, General Carlos
Prats, and his wife in September 1974 in Buenos Aires. Later, in 1976,
the former vice president of the republic, Orlando Letelier, was assassinated in Washington, DC. Much later, in 1996, when the commission
appointed by the democratically elected government submitted its report, it provided a careful accounting for 2,115 individuals who had
disappeared or been killed (Chile, Corporación Nacional de Reparación
y Reconciliación, 1996). Since many deaths were never accounted for
and disappearances never solved, the general estimate of 3,000 people
(in a population of about 12 million) is probably an understatement.

After the initial wave of murders of known supporters of Allende,
the disappearances, torture, and killings included a wide range of people who, in the mind-set of the military and DINA officers, were subversives: prominent among them were intellectuals, journalists, students,
trade unionists, labour lawyers, some medical professionals, social
workers, and artists. In addition to these groups, poor people in shanty
towns around Santiago and other cities, and workers who might have
been sympathetic to the Popular Unity Party, were picked up on the
streets or at their places of work or residence. Individuals were bullied
and taken into custody, never to be heard from again, or soldiers simply killed them on the spot. Javier Martínez and Alvaro Díaz (1996:
12–13) observed that, in the early days of the new regime, the "leadership contest ... was marked by attempts to give the greatest demonstra-
tion of commitment to the reactionary consensus, and this became a
competition as to who could best represent authoritarian extremism.
For Chilean society, the consequence of this was years of terror."

The role of the DINA is of particular interest. Hannah Arendt argued that a secret intelligence service and concentration camps were
essential terrorist tactics. We have not encountered these tactics in all
the cases we've examined, however: they existed in the USSR but were
not much in evidence in Armenia and central Africa. In all those
cases, the policies were designed to eradicate the population, not sim-

ply to intimidate people by using selective eradication. In Chile the objective was to intimidate, and it was ideas more than people, and leaders more than followers, that the government wanted to eradicate. It wanted the population to abandon support for land reform, military reform, reforms for workers, and other liberal or liberal-left ideas, and the means to achieve this goal was selective murders by a special forces team answering only to Pinochet. The junta organized the DINA to conduct clandestine activities and charged its Operations Department with the task of purging the left (Ensalaco, 2000: 57–8). This department had several subgroups with specific missions, and the head of the DINA, Manuel Contreras, established a regional intelligence unit called Operation Condor, charged with the task of tracking subversives outside the country. It was linked to similar police units elsewhere in Latin America, and to neo-fascist and extreme anti-communist organizations in Europe and North America. This organization was responsible for the assassinations of Prats, Letelier, and others, and brought unwelcome world attention to the *modus operandi* of Pinochet's dictatorship. Contreras was finally dumped by Pinochet under pressure from other countries and from his own armed forces, which had not appreciated the interference of the secret police in their work.

The pervasive anti-communist ideology blended well with the forces' sense of their own importance as saviours of the nation. The armed forces in Chile had conducted a few battles in this history, mainly against indigenous people whose land Europeans coveted, and a few skirmishes with neighbouring countries over borders. But, like most of the armed forces of the continent, they had much larger institutional egos than actual records for bravery.

It was not until 1983, when the powerful Confederation of Copper Workers called for a strike, that citizens began speaking out and staging "pots and pans" demonstrations in the streets. These protests did not result in a new coalition of forces because diverse sectors of the opposition were still plagued with ideological differences. The Chilean Catholic Church (unlike its Argentine sister institution), and particularly the Vicaría de la Solidaridad in central Santiago, became the major institution opposing the government. It maintained a list of human rights violations, enabled potential victims to escape, registered complaints, and helped the relatives of victims. Pinochet agreed to allow for a limited form of democracy, but the population voted against him in a referendum in 1988. He retired as president, but retained his dominant role as chief of staff. Still in control of military forces, he established a new constitution that ensured amnesty for himself and his followers and appointed himself and his supporters to lifetime Senate positions, where they could prevent any changes to the constitution. In 1998 he was detained in Britain under international criminal law, but both Britain at that time and, later, Chile, declared him mentally and physically unfit to stand trial for crimes against humanity. In July 2002 he resigned his lifetime seat in the Senate, saying he had served his country well and had nothing to regret.

Chileans' Opinions about Causes

In 1997, before the detention of Pinochet in London, and again in 1998 while he was detained, William Marchak and I interviewed a number of Chileans about their experiences and observations during the military regime. We heard strong opinions from both the left and the right in a country that, to this day, remains politically divided: human rights organizations represent families whose members disappeared, suffered torture or death, and survivors who were incarcerated and tortured; and right wing think tanks claim to represent businesses, military forces, and some Catholic groups. Because of the terms of the granting agency for this research, we cannot divulge names or other identifying information about our informants, so the names given below are aliases. These observations and opinions, however, were typical of the comments we heard and recorded.

SR ERNESTO GALVEZ: Here, as in the Argentine and Brazil, the problem is that the state ended up organizing the civil society rather than the other way around, and the state is authoritarian. There was a powerful oligarchy, in the first place associated with the Spanish monarchy. After independence, they ended up building financial capital with the help of the military. So the military always was the powerful ally of the oligarchy ...

Question: Why was there so much disorder under Allende? Who initiated that disorder?

Well, what is known because of the Church Report,* which acknowledges the U.S. decision to demolish the government of Allende, is that there was a direct financing of the opposition.

---

*   United States: Senate Select Committee 1975a, 1975b.

SR JORGE CHAVEZ: All the big Chilean businessmen, I also think that a great part of the medium-sized businessmen, identified with the policies of General Pinochet. The business world considers Pinochet the creator of the Chilean economic model which has had so much success. And this applies not only to Chilean businessmen but also the representatives of the big foreign companies who have invested in Chile over the years ... The media in this country, fundamentally the two newspaper chains, that of *El Mercurio* and that of *La Tercera*, were clearly in this position. The Confederation of Manufacturing and Commerce, which brought together all organizations of farmers, miners, industrialists, tradesmen, were in this position.

I think there is an agreement of honour among the military to deny what happened ... This goes together with what the business world and the right think, and above all, feel, that the Armed Forces saved Chile from communism.

SRA DOROTHEA LAPHAM: Before Allende came to power, there was much poverty, but [the government] between 1970 and 1973 tried to reduce it. At least the poor people had something to eat. They had more access to education, health, a little at least. The rich people were afraid. There was a thing called the Campaign of Terror. Before the coup, they were talking of a Plan z. It was about the poor killing the rich. The rich claimed there were lists to kill them. They were all first on the list of course ... So that explains a little the acceptance of the coup.

The Introduction of Neo-liberalism

As noted above, there is no indication that the coup was motivated by any clear economic doctrine other than generalized opposition to the changes advanced by the Allende government and anti-communism. More by chance than by planning, about a year after the coup the alumni of the University of Chicago passed around a proposal for economic reform that would sit well with conservatives, though contrary to the interests of the landed oligarchy. This plan became known as the "new right," or "neo-liberal," economics. By this time Pinochet had exhausted alternative possibilities: his first minister of the economy had been a structuralist, and the economy did not revive; his second alternative was to pursue policies promoted by the major economic actors in the society, but since their interests were divergent, it was hardly surprising that they were unable to put forward a jointly agreed-upon strategy. He gave the "Chicago boys" free rein, and they produced a capitalist revolution in a country that had been quasi-feudal in much of its territory before then

(Martinez and Diaz, 1996). The "new right" was not embedded in the ideology of the military state at its inception, nor did it become such until well into the 1970s, but by the 1980s, when the country began to prosper, the dictatorship became known outside the country as the government that ushered in a new economic formula. Further, this statement is frequently accompanied by the old saw: "If you're going to make an omelet you have to break a few eggs." The Chilean eggs were broken before, and for different reasons from, the onset of a new economic plan. Martinez and Diaz (1996: 2), who have examined what they call "the Great Transformation" in Chile, argue that

Certainly the most fundamental stage of economic transformation in Chile took place *during* the military dictatorship headed by General Augusto Pinochet and was promoted and imposed by the economic team chosen and supported by the military. Yet the military dictatorship emerged in Chile as a reaction to the unmanageable situation brought on by the social struggles that accompanied the reforms of the government of Salvador Allende. The junta's claim to legitimacy was based on the restoration of political order, not economic transformation. Only later, as a result of the radical nature of the military intervention – and following the historical patterns of the few military interventions in Chilean politics – did the necessity emerge for an equally radical economic program ... it was not so much the regime's use of force, but rather its autonomy from the immediate interests of the social groups that had brought it to power, that permitted the Pinochet government to carry out a complete restructuring of Chilean capitalism.

It is worth noting, incidentally, that while Pinochet's government gave the economists much leeway, and even while neo-liberalism advocated privatization of industrial properties, the government retained the major copper enterprise, CODELCO, nationalized by its predecessors. CODELCO's constitution states that it must pay 10 per cent of its gross revenue to the armed forces every year; thus, the military retains a measure of independence from the government, long after the return of democracy in Chile (Marchak and Marchak, unpublished field notes, 1997).

EXTERNAL INFLUENCES

The Cold War formed a context for postwar Chilean development, as for other Latin American countries. The battle between the left and the right in Chile attracted the attention of the United States years before the showdown in 1973. The CIA contributed more funds per voter in Chile during the 1964 election than the two leading contenders spent on their campaigns in the United States' election of the same year (Valenzuela, 1978). Seymour Hersh (1983: 260–1) argues that "at least $20 million in support of the Frei candidacy – about $8 per voter – was funneled into Chile by the United States in 1963 and 1964, much of it through the Agency for International Development (AID)."

Covert activities under the Nixon administration finally attracted the attention of the US Senate Select Committee on Intelligence Activities (1975a, 1975b), chaired by Frank Church, which investigated American activities in Chile from 1964 to the coup in 1973. The CIA conducted "a variety of covert activities in Chile," according to the Senate Report (1975a: 26–9), and its "propaganda projects probably had a substantial cumulative effect over these years, both in helping to polarize public opinion concerning the nature of the threat posed by communists and other leftists, and in maintaining an extensive propaganda capability." The Senate reported that the CIA spent up to $1 million on covert action before the 1970 election, and funds were allocated by other US agencies and multinational corporations. International Telephone and Telegraph alone contributed some $350,000 to the anti-Allende campaign, and matching funds came from other US businesses in Chile. Among the covert activities in the run-up to the 1970 election were "spoiling" operations, designed to undermine the coalition of leftist forces. The leading conservative newspaper in Chile, *El Mercurio*, published "more than one editorial per day based on CIA guidance" (1975a: 30–3). The Senate argues (34) that the " 'scare campaign' contributed to the political polarization and financial panic of the period."

Allende's victory in 1970 flew in the face of these extraordinary efforts by the United States to elect its preferred government, and the CIA and other US groups initiated a propaganda campaign and an economic offensive. President Nixon instructed the CIA to organize a military coup d'état (Senate Report, 1975a: 38), without the knowledge of the Departments of State or Defense and without informing the US ambassador in Chile. Despite these efforts, Allende was confirmed as president in October 1970. In the following months, the United States "cut off economic aid, denied credits, and made efforts – partially successful – to enlist the cooperation of international financial institutions and private firms in tightening the economic 'squeeze' on Chile" (41). The squeeze added to crippling strikes in the mining and transportation sectors, enabled by US funds. American AID assistance to Chile totalled $3.3 million during Allende's presidency, compared to nearly $70 million annually during most of the 1960s. Throughout Allende's short stay in office, the US maintained "close contact with the Chilean armed forces," yet the Senate Committee claimed "there is no hard evidence of direct US assistance to the coup" (42).

Other reporters go further than the Senate, which had to rely on the CIA for information about itself. Hersh (1983: 258–96) argues that many more millions of dollars were spent and much plotting was undertaken to oust Allende. Mary Helen Spooner (1994) supports this view. She also claims (93–5) that $41.6 million was given to the right-wing newspaper *El Mercurio* (denied by the newspaper, 6 December 1975) and that Chilean Central Bank figures indicate that Chile's foreign reserves shrunk from $393.8 million in 1970 to $12.9 million in 1973.

In 1970 the United States staged an unsuccessful attempt to abduct the commander of the armed forces, General René Schneider, who was killed in the skirmish. This action and others initiated by the Nixon administration were condemned by the US Congress, which had earlier demanded a stop to US interference in Chilean affairs. The world at large learned of the US role through the movie *Missing*, which was primarily about the United States, not Chile, and through the Senate hearings and report.

After the coup, the Nixon and then the Ford administrations arranged for commodity credits for the military regime. Chile, in turn, agreed to compensate North American companies harmed by previous government policies. Debt payments were rescheduled and aid packages were provided. This cooperation enabled Pinochet to violate human rights with impunity. US support did not cease until the human rights activist, Orlando Letelier, was killed by DINA officers in the United States.

12

Cambodia, 1975–79

The West learned of the Cambodian genocide from journalistic reports based on interviews with migrants in Thai refugee camps. During the initial period of the revolution, the migrants were urban, middle-class, educated people and officers in the army of the republic who had reason to believe that their lives were endangered by the victory of the communists. In the later periods, when Pol Pot's army was retreating to the forests of the north, the refugee camps were filling with a wider range of Cambodians – though, as it turned out, far fewer than Western observers had anticipated. Most of the accounts dwell on what a popular American film described as "the killing fields," where an estimated 1.8 million men, women, and children were said to have been murdered by Pol Pot and the Khmer Rouge (KR) in a brief period of utter and absolute terror between 1975 and 1979. However, readers should be warned: the estimate and the validity of Western journalistic accounts are disputed. Michael Vickery (1984: 187–8), an outspoken critic, argues that the executions would have been closer to 300,000 than to 1.8 million, though he agrees that another 300,000 to 400,000 must have died from starvation and physical exhaustion. Disputed numbers of victims notwithstanding, all reporters acknowledge that the Pol Pot regime spawned a particularly violent episode in human history.

In addition to the deaths, another 850,000 Khmer refugees fled the country between 1975 and 1981 (this number includes refugees from the Vietnam period). Just under 40,000 of them returned after 1979. Over 100,000 moved to third countries, and in 1982 about 350,000 remained in refugee camps (Kiljunen, 1984: 47).

The Cambodian experience was not directed at a particular ethnic group, although both the regular army and the revolutionary army killed Thai and Vietnamese foreigners in substantial numbers. The focus of the revolutionary army in power was not the foreigners but Cambodians deemed to be members of a despised class. This massacre was a class struggle, and the revolutionary army saw it as such.

HISTORICAL CONTEXT

The Khmer people of Cambodia are ethnically different from their Lao, Thai, and Vietnamese neighbours, and throughout their history they have been hostile to those neighbours. They were dominant in Southeast Asian affairs from the early ninth to the mid-fifteenth century, but local wars weakened their leadership and they lost control of much of their territory. They became a French colony in 1867 and remained so until the 1954 Geneva Accords. From 1955 until 1970 Prince Norodom Sihanouk controlled the country, first as king (he was crowned by the French in 1941) and then as the elected premier.

Sihanouk incurred the suspicion of Americans when he instituted a policy of neutrality encased in Cambodian law in 1957, yet simultaneously initiated trade and assistance relationships with China and North Vietnam. He maintained the traditional enmity with Thailand and South Vietnam. In 1958 the American Central Intelligence Agency (CIA) gave funds to a group in opposition to Sihanouk, the Khmer Serei (Deac, 1997: 35–6). Similar funding and encouragement were given to other right-wing opponents of Sihanouk over the following decade. Such actions, designed to offset Sihanouk's "left leaning neutrality," as the Americans called it, led to the supposition that the United States backed the overthrow of Sihanouk by Lon Nol, head of an opposing elite, in March 1970. Whether the US had prior information remains unclear, but US policy was subsequently directed towards destroying communist forces in Cambodia. Throughout the civil war from 1970 until American forces were obliged by the US Congress to withdraw from Cambodia in 1973, Lon Nol had American support.

Karl D. Jackson (1989b: 4–7) argues that both the Sihanouk and the Lon Nol governments were, like most governments throughout Southeast Asia, corrupt, nepotistic, hierarchical in organization, and inequitable in distribution of opportunities and wealth. Buddhism supported the ruling cliques through the concept of karma: the only way to gain status, power, or wealth was to be born into one of the ruling families. Governments were essentially bureaucratic departments within the hierarchical political culture, and politics consisted of exchanges between competing elites with little or no input from, and even less concern for, people who were outside the ruling cliques. The majority of the population remained in rural areas as a traditional peasantry. By the end of the 1960s, urban centres and semi-urban regions contained about 21 per cent of the population; Phnom Penh, the capital, held 10 per cent of the population. Since commercial employment did not grow at anything like the same rate, and there were few industries, this concentration represented an increment in unemployed, semi-literate people who aspired to the bourgeois lifestyle seen in Western movies, but which was unattainable for most. With the onset of war in 1970, urban immigration increased. Bombing in the rural regions, especially by Americans in 1972–73, increased the impoverished population that could no longer survive in the country (Vickery, 1984: 25).

Communism in Cambodia had its start in the First Indochina War and the founding of the Indochinese Communist Party by Ho Chi Minh in 1930 (Carney, 1989: 13–16). Though weak in its earlier stages, the Communist Party had established a small and dedicated army by the late 1960s under the direction of Saloth Sar. Later known as Pol Pot, Sar had been trained in the French Communist Party during the 1950s, as had Khieu Samphan, the chief ideologue for the Pol Pot regime. The People's Army of Vietnam (from North Vietnam) and the People's Liberation Armed Forces (the Viet Cong guerrillas) were already in the border areas of Cambodia in early 1970, and by their own account were using Cambodia to access supplies and provide sanctuary to their troops (Carney, 1989: 19, drawing on documents of the revolutionary government in 1978). They were also, clandestinely, providing training to Khmer revolutionary forces and ethnic Vietnamese born in Cambodia. The fall of Sihanouk in 1970 was not easily accepted by the peasantry, and the overthrow of his government led to uprisings against the Lon Nol government. Repression followed and, as political positions within the society became increasingly polarized, peasants in some areas of the country joined the KR forces. The Communist Party remained a secretive organization, however, and did not become openly associated with the leadership of Democratic Kampuchea until 1977.

The revolutionary force was not, like Lon Nol's group in the battle against Sihanouk, yet another elite competing for power. They were peasants, workers, and intellectuals who spoke of radical egalitarian objectives – a transformation of society in which the current elites, religious functionaries, professionals, and bureaucrats would be re-educated as workers in the fields. They were prepared for a prolonged civil war. By 1970 the Khmer contingent had become strong enough to fight its own battles; indeed, by this time the Khmers and the North Vietnamese were on increasingly unfriendly terms. The KR, though strong, was never a unified army. For reasons of security as well as its diverse roots throughout the country, the KR remained a decentralized organization with numerous semi-autonomous segments.

While the acknowledged rift in the communist camp between Khmers and North Vietnamese was attributed to ideological differences, the traditional enmity between Vietnamese and Cambodians on the government side was also erupting in conflict. Lon Nol's government evicted some 190,000 South Vietnamese in 1970–71. Thousands of others were massacred (Deac, 1997: 74–5). Yet South Vietnamese forces were an essential support for the disorganized and ill-trained Cambodian forces against communist forces. By late 1971 there were still some 11,000 South Vietnamese troops in southeastern Cambodia, and a civil war was in full force throughout the country.

From 1971 to 1973 American armed forces bombed the Cambodian side of the border with Vietnam. The Pentagon initially claimed that US participation had been "without [its] prior knowledge or consent" and that, while it did not wish to widen the Vietnam War, American incursions would "continue for self-defense purposes" (Deac, 1997: 71). The North Vietnamese reacted by substantially intensifying their offensive, and American bombing intensified. The Nixon government then claimed that Cambodia was the "headquarters for the entire Communist military operation in South Vietnam" (Deac,1997: 77) and, even while withdrawing troops from Vietnam, increased the bombing in Cambodia. Naval and armed forces were added to the US contingent to clear the Mekong river area, and the US incursions spread out beyond the original targets. In 1972 the Pentagon announced that it would employ the "full range" of air power in Cambodia and launched a major offensive, no longer pretending that its actions were merely defensive.

In January 1973 the United States and North Vietnam signed the Paris Peace Accords, and US forces withdrew completely from Vietnam. The terms of the treaty forbade interference in the affairs of other countries. Even with this agreement and United States Congressional prohibitions on further incursions into Cambodia, American forces continued to engage in an intensive bombing campaign in Cambodia until mid-August, when the US Congress successfully stopped funding to US military forces in Cambodia, Laos, and the Vietnams. The North

Vietnamese also withdrew from Cambodia in 1973, following a formal transfer of military authority to the Khmer group.

American air attacks caused casualties and prolonged the war. Moreover, the bombs "accelerated the collapse of rural social order, brought in many new recruits, and strengthened the hand of Pol Pot" (Deac, 1997: 166). In addition, Prince Sihanouk, now an asset to Pol Pot, came out of exile in Beijing in February 1973 to "march" in a convoy of Soviet vehicles to Cambodia via the Ho Chi Minh Trail.* At about the same time, KR extremists slaughtered or evicted ethnic Vietnamese and Chams in the 80 per cent of the country they now controlled – a replay of the massacres sponsored by the Lon Nol government in 1970. In mid-April 1975 the KR army took over Phnom Penh.

The conflict between Vietnam and Cambodia continued under the new regime, and after the takeover of Saigon by the Communist forces. The Vietnamese claimed that the KR were attempting to recover territory in Vietnam that had been lost in earlier centuries. They launched a major offensive late in 1978, captured Phnom Penh in January 1979, and ended the Pol Pot regime.

POLITICIDE

Our state of knowledge about what precisely happened between 1975 and 1979 is poor. Foreign reporters left Cambodia as the revolutionary army entered Phnom Penh. Reports from refugee camps reflected the class bias of informants and did not provide adequate information on events in different parts of the country nor over the duration of the regime. As well, this whole event occurred in the midst of the Cold War and immediately following the defeat of the United States in Vietnam. Much of what the West learned, as a consequence of selective information and even more selective reporting, was of dubious accuracy. While sceptics argue that far fewer executions took place than were claimed, there is agreement about the brutality of the regime during its forty-four months in power.

Before the fall of Phnom Penh, the KR already controlled village councils throughout the rural regions and had begun the collectivization of farms. Some of these areas had been taken over in 1971–72 by

---

* Sihanouk was subsequently used for public relations exercises, then imprisoned in Cambodia. He learned in the 1980s that many members of his family, including five of his children and fourteen grandchildren, had been killed by the Khmer Rouge.

North Vietnamese forces and were subsumed under Khmer power when the Vietnamese left in 1973. As the Khmers gained territory, they also exerted ever stronger controls on the population. Land ownership in these areas was abolished in 1973, and the economy was demonetized. Private property was confiscated and, in some regions, villages were destroyed and the people forced to live in dormitories. Populations were moved from urban centres to collective farms. Some reports claimed that women were forced to wear black clothing and no jewellery. Food rations were severely curtailed, and critics were jailed or executed (Carney, 1989: 30). Many people fled these regions: some moved into South Vietnam, and others tried to survive in the regions still controlled by the government.

Immediately after the fall of Phnom Penh in 1975, the KR ordered the population to evacuate the city. Since it was under the control of several different zonal forces arriving from diverse regions of the country, these orders were contradictory in content. In at least one zone, inhabitants were told to leave the city immediately and by foot; they had no time to gather their goods or arrange their affairs. In another zone, according to refugees, they had a full day and were permitted to pack their goods in their own cars and leave by road (Vickery, 1984: 69–75). There were several reasons for this evacuation. Most immediate, there was insufficient food to maintain unproductive urban dwellers. The army did not know how to maintain the infrastructure of urban centres, and these dense clusters of hostile population were a security risk. The peasants who formed the majority in the army were shocked by the prosperity and debauchery of the cities, and possibly envious of city dwellers as well. Finally, the ideology of the KR dictated that all people should be working on the land, that there should be no differences between groups in a classless society, that wealth leads to corruption, and that self-sufficiency was the goal of a virtuous society.

The KR sorted all the evacuees into groups, and each one received predetermined forms of treatment. They murdered some army officers, many bureaucrats and landowners, and selected groups of factory workers, educated professionals, Moslems, and Buddhist monks. The Buddhist monkhood as a whole was dispersed (Jackson, 1989b: 51; Carney, 1989: 33, no. 21; Ponchaud, 1989: 164–5). The KR demolished the Central Bank and Christian churches and disbanded the communications media. They abolished money, closed schools and libraries, and burned the books. Many hospitals were closed or demolished, adding further stress to a deteriorating health-care system.

Vickery (1984: 77–8) notes that some hospitals had been destroyed in the war, and there had been a steady exodus of doctors and other medical personnel who could obtain employment outside the country. Under the revolutionary army, "probably about half the doctors remaining in Cambodia in April 1975 perished" (144).

The urban émigrés were moved, mostly by enforced marches, to agricultural regions, where they were obliged to work in the fields alongside peasants. In some regions they were treated with contempt, given the most demanding tasks, provided with insufficient food, and essentially killed through exhaustion and starvation. Not all peasant communes were as harsh in their response to the newcomers. Vickery, while arguing that the regions were very different in their treatment of city people, estimates that some 300,000 to 400,000 people died from starvation. Other estimates are generally higher. A Finnish investigative group noted that supervision on collective farms was performed by very young peasant boys who had been taught that urbanites were treacherous (Kiljunen, 1984: 17): "[The boys had] an absolute power which could lead to random executions for the merest show of insubordination."

From the beginning, the population was grouped into three categories. The first consisted of individuals who were of the proletariat and who had cooperated with or become members of the revolutionary army. In general, these were the poorest and most uneducated segments of the rural population, and many were little more than children. This group was given full food rations and opportunities to hold political offices. A second group consisted mainly of rural people as well, but they had not previously joined the KR. They could hope that, in future, they would be given full rights. Some urban people were included in this group, those deemed to be capable of transforming themselves. The third group had no rights: the surviving landowners, army officers, and other urban people. In the more rigorous regions where the ideological position against urbanites were strongest, these rightless people were given a near-starvation diet and forced to work until they dropped, or they were killed outright.

The question arises as to why starvation was rampant in the country as well as in the cities. According to some of the reports at the time, it resulted from KR policies of self-sufficiency. As the cities disintegrated and the skilled urban workers dispersed, knowledge of how to run a system for creating and distributing even basic necessities diminished. In short order, there was widespread starvation, yet the Khmer Rouge refused offers of wheat from Canada and food supplies from other countries, asserting that they would prefer to be "masters of our destiny and to rely on our own strengths, on our own resources" (Jackson, 1989b: 49). In similar vein, they refused all foreign medical supplies, claiming that their medical needs could be produced from local herbs. Among the causes of deaths in 1975 and 1976 were epidemics. Finally, in late 1976, the government purchased DDT to combat malaria.

Vickery disputes these explanations (1984: 78–80). He argues that the portrayal of pre-revolutionary Cambodia as a peasantry of independent and self-sufficient producers is seriously flawed. In his view, there was one major rice-growing corridor through the centre of the country. Other regions were not blessed with sufficient good soil and water for agricultural production, and many people lived by fishing, hunting, and rooting for food in the forests. As the population expanded, the amount of food available from local sources became insufficient, and hunger had become widespread before the war. Further, the cities were attracting people from the countryside, as has been the case in every developing country. But in Cambodia there was little industry to absorb the migrants. Then the war exacerbated the problems: migrants now included huge numbers of country people whose villages had been bombed. There were many deaths during the war – estimates vary between several hundred thousand and over a million between 1970 and 1975. As Vickery puts it, "whatever else it may have been, [it] was also a war between town and country in which the towns fought increasingly to preserve privileges while the rural areas suffered" (24–5). Later, in his summary of conditions between 1975 and 1979 in Democratic Kampuchea, he acknowledges that deaths from hunger or from illness exacerbated by hunger exceeded executions for the most part, but were nonetheless avoidable "simply by giving people the freedom to forage for themselves" (144).

Deportees from the cities, and particularly from Phnom Penh, were moved a second time after the first migration, from the densely populated southern regions to more northern and less heavily populated zones. Some of these migrants encountered extremely harsh conditions in forest areas they were forced to clear. There, death from malaria, starvation, or exhaustion was commonplace.

Sar, Ieng Sary, and Son Sen were the three major figures in the revolutionary army, becoming, respectively, the premier, deputy premier in charge of foreign affairs, and deputy premier for national defence in the new government of what they called Democratic Kampuchea in 1976. Khieu Samphan and Nuon Chea were other important figures of long standing and, like the others, they were returned intellectuals. Several other leaders of the pre-1975 victory disappeared from public view, along with Sihanouk and his mock cabinet.

These returned intellectuals, having read not only Marx and Mao but also Frantz Fanon and other "dependencia" theorists of the 1950s and 1960s, were the leaders of the movement. But the bulk of the soldiers were peasants from the countryside. The revolutionary army was a complex, though small, army consisting of about 60,000 men when it took over Phnom Penh. A contingent of its fighters had been trained in Hanoi, and these soldiers had been integrated into the indigenous forces, but tensions remained over their relationship to soldiers who had been trained in Cambodia. In addition, there were still ethnic Vietnamese in the revolutionary army, though they, along with the Hanoi fighters, were purged soon after the revolution. Beyond those special groups, there were different regional contingents, each with a high degree of autonomy and operating in diverse ways even when there had been consensus (as in the decision to evacuate the cities) about major policies. In addition to regional differences, there were conflicts between the top leaders and others in important positions within the Communist party or the Democratic Kampuchea government (the two were separate organizations). Vickery (1984: 148–50) says that the policies initiated by Pol Pot were at odds with the views of many veteran communists and leftist intellectuals. After the victory, these factional wars became critical to the whole situation. Pol Pot's group began to purge those whom they saw as dissidents and opponents, and, after 1978, other groups moved against Pol Pot. As the war with Vietnam intensified, groups with less hostile responses to Vietnam may have become dominant, though sources are not in agreement on this point.

Jackson (1989b: 54) describes the revolutionary army at the local level: "Khmer Rouge soldiers ordered about and terrorized individuals who had formerly been respected because of age, wealth, office, Western learning, or adherence to the way of Buddha, and this new-found power must have been intoxicating for many Khmer Rouge who had been poor, illiterate villagers before the revolution and remained scarcely more than children in age even as they wielded absolute power over their elders."

A US State Department publication in 1976 argued that the revolution was carried out by "a small group of dedicated cadres, despite the absence of grievances sufficiently serious to motivate the peasantry to participate" (Quinn, 1976, as cited by Vickery, 1984: 87; see also Quinn, 1989a, 1989b). This view is dismissed by other writers. They note that peasant participation and support for the revolutionary forces was widespread, though greater in some regions than in others. The substantial difference in perspectives may be attributed to the beliefs in place at the State Department, the Cold War, and the particular refugee groups interviewed by the authors.

The victims, initially, were the urban middle class and foreigners, who occupied high positions in cities, and, later, Vietnamese in the revolutionary army and peasants or workers who failed to satisfy the cadres in their regions. The first group included government functionaries, professionals, landowners, skilled workers, Buddhist monks, Cham, and ethnic Vietnamese Khmers. Vickery (1984: 26) describes them in harsh terms: "These were the people – spoiled, pretentious, contentious, status conscious at worst, or at best simply soft, intriguing, addicted to city comforts and despising peasant life – who faced the communist exodus order on 17 April 1975." Their horror at being forced out of the city and into hard work was, in his view, heightened by the fact that the orders were issued by illiterate peasants.

Victims in later stages included cadres and workers. As seems to occur in all successful revolutionary movements, internal rivalries and sharp differences of opinion began to erode relationships between different factions of the army and the government. In 1978 a dramatic change in policy took place. Some of the cooperatives were told to eliminate distinctions between peasants and displaced urbanites working with them. This order erased privileges and created new and harsher conditions for the peasants, who reacted with hostility. Some of the intellectuals were permitted to return to less menial tasks. Presumably these changes were related to the increasingly likely prospect of a Vietnamese invasion, during which some of the urban evacuees might have been useful allies.

Assuming that the initial victims were active supporters of the Lon Nol government, their shared view of the revolutionaries would have been, at best, disparaging. All the writers on the subject note the antagonism that urban dwellers had towards peasants long before the peasant revolution transposed their social positions. Their views of what happened were prominent among the early refugees and, in turn, in the Western press. Not surprisingly, the Western media viewed the revolutionaries as Marxist communists, rarely making distinctions between that position and the actual statements and actions of the revolutionary government. As well, Western journalists concentrated on sensational stories, often missing the meaning of what even the refugees said, in part because they did not know the country's geography, regions, diverse population, or cultures. The ideology of Western anti-communists permeated the West's version of the revolution.

Since the victims of subsequent purges included party members and faction leaders, their ideological perspectives were obviously at odds with those of the Pol Pot faction. As Pol Pot himself began to lose control after 1978, the government initiated talks and indicated greater solidarity with the Vietnamese. This accommodation indicates that the extreme levelling to the lowest position in society was no longer viewed by top strategists as the ideology of the movement.

EXTERNAL INFLUENCES

The war in Cambodia and its aftermath were heavily influenced by external powers. A complete study of these influences would have to include the long period of French influence throughout Indo-China. The region's royal or elite families retained control of their countries during the mid-twentieth century in some part, at least, by virtue of French support for puppet governments. When the French were defeated, the Americans came in, persuaded they could prevent the region from "falling to the communists." Any attempts by governments or opponents to existing elites to democratize the countries had been effectively squelched, so communist takeovers were virtually the only form that genuine opposition could take. During the 1970–75 war, the United States and the North Vietnamese, Thai, Indonesian, and Chinese governments were all involved in Cambodia's affairs. The United States provided $1.18 billion in military aid and another $503 million in assistance to the Lon Nol government (Carney, 1989: 31). American bombing had a long-term impact on the countryside and on the rural population. Thailand and Indonesia provided training for government troops. Japan and some European countries provided financial aid. China provided foreign support to the insurgents, along with ammunition, tactical aid, and a home for Sihanouk and the royal government in exile. Sihanouk's efforts on behalf of the insurgents against the Lon Nol government included many visits and petitions to other countries and to the United Nations, thereby engendering a world opinion that reduced the support for the Lon Nol government, though, in the midst of the Cold War, it did not increase understanding or support for the revolutionaries.

13

Argentina, 1976–83[*]

Most Latin American countries have been cursed with a history of military takeovers. Military forces, born in the Spanish conquest and renewed in the wars of independence, have had far greater independence from civil authority and much more influence on Latin American societies than on those in Europe and North America. The chapter on Chile profiled a strong military force that had influenced, but had only once before and then for only a year, taken control of the government. In 1973 it inflicted a coup on a leftist government and imposed terror on the population. In Argentina the first military coup and government after the establishment of democracy occurred much earlier in the country's history, in 1930. But the military coup of 1976 was different from its many predecessors: it ushered in a government that killed or "disappeared" an estimated 30,000 citizens before it collapsed in 1983.

The Argentine military forces had developed considerable autonomy, though we cannot take for granted that they operated at the behest, or even in support, of a class of domestic capitalists. Their relationship to external capital was also somewhat ambiguous. At the same time, they clearly saw themselves as acting in the long-term interests of capital as a system apart from particular class alliances. Indeed, their own explanation for the military dictatorship of 1976–83 was that they had to save the country from communism.

---

[*] This chapter is based on the research that William Marchak and I did in Argentina in 1996–98, much of which is reported in *God's Assassins: State Terrorism in Argentina in the 1970s* (1999).

HISTORICAL CONTEXT

Argentina began as a Spanish port along the River Plata, governed by military forces. It eventually expanded into a large colonial territory with rich ranchlands and grain-growing areas. It became an important exporter of beef and wheat, and its port city, Buenos Aires, and interior cities grew into substantial trading centres. Its agricultural lands were quickly dominated by huge estates owned by private families whose joint interests were looked after by an oligarchic government. Something approaching democracy finally caught up with the inhabitants of the country, obliging the government to enact electoral reforms in 1912 that included secret ballots and universal (male) suffrage. However, much of the population had not become Argentine citizens. Indeed, most urban entrepreneurs and business people retained their citizenship in their European countries of origin, and few participated in the political life of Argentina. For much of its post-Spanish life, Argentina was an unofficial colony of other European powers, an area where fortunes were made, but not a society in which members took their citizenship seriously.

During the second decade of the twentieth century, the army twice defended oligarchic interests in bloody massacres of workers – in Semana trágica in 1919 and in the Patagonian Rebellion in 1921–22. Repressive action against workers was commonplace for the next several decades. Extreme right-wing movements emerged in the country during the 1920s (Deutsch, 1993), leading, eventually, to the overthrow of the democratic government in 1930. To this point, the military forces acted in the interests of the agro-business oligarchy and other business interests.

In 1930 the Supreme Court of Argentina ruled that the armed forces could legally oust an elected government because they alone would be in a position to protect life, liberty, and property if the established order broke down. This order gave them a privileged position from which they ruled the country directly or indirectly to 1945, and again from 1955 to 1972. The cause of the initial coup is significant in light of later history: the army was fearful that a reform-leaning government, far from radical left though called the Radicals, might upset the status quo. The status quo was a hierarchical, authoritarian society, dominated ideologically by the Roman Catholic Church and economically by an agrarian-based oligarchy. The army had, up to that point, worked closely with the oligarchy, but during the next fifteen years it developed its own momentum. After the 1930 coup, Argentina experienced a situation that became

increasingly common: a declared state of siege, dissolution of trade
unions, deportation of unnaturalized union leaders, arrest of many others, and suspension of the few civil liberties that existed. Within a year,
the government was toppled by yet another coup, and coup followed
coup. Throughout all this turmoil, the army retained de facto control,
even when civilian governments had been elected in exercises with restricted franchises and civil liberties were absent.

In the 1920s Argentina had a per capita income which rivalled that
in many European countries. Growth rates were similar to those of the
other resource-based, immigrant countries, Canada and Australia, and
the country suffered much less from the global depression than either
of those rivals. The landed oligarchy moved into export business and
then expanded beyond farm produce to create new industries. External
capital came into the country, and by the mid-1940s there were manufacturing industries in the province of Buenos Aires and in interior
locations. These growing industries provided employment to a rapidly
growing industrial labour force. Import substitution policies had been
introduced with some success in the 1930s.

Juan Domingo Perón, the minister of labor in the early 1940s within
a military government, recognized the potential political clout of the
working class if it were organized. He and his second wife, Eva (Evita)
Perón, began to organize state-centred unions where both employers'
and workers' representatives bargained through state agencies. The military, no longer able to control organized labour, allowed elections to
take place, and in 1946 the military backed Juan Perón's successful bid
for the presidency. A roller-coaster ride carried the country through the
next decade. Juan and Evita Perón dominated not only Argentine politics but also the culture and every other facet of the society. Unions became fat with obligatory dues and huge memberships. They bargained
through the state rather than directly with employers; in this way, Perón
continued to keep them under his personal control. Working people
prospered with wage increases, improved working conditions, and escalating bargaining power. The social policies of the Peronist government
required the state to employ many new civil servants, and they, too,
were unionized and well paid. But the economic pie did not continue to
grow. The domestic market could not support further import substitution, and both domestic and foreign companies were resisting spiralling
costs. The gap between the wealthy and the poor had narrowed, but
foreign-owned companies began to pull out and Argentines with money
banked it outside the country.

After Evita's death, Perón, with the solid backing of organized labour, continued to rule the country for a short time. However, both the
strong Catholic Church and the military grew weary of his populism.
He had taken to attacking the church, attempting to substitute Peronism in place of Catholicism. The cult of (Santa) Evita (as she was
known) had become popular, and the military could not control their
man anymore. So, in Argentine style, Perón was displaced by another
military coup in 1955, and the army resumed its role as government or
controller of government until 1972.

The post-Perón period was often brutal as the military forces set out to
reverse history. Peronist unions were still powerful and continued to negotiate wage demands from a position of strength, but they were beginning to be challenged by new organizations in foreign-owned automobile
and other manufacturing sectors and by groups to their left, politically,
with different ideological positions. Some of the union leaders in traditional sectors had become so wealthy that they lived in mansions with
the accoutrements of an aristocracy. They maintained body-guards, and
more than a few leaders were assassinated during internecine battles for
control of the union movement. Peronism (under the political label, Justicialism) refused to bow out gracefully, though Perón himself reclined in
splendid luxury in Spain for eighteen years. When Justicialism was
banned, it became even more popular. Perón continued to advise his
faithful followers, even to the point of ordering ostracism or assassination for union leaders who tried to break out of the Peronist mould. As
economic and social conditions deteriorated in Argentina, he began to
incite his student followers to stage a revolution.

Between military action against them and their internal battles, the
unions did not mount concerted confrontations with governments until
the late 1960s. A week-long general strike in the major industrial town
of Córdoba ushered in a period of bloody battles in the streets and engaged a large part of the population. Many students took up the cause;
both the elite schools and the universities became embroiled in the
romance of a student revolution to rid the country forever of military
dictatorships. A few student leaders went to Cuba to learn tactics and
returned as "Guevarists" (after Ernesto "Che" Guevara, the hero of
the Cuban revolution and an Argentine by birth). Most students who
participated were convinced of the need for the revolution, but few had
any idea how to go about launching such an event. They were too
young to have experienced the Perón period, but they were devoted to
what they believed were Perón's ideas and marched to songs eulogizing

Evita and Che. They expressed the hopes of a generation of middle-class youth, intelligent, well-educated, and determined to change the world they inherited. That world was run by an overbearing army and strongly influenced by an autocratic Catholic Church. A large number of these students and young faculty pinned their hopes on the return of Perón.

Finally the military, unable to contend with the conflict and becoming increasingly brutal in its attempts to maintain control of the population, agreed to let Perón back into the country and to allow him to run for president in the 1973 election. Students and workers were ecstatic when he won, but these two groups were at odds with each other. The students thought they were the vanguard of the revolution; the workers considered the students to be naïve upstarts. Between the two increasingly militant groups, there were loosely organized groups of social workers, lowly priests, and students whose main objective was to improve the living conditions for the poor. Perón played each group against the other, using them, abusing them, and finally casting out the students, calling them "beardless ones" at a public rally of thousands of supporters. In their place, he embraced the unions, put forward a reactionary program, and initiated the paramilitary forces against those he considered to be subversives.

The students dispersed, then reorganized as clandestine guerrilla groups. Though they used the rhetoric of Marxism, few had serious knowledge of the source, and the largest guerrilla group, the Montoneros, was actually led by individuals whose background was in extremely right-wing (even Nazi-like) Catholic youth clubs. During the remaining months of Perón's life, and throughout the twenty-one-month duration of rule by his third wife, Isabel, Argentina was beset by a continuing battle, sometimes in the open streets and, sometimes in the shade, between paramilitary groups covertly organized within her government and student guerrilla forces, a period now designated "the dirty war." The economy was beset by inflation, unemployment, and departing industries. The upper class continued, as it had done traditionally, to deposit its wealth outside the country.

While the dirty war contaminated all interactions, making ordinary life unpleasant and, for many, very dangerous, the military forces planned a takeover with a difference. They used their four years absence from government to prepare the repression in infinite detail, and by the time they took over in 1976 they had already set up concentration camps replete with the instruments of torture and murder.

Long before the coup, many of the student activists and union workers had been killed by the paramilitary forces (known as the Triple A,
for Argentine Anti-Communist Alliance). The People's Revolutionary
Army (ERP), which had attempted to take over the northern province
of Tucumán, following the Che Guevara theory of establishing "foci"
revolutionary regions, was thoroughly routed by the army a year before the coup. This defeat virtually destroyed the only genuinely Marxist guerrilla group. It had never been large and had no previous
experience of war (Andersen, 1993; Marchak, 1999). Most of the leaders of the Montoneros were killed in ambushes before 1976, and those
who survived had fled the country. In retrospect, there is considerable
suspicion, and some evidence to support the belief, that the one surviving leader of the Montoneros (Mario Firmenich) was, in fact, reporting
to the army's intelligence service throughout these months (Andersen,
1993; Gillespie, 1982, dismisses this theory but his publication preceded later information; Marchak, 1999, outlines the evidentiary basis
for the claim).

POLITICIDE

The coup in March 1976 was expected and welcomed by the vast majority of the population, fed up with corpses on the streets, bombing of
public places, kidnapping of company executives, and disappearance of
journalists. Newspaper editorials cheered and assured the reading public that the military leaders were trying only to restore peace and stability to a much-distressed country.

Yet at the moment the coup occurred, a search was under way for
those whom the military had already designated as "subversives" –
union leaders and many rank and file members, student leaders and
other students, social workers and priests who had worked in the
slums, labour lawyers, journalists and other writers, professors of
social sciences and humanities subjects, psychoanalysts and psycholo-
gists (of whom there were an extraordinary number in the major
cities), and many others in the liberal professions. Persons under the
age of thirty were suspect regardless of their occupations. Any male
who wore green clothes (the preferred colour of revolutionaries) or
who had longish hair or a beard was a likely suspect. High school students in one town who had protested a rise in bus fares were rounded
up and incarcerated, all but one disappearing forever. The one who escaped provided information to the Commission of Inquiry in 1984;

the event was turned into a chillingly truthful film entitled *La noche de los lapices* [The Night of the Pencils].

It was clear that detailed plans for this coup and the terror that followed had been worked out well before the operation. Concentration camps had already been established, and armed men had been taught how to torture victims. Within the first few weeks of the coup, thousands of suspected subversives had been rounded up, taken to detention centres and concentration camps, and tortured. Some had already been murdered. Thousands more were kidnapped as they made their way to work or school, and many were taken from their homes by plain-clothes policemen who forced them at gunpoint to surrender. While those who were known to have been Montoneros or other guerrilla activists knew they were on the hit-list, many were picked up who had no record of subversive activities or whose subversive activities amounted to caring for the poor. Those who could escape went into exile; others spent the next seven years in hiding or constantly on the run. In addition to the physical assault on citizens, the armed forces intervened in universities (putting military personnel into administrative positions and even into classes), burnt books, destroyed libraries, and closed theatres and other cultural centres where ideas were spawned and disseminated. Unions were also intervened, and many union workers were abducted or killed outright. The terror diminished over time, though it never stopped while the military forces were in power.

The combined military forces of the army, navy, and airforce, together with the provincial and municipal police forces, were organized for this period of terrorism. The organizers were the chiefs of the three armed services and some major city police chiefs. The total area of the country was divided into sectors under separate control of one of the armed forces, leading to some differences in the way prisoners were handled and to some communication errors that occasionally allowed intended victims to escape. The operations in some cities (Córdoba, Rosario, and Tucumán, for examples) were particularly brutal, in each case led by individuals in the armed forces who acted as *caudillos* (a term for "strongmen" going back into early Argentina history) in their territories. Groups of armed men were used everywhere to pick up intended victims. Usually these men wore no uniforms when they entered homes and offices by force and kidnapped the victims. Some victims were abducted on city streets in full view of spectators, and they sometimes called out their names to passers-by in the hope that someone would remember who they were before they disappeared forever.

The torturers were also members of the three armed forces or police forces. The police forces, in particular the police attached to the Province of Buenos Aires, were reported to have been especially vicious and to have used torture before the military regime as well as during it. There was also an intelligence service within the armed forces, charged with the task of collecting information from the victims under torture and from other sources, in order to find new victims. This service reported to the junta, but there is no indication that it was "owned" by any one member of the junta or that it had exclusive privileges or access to the presiding generals (unlike the relationship between the DINA and General Pinochet in Chile). Although one general, Jorge Videla, presided over the seven-member junta for the initial five-year period, he did not become a lone rider as did Pinochet. The three forces were not perfect comrades-at-arms, and internal jealousies, conniving, and stage-stealing became so extreme by 1982 that the junta was imploding. Had it not been for the plans to promote an assault on the British-held Malvinas (Falklands), the junta might not have been able to hold on as long as it did. It should be noted that, in spite of the disappearance of middle-class children and many others, the population rallied to the cause of taking the Malvinas, and, for a brief belated honeymoon, the armed forces enjoyed popular support. It faded when they proved themselves to be incompetent at the war game.

The military definition of a terrorist was, in the words of General Videla, "not only someone with a gun or bomb, but also anyone who encourages their use by ideas incompatible with Western Christian civilization" (*Clarín*, 1977, as quoted in Frontalini and Caiati, 1984: 24). Before the coup, Videla expounded a little further, noting that "as many persons must die in Argentina as are necessary to guarantee the country's security" (Hodges, 1991: 192–3). On another occasion, Videla said: "I want to clarify that Argentine citizens are not victims of the repression. The repression is against a minority that we do not consider Argentine" (*La Prensa*, 1977, cited in Frontalini and Caiati, 1984: 22). General Roberto Viola, another powerful member of the junta, defined terrorism as "any concealed or open, insidious or violent action that attempts to change or destroy a people's moral criteria and way of life, for the purpose of seizing power or imposing from a position of power a new way of life based on a different ordering of human values" (Frontalini and Caiati, 1984: 75). "Such statements, repeated frequently with minor variations, made it clear that the objective was not merely to rid the state of particular individuals but also to destroy institutions, ideologies, books, and ideas of any vintage or origin that offended or ran contrary to the ideologies and ideas of the generals. Universities and trade unions were major sources of these contrary ideas" (Marchak, 1999: 150–1).

The intended victims were union leaders, intellectuals who were critical of military rule, students and others who had joined the Montoneros and other underground guerrilla groups, and priests who had become affiliated with the "Third World" or "liberation theology" movement. These individuals may have shared ideas about social change, but in many respects their interests, values, and *modus operandi* were very different. In particular, the students and unionists were not in agreement in much of the country, though there were some locations where they worked together. Students saw themselves as the vanguard of the proletariat, and the proletariat's own leaders were not interested in giving them that priority. Democracy was not a value for any of these groups because the word was associated with American imperialism, rather than reform. The unions were not democratic, but tended to be hierarchical and corrupt organizations. The guerrilla forces were organized as small armies, also hierarchical and authoritarian. The priests had to contend with an authoritarian church that steadfastly opposed them and turned them in to the military when it suspected them of caring too much for the poor instead of preaching to the rich about sin. Even within groups there were schisms: unions of different groups were in conflict with one another; the ERP, or revolutionary army, was in conflict with the Montoneros, and so on. In short, though all these groups sought major social changes, they were not united organizationally or ideologically.

Some of the former revolutionaries were convinced that the military operated in the interests, and at the behest, of the agrarian oligarchy, combined with the upper echelons of the commercial and industrial classes (Marchak interviews, 1996, 1997). More of them were convinced that the United States was behind the military, ensuring that no communists gained power. Others, even when sharing those views, lived with a great deal of remorse. They said they had begun to realize, long before the end of the terror, that the Montoneros was not a revolutionary organization, certainly not a Marxist one. Some already had suspicions that some of its leaders were double agents, or at least had been persuaded to turn in their younger and more vulnerable followers. Some also admitted that they had been part of the kidnapping of American company executives and similar types during the 1974–75 dirty war, and that at the time they saw such actions as revolutionary, but now they saw them as futile, if not worse. They simply tried to get through each day, trying to cope with the tragedy of their many fallen comrades and their sad memories.

Military officers who had been active during the government of the military junta were adamant in their interviews that they had saved the country from a communist takeover. In their view, and in that of spokespersons for the conservative church, the students and others had been led astray by Third World priests and Marxists, and there was no choice but to kill the revolution before it destroyed Argentina. One of the officers we interviewed also observed that the major world powers used the "Third World" as a surrogate pasture where they fought out their own ideological differences, letting the poor citizens of other countries take the casualties (Marchak, 1999: 278–9).

One of the military interviewees responded to a question about the armed forces' estimation of guerrilla strength in 1976 in these terms: "The guerrilla has the characteristic of fighting with all available means, all imaginable methods, and in all kinds of terrain. It is a multi-faceted and multidirectional subversive phenomenon." In response to the question, "Was the army struggling against ideas or against arms?" he said: "Both ... the purpose of the guerrillas was to change the political system in Argentina. They wanted to take power, to establish a socialist and Marxist government like the one in Cuba ... So the fight was against the revolutionary ideas which they wanted to implant, and they wanted to establish socialist, Marxist governments in the region, not only in Argentina. And it was also against the arms which supported those ideas" (270–1).

A conservative Jesuit priest had similar ideas. We asked him: "You've used the word the enemy. Who was the enemy of the church?" He responded: "The enemy was Marxism. Marxism in the church, let us say, and in the mother country – the danger of a new nation." We pressed further, asking if he meant Marxists even if they had no weapons. "It wasn't just armed guerrillas?" we asked. He responded: "That is correct. It was not just armed guerrillas" (241–3). This same priest spoke strongly when we asked if he thought the military had chosen the best way to solve the problems. "No, I must say no," he said. "It was done so badly that the military junta was brought to justice. When the anti-military won, the military were judged. They did it very badly.

They did not manage it like Pinochet, who remained on top ... they did not eradicate the problems." When we asked who he was referring to as the anti-military, he responded:

Well, in a way, to the groups that defied the military prior to their fall, to the ones who allowed the guerrillas to do what they did, the ones who opposed the military authorities, those who did not agree with the eradication of the guerrillas. In other words, the ones in total opposition without mitigation. You see, before the military regime fell, there were people who had looked kindly on subversion, without themselves being subversive. They are the ones who gained power after the military departed. The military government was unable to create a community. They tried to follow Pinochet's example, but it was a disaster. They did not know how to do it as Pinochet did.

Personal Experiences of Victims

The stories of some of the surviving students who tried to stage a revolution are tragic because of their thwarted idealism. Here is one excerpt:

I was seventeen when the military killed people in Trelew in 1972. At that time being an activist was normal. We all believed that Argentina was going through the same process as that of May, 1968, in France, and the revolution of 1959 in Cuba. The role of Che Guevara gave us a sense of belonging. For us teenagers it was very important that he was an Argentine. We felt that we were part of the revolutionary history of Argentina. There was no possibility of being young and not being an activist; it was like a destiny. In 1973, when I entered the university, almost all my life had been under military control, so I felt that our generation was part of a critical moment in our history. Also, we thought we were freeing literature in Argentina, because we were reading Marx and Freud and Lévi-Strauss. [She joined the Montoneros.]

...

I thought that the project was for the people, that we had to do anything for them. I trusted the organization [the Montoneros] even if later I didn't trust the leaders ... I thought that the only way I could survive was to be part of the situation. I called three times a day to know where I could walk in the city ... I myself, with my first husband,* had gone to a working-class district in 1974 to

---

* The activists typically married at very early ages, as part of their pledge to be loyal servants of the revolution.

do social work, and in 1977 we returned to that place. There was nobody left. Everybody had been killed, the houses bombed. We stayed there, hiding, but there was nothing left of the district, only the parents of our friends who had been caught. We stayed [there], hiding, and trying to reorganize our lives for the next two years. Isolated, because we couldn't visit our families. We couldn't do anything else. We were hiding. (Marchak, 1999: 181–7)

Other stories are tragic in a more classic sense:

My husband continued to work with the Montoneros, but now his work was clandestine ... In February, 1977, my husband disappeared. During the year before he disappeared, it was very hard. Compañeros were kidnapped every day. We were never completely clandestine, but we moved constantly because any of our compañeros who were abducted or imprisoned might identify us under torture. I slept in the street many times, pregnant, and with my two-year-old son, and sometimes friends would come to tell me that someone had been killed. Sometimes we travelled all night on one bus and then, when we got to the terminal, on another bus. Or stay the whole day in the zoo, pregnant, and with my oldest son, waiting from morning to night until they closed the zoo and someone would take me to sleep somewhere. It was very horrible, very dangerous. Then, on February 20, a Sunday, my second son was born. The following Saturday they took my husband away ... Then they broke into the house where I was staying. I had just finished breastfeeding the baby. I pulled up my slip, I put him in the crib, and at that moment they suddenly entered. They kicked me, they opened the stitches from the birth, and other things. Then they had my newborn baby on the floor, they grabbed him by his feet, with his head toward the ground, and they put a gun in his mouth. They broke everything, they checked everything, looking for things. They said they were under the authority of the superintendency of federal security. And, well, they had me on the floor. To have to remember that day exactly makes me feel terrible. It was very terrible, very frightening. (170–2)

She learned many years later that her husband had already been killed by the time she attempted to find him at the notorious detention camp, the ESMA, run by the navy, on the outskirts of Buenos Aires. But the priest of the ESMA told her nothing and instead tried to get information from her about her husband's friends.

Other personal stories are as hair-raising. A reign of terror creates a fear that is unbearably painful, and much of the population is caught up in it whether as victims, the parents and children of the victims, or potential victims living in daily terror that someone they know had their name innocently scribbled down in an address book. The youth of Argentina got into the habit of not keeping telephone numbers of their acquaintances. Indeed, they and many others got into the habit of not making friends, of maintaining an aloof stance because there was no way of knowing who could be trusted, or who would be caught next and tortured.

The largest single group of victims were union members, many of whom were designated leaders in the union movement. At the beginning of the repression, leaders of Peronist unions were targeted, but soon all unionists were in the same danger. Some were killed outright, and others disappeared never to be seen again. Still others were jailed without charge or any knowledge of how long their incarceration might last. This testimony comes from one survivor who was jailed without charges for many years:

One day we were being searched in the patio of the jail. It was a very cold morning, we were naked, and we were being hit with sticks. They hit [one of the prisoners] and he fell, and then, because he could not get up, the officer pulled out his weapon and shot him in the head. Another prisoner was taken out of jail and they [the military captors] applied the "law of flight," which means they claimed he was killed while trying to escape. And there was a case of a *compañero* being stretched out and beaten all night until he died. This could have happened to anyone regardless of any degree of political participation. Who knows what criteria were in effect? These were judgments made only by the security force. (90)

Termination of the Military Regime

The economy had perked up for a short while, then declined, and by the 1980s the country was again in deep economic trouble. The military forces staged a war against Britain, expecting that the United States would support them and that Britain would not consider it worthwhile to oppose them militarily in the Falkland/Malvinas Islands. They misjudged both countries. Their humiliating defeat brought them home in ridicule, and they were obliged to hand over government to civilians by the end of 1983. Though Argentina has never managed to extricate itself fully from that terrible period, it is one of the few countries, and the first after Greece, to establish a "truth commission" – an investigation into the disappearances and deaths of citizens, and, for a time at least, the incarceration of military officers responsible for the terror of 1976–83 (Argentina, Comisión, 1985).

EXTERNAL INFLUENCES

There seems to have been no direct interference in Argentina similar to that in Chile by the United States or any other external power. There were indirect influences in the form of the IMF, the World Bank, aid programs, American-style business unionism, and direct investment and management of private-sector firms. The automobile and other manufacturing industries were dominated by European and American automakers. There was also the long-term participation of officers in training schools in France and the United States, where the suppression of communists and indoctrination against communism were prominent. France was an important country for Argentina because more of its officers had trained there or under French military officers who had learned techniques of anti-guerrilla warfare in Algeria and Indo-China (even though France was the defeated power in those wars). Also, Argentines were more likely to speak French, or to learn it quickly, than English.

The USSR was an influence of another sort. In spite of the extreme anti-communist rhetoric, the military forces discovered that the USSR was a big market for Argentine wheat after the United States, under Jimmy Carter's administration, attempted to cut off wheat shipments there. In return for wheat, the USSR played another role in Argentina's life: it prevented the Human Rights Committee of the United Nations from investigating Argentina's record for many of the early years when the record was most devastating (Guest, 1990).

Although Amnesty International and other human rights groups, alone with unions in Italy and elsewhere, visited Argentina and did their best to expose the atrocities, the external world was not interested in intervening in the affairs of what it considered to be a sovereign country. Although Carter's government pursued human rights violators and imposed sanctions, it was unable to mobilize even its own bureaucracies, let alone its leading corporations with interests in Argentina. Eximbank continued to provide generous funds to the junta. Early on, the State Department tried to stop financing of hydroelectric turbines while human rights abuses were continuing, but business lobbyists persuaded it to withdraw its objections. The World Bank awarded extraordinarily large loans to the junta during its tenure. And Argentina was a principal beneficiary of the US Generalized System of Preferences. After the 1980 election in the United States, and under the leadership of Ronald Reagan, all attempts to influence other countries with respect to human rights ceased. Human rights violators were then identified as anti-communists, and the label apparently justified their actions, irrespective of cause.

14

Yugoslavia, 1990–94

To this point we have considered cases of state terrorism. As the reader will have realised, the cases are extremely varied, yet they have in common certain features: a crumbling political fabric, a weak institutional basis, a move towards centralization of power, and an ideology consistent with the cultures of perpetrators of state crimes but justifying privilege and power by some over others. Some cases rest on ideologies of differences between ethnic and religious groups; others on differences by class and status. In Chile and Argentina a struggle over control of the state between opposing groups with very different political utopias resulted in terrorist military governments. We will now consider one case where the state simply broke down altogether and rival factions declared war on one another, committing genocide along the way. Such cases are difficult to make sense of because the perpetrators are not unambiguously defined, the victims often exchange places with the perpetrators, and the motivations are at best murky. I see these situations as anarchic, and in that condition people tend to revert to crude behaviour unbridled by the fetters of society and culture. But there is one factor that interrupts that line of thought and it is history – or, perhaps more accurately stated, history as interpreted through the filters of folk memory, nationalism, ethnicity, and religion. The combatants are not acting in a vacuum even in the midst of apparent anarchy. They are piloted by memories, even memories handed down by earlier generations, and the pilots send their loads on murderous missions by way of belated retribution.

HISTORICAL CONTEXT

Marshall Tito died in May 1980, leaving a political vacuum in the Yugoslavia he had re-established and in large part created in 1945. The country stumbled along with an impossible coalition in place of either a strongman like himself or a democratically elected parliament. Then, in the 1990s, the country simply disintegrated. The army became a force for one of the component states of the former union, Serbia, and it launched a series of wars throughout the rest of the territory, especially in Bosnia-Herzegovina. Our objective here is to understand not only why it disintegrated – that might not be so puzzling – but why its disintegration involved atrocities amounting to massive crimes against humanity. The Bosnian war followed the war in Croatia, and both followed increasingly hostile interactions between these states and Serbia. Before I go into more depth on Bosnia, I will provide a brief history of the preceding events because the Bosnian crisis did not stand alone.

Prior to 1918, advocates of a union of South Slavic peoples had little serious hope for change. Slovenia, Croatia, and Bosnia-Herzegovina were components of the Austrian Empire, while Serbia belonged to the Ottoman Empire. Even then, however, the Croatian claim to the right to self-determination, based on its version of ancient territories, included the whole of Croatia, Slavonia, Dalmatia, and Bosnia-Herzegovina. Serbian national liberation ideology simultaneously claimed the right of Serbs living in the same regions to be united with Serbia. The two major peoples nonetheless shared a language (though with two alphabets) and culture and had similar ancient origins. Serbian military success in the Balkan Wars of 1912–13 intensified the desire among Serbs for an independent state, the more so after they recovered Kosovo-Metohija. However, there were young Serbs – those who assassinated Austria's archduke in Sarajevo, most notably – who hoped to displace the heavy hand of the Hapsburg Empire so that a South Serb union could be effected. Austria obliged the Croats and Slovenes, instead, to fight against the Serbs. The conclusion of the First World War brought about the end of both the Austro-Hungarian regime and the Ottoman Empire and allowed for the creation of a South Slav union, Yugoslavia, dominated by Serbia as the strongest military force in the region.

The first Yugoslav state was born in 1918, a sprawling, multinational, multi-religious country in highly diverse geographical and ecological settings carved out of the dismembered empires. It included the independent kingdoms of Serbia and Montenegro; the former Austrian territories of Croatia, Slovenia, and Dalmatia; Macedonia, ruled by Turkey until 1912; Vojvodina and Croatia-Slavonia, previously governed by Hungary; and Bosnia-Herzegovina, which had been shifted from Ottoman control to that of Austria-Hungary in 1878. The religions of the new Yugoslavia were Eastern Orthodox (47 per cent of the total), Roman Catholic (39 per cent), and Muslim (11 per cent) (Cohen, 1993: 13). The Serb population was dispersed between the various territories, and Serb leaders of the time, and throughout the existence of the union, resisted a full federal system of government. Croatian and Slovene leaders simultaneously resisted control by Serbs, some of them arguing that while they were Europeans, the Serbs were Asian in outlook. Montenegrins, Macedonians, Albanians, and Hungarians were not recognized within the federation (Cohen, 1993: 15). The union never coalesced during the inter-war years, and an accord of 1939 recognized a "Croatian nation" as a hybrid government, neither entirely autonomous nor subject to the Yugoslavia dominated by Serbs that was still in place. The Second World War interrupted further negotiated changes.

Nazi Germany and its allies occupied Yugoslavia in 1941. They established a state of Croatia, including Bosnia-Herzegovina, wherein a paramilitary unit, the Ustashe, undertook a campaign of genocide against Serbs, Jews, Gypsies, and other non-Croats living in Croatia and Bosnia-Herzegovina. Reciprocal and independent atrocities were launched by Serbian Chetniks (guerrilla fighters) against Croats, Muslims, and others, though the Ustashe atrocities, which included concentration camps and all the technology of the Nazi period, were not matched elsewhere in the former Yugoslavia. Towards the end of the war, the Partisans (Communist guerrilla fighters led by Tito) added their own brutalities to the mixture, killing the remnants of the Ustashe and any others they perceived as real or potential enemies, including the remaining Chetnik forces. Of the Ustashe brutalities, Smilja Avramov (1995: 1) observes: "In terms of the number of victims involved and the brutality of the methods used to kill them, the genocide of Serbs, Jews, and Gypsies which occurred in the territory of Yugoslavia in the course of the Second World War must be recorded as one of the most monstrous events of recent history ... To this very day it remains a festering sore in the hearts of those on whose behalf it was perpetrated and in the hearts of the remnants of the groups who were its victims."

Apart from blaming Croats for the brutalities of the Ustashe, Avramov and other Serb writers do not provide much of an explanation. Aleksander Pavkovic (1997: 37) argues that these events may be understood in terms of the divergent national myths of Croatians and Serbs

already fully developed by the 1940s: "In the Ustashe's view Yugoslavia was an artificial creation which the Serbs imposed on the Croats to
deny them their freedom; therefore, to attain their national liberty the
Croats have to destroy this state and to free themselves from Serb domination. But the Serbs had not only robbed the Croats of their historical
liberties but they also contaminated, with their presence, the purity of
the Croat race ... Like the Jews to the Nazis, the Serbs were for the
Ustashe not only exploiters but representatives of degraded humanity."

The wartime massacres were, inevitably, part of the living and inherited memory of the people who became the second federation in Yugoslavia. The number of people killed in that period is debated, as these
matters so often are. Franjo Tudjman, who became the president of
Croatia at a later time, claimed that no more than 40,000 had died in
Ustashe camps. Independent sources in Germany and Italy indicated a
death toll closer to some 500,000 Serbs and an unknown number of
others (Avramov, 1995, citing various sources). Bogdan Denitch (1994:
32–3) argues that the "numbers have been distorted and politicized beyond all resemblance to reality by revenge-seekers" He estimates that
the total number of victims in the notorious Croatian death camp of
Jasenovac could not have exceeded 100,000 casualties – a terrible figure, but considerably less than the estimates by Serbian nationalists.
What matters for an understanding of the genocidal events fifty years
later, however, is not truth, whatever the truth might be, but folk memory carried on through the generations.

The memories notwithstanding, Josip Broz (Tito) was able to re-establish Yugoslavia in 1948. Tito's Partisans claimed to have struggled
against the ultranationalists in all camps as well as the Nazis, blamed
the wartime atrocities on the Nazis, and promised to respect ethnic and
community differences while seeking a socialist economic future in a
federal state under the banner "Brotherhood and Unity." Although the
initial one-party government he established was based on the notion
that ethnic conflicts and national aspirations could be defeated by ignoring them, the memories did not wither away, and Tito finally established a federal form of government in the early 1960s. Provincial
governments gained considerable autonomy. Tito was careful to balance representation in the federal structure and to grant equal powers
to the provincial organizations. Serbs, distributed throughout several
regions, actually constituted the largest proportion of the population at
about 36 per cent, compared to just short of 20 per cent for Croatians,
and a 8.9 per cent for Muslims. (Muslims were defined as an ethnic

group, though they were, in fact, Serbo-Croatians with an Islamic religion) (figures from the 1981 census: Denitch, 1994: 29).

During Tito's governance, Yugoslavia gradually emerged as a non-aligned territory, anti-Stalinist but communist, developing a model of self-governing federated territories. Its experiments with autonomous worker-controlled industrial and agricultural economic units were widely admired and, despite the continued surveillance of secret police, imprisoning of dissidents, corruption at the centre, and ambiguity about the meaning of Yugoslav unity, the country achieved more peace than any of its parts had experienced hitherto.

There were, however, continuing problems. The various regions did not benefit equally from economic decisions, and resentments by both the richer regions that were obliged to share their wealth and the poorer ones that perceived exploitation bedevilled their relationships. Profound economic differences could not be overcome: Slovenia, for example, had one of the highest per capita incomes in Europe, while Kosovo and Macedonia were among the poorest (Liotta, 2001: 65). Croatian nationalism was a continuing problem and it erupted in 1972, capped by a crackdown under Tito's rule. The crackdown also affected other regions where reform movements were interpreted as nationalist movements. In the opinion of sociologist Bogdan Denitch (1994: 56): "That effectively removed the brightest and the best of the young postrevolutionary generation of Yugoslav leaders ... An entire generation of liberal Communist reformers was eliminated from political life for two whole decades. To make things worse, this generation had shown that it could cooperate to an extent that was not duplicated by their successors. In addition to purging the 'liberal' Communist reformers, Tito's crackdown fatally and permanently alienated a whole generation of non-Communist moderate nationalists and democrats."

Tito's brand of communism began its slow decline after 1972. In addition to long-standing ethnic animosities, the country was losing its economic viability. The external world had changed, but Yugoslavia had not. External debt was accumulating, and Yugoslavia did not have a convertible currency. It relied heavily on imports and had not managed to develop an independent industrial capacity. Growth rates declined, and unemployment rose throughout the 1970s and 1980s. The lid was kept on by encouraging Yugoslavians to become "guest workers" in Germany, where they earned enough to sustain their families at home. The political structure, combining a highly centralized federal state with some decentralized decision-making at the provincial level, did not lead to economic solutions. Popular discontent was expressed in strikes and demonstrations. Political leaders were blamed, and the diverse regional party organizations became increasingly autonomous, unwilling to maintain their allegiance to the central government. Though the Yugoslav Federal Assembly attempted to open up the economy and implement various reforms demanded by diverse regions of the country, one scheme after another disintegrated; politicians were replaced, but new ones were equally unable to solve either the ethnic tensions or the downward economic spiral. The various crises led quickly to the delegitimation of the Communist Party.

Gradually the country lapsed into regional and ethnic discontents. Nationalist resentments simmered under aging party leaders and, after Tito died and the elder statesmen of his generation faded away, the conflicts were openly expressed. The Albanian situation in Kosovo deteriorated quickly. An underdeveloped province, 77 per cent Albanian and the remainder Serb and Montenegrins, the three ethnic groups became increasingly hostile towards one another. In 1981 the Kosovo Albanians rioted, demanding what they claimed were historic rights to self-determination. They, like the Croatians and Serbians, had a myth of origins; in their case, the claim was that Albanians from the ancient tribe of Illyrians had settled in the Balkans before the South Slavs (Pavkovic, 1997: 86–7). But Kosovo was not alone: other provinces were also becoming impatient with a union they perceived as increasingly Serbian-dominated. And many Serbs, simultaneously, perceived themselves as victims of a union that ignored their numerical majority and their ancient history. Serb nationalist themes and revivals of religious rituals were used to portray the rights and demands of Serbians. Slobodan Milosevic, assuming leadership of the party organization in Serbia in 1984, increased Serbian demands

Slovenian political leaders were considering reforms, and relations between Serbia and Slovenia deteriorated to the point that Serbian communist leaders terminated links with Slovenia in November 1989. The unravelling of the one-party federal state was now under way, and it came to an abrupt finale in 1990 when the League of Communists failed to arrive at a consensus. In 1990 Slovenia held a successful multi party election. Shortly afterwards, Croatia held less-successful elections, with the ethno-nationalist party led by Franjo Tudjman taking a clear majority of the Croatian votes and the Serb-dominated parties providing a protest vote. Albanian Kosovars moved in the same direction. Milosevic's response was threatening, and Kosovar resentment festered. Attempts by the still existing but no longer functional Yugo-slavian central party to overcome the proliferation of ethno-nationalist parties and movements had utterly failed.

As the separating regions multiplied, the issue of Serbian minorities in all the non-Serbian states became paramount. Over a third of Serbs resided in other provinces. In Croatia, Serbs were an absolute majority in eleven communes, and a relative majority in another two; in all of these, Serbs, who had previously been favoured in the federation, were now marginalized, and unrest among them intensified after the election (Cohen, 1993: 126–35). In Bosnia-Herzegovina (BH), Serbs made up a third of the population of 4.36 million, Muslims nearly 44 per cent, and Croats another 17 per cent. Muslims in BH comprised 84 per cent of all Muslims in Yugoslavia (Meier, 1999: 195). Again, as in Croatia, Serbs were concentrated in particular regions, and, again, the Serb majorities in these regions demanded their own border state or some form of incorporation into the Serbian republic. The 1990 elections in BH disintegrated into ethnic competitions. During the early months of 1991 the leaders of the various provinces-cum-states met several times, but their respective wishes and demands were incompatible. Proposals for reforms to keep them together in some kind of union all failed.

The breakaway provinces of Croatia and Slovenia created paramili-tary units, and when these Croatian forces attempted to stop Serbian revolts in Krajina, a predominantly Serbian region of Croatia, the Yu-goslav military force was called in. Tudjman angrily denounced their participation as an attempt to "install a centralist unitarist Yugoslavia, and return to communism" (Cohen, 1993: 201). Milosevic and the army leadership demanded that the northern provinces disband para-military units. They were rebuffed, and the president of the federation resigned, saying he could not accept a "vote of nonconfidence" in the military. Milosevic, as president of Serbia, attempted to take over con-trol of the army but failed. In the early stages of this mounting conflict, the military establishment of Yugoslavia still saw itself as the saviour of the country, destined to use force if necessary to protect "socialist self-management" against multiparty pluralism and ethnic nationalism. It was unwilling, however, to interfere in what its commanders regarded as purely political issues (Cohen, 1993: 87–8).

Slovenia moved steadily towards complete independence. The Slov-enian government withdrew its contingent of troops from the Yugo-slav army and, when federal military forces moved to secure control over Yugoslavia's borders in June 1991, they were defeated by the paramilitary forces already organized in Slovenia. Unlike other provinces, Slovenia had no minority Serb population, so it posed less of a threat to Serbia than did Croatia and Bosnia.

In May 1991 an overwhelming majority of Croatian voters supported the creation of an independent country, but Krajina Serbs boycotted the referendum. The Yugoslavian government, with Serbian support, insisted that unilateral declarations were unacceptable, and tensions mounted. A clash between Croatian and Serbian police claimed more Croatian casualties, and the Croatian government mounted an international campaign in which it claimed the Croats had been tortured. By September 1991 the Yugoslavian army, now fragmented and with no clearly defined Yugoslavia to defend, mounted a concentrated assault against Croats in the areas with substantial Serb populations, including the cities of Vukovar and Osijek and the area around Dubrovnik.

The outcome of this stage of the war is interpreted very differently by various commentators. Indeed, from this point on, virtually every claim has a counter-claim, and the propaganda war may well have been greater than the military war. In internal war, unlike state terrorism, there is no single perpetrator of bestiality. And though states hide their sins in twilight wars, warring factions in internal wars are even better at manipulating the mass media. In this war, most external media observers had virtually no knowledge of the country or its long history of hostilities. There were numerous instances of the media accepting the version of events that one or the other side gave – showing bodies the Croatians claimed were innocent victims of Serb attacks, for example – and then being obliged to retract in the face of contrary evidence, such as that the bodies were in fact Serbs killed by Croats. Villages were sacked and razed, children raped and their parents tortured, but in Croatia the share of these terrible events committed by Serbs or by Croatians remains unclear. On one point the observers tend to agree: that the Yugoslav army had been transformed into an "an essentially Serbian-run and Serbian-manned military force, which became almost completely autonomous from civilian and federal control" (Cohen, 1993: 226).

Pavkovic (1997: 142) observes that the war in Croatia demonstrated that what was left of the Yugoslav federal army had neither the popular support nor the military capability and manpower to rule over non-Serb areas. It also proved that Croatian militias were unable to defeat Serb insurgent militias, which were still armed and supported by the (former) federal army. Propaganda, indoctrination, and hate were what kept them all going by the end of 1991. There were atrocities and barbaric incidents. Both sides had become adept at portraying the other as evil, and themselves as peaceful. The external media, often taken in by fraudulent claims, could not be depended on to provide an entirely objective or factual account of the war in Croatia in 1991–92.

The war in Croatia continued with intermittent outbreaks of hostilities throughout the early 1990s. In 1995 Croatian troops recaptured the rebel-held Krajina area, which had already undergone the opposite ethnic cleansing by Croatian Serbs four years earlier. The European Commission on Human Rights, UN observers, Helsinki Watch, and other groups all reported atrocities and subsequently accused the Croatian government of attempting to cover them up. Franjo Tudjman promoted one of the men already indicted by the International War Crimes Tribunal in the Hague, sending out his message of indifference about world opinion (Cushman and Mestrovic, 1996b: 16–17).

The world, introduced to these attacks via television and newspaper accounts, called them "the Balkan wars," as though they were similar to the wars of 1912–13 between Russia and Turkey for control of the region. But, the wars, beginning in 1991 in Slovenia and proceeding through Croatia and Bosnia, and ultimately in Kosovo, did not actually touch the soil in Serbia, Greece, Bulgaria, or other regions of the Balkans. In all these wars the former federal army was intent on killing civilians rather than the soldiers of other armies (Cushman and Mestrovic, 1996b: 3–4). The soldiers themselves were without any clear direction, and they tended finally to defend their own little stretches of homeland. The wars had disintegrated into petty hatreds between ethnic/religious groups, each with its own mythic history and claims to historic rights.

GENOCIDE/POLITICIDE AND WAR IN BOSNIA-HERZEGOVINA

As noted earlier, Muslims in Bosnia-Herzegovina made up nearly 84 per cent of all Muslims in the former Yugoslavia. (Muslim was regarded as an ethnic identity for purposes of the census and did not necessarily imply a religious connotation.) The Croatian population had two parts: one was integrated into central Bosnia and had high intermarriage rates with Muslims; the other resided primarily in the former Herzegovina region, where they had little contact with Muslims. The latter group wanted a union with Croatia. The Serbian population, comprising 31 per cent of the population, wanted a union with Serbia, and its leader Radovan Karadzic, following Slobodan Milosovic, was unbending in his demand for union. Each of these groups insisted that its ancestors had been in the regions before the others.

The state's first democratic elections were scheduled for November 1990. The contesting parties each represented their ethnic and religious groups. In spite of their cleavages, Bosnians were able to maintain some degree of internal cooperation through 1991. The Muslim majority in Parliament expressed confidence that the federal army of Yugoslavia would protect the democracy if required to do so (Meier, 1999: 206–7). Their optimism was misplaced, however: the federal army, now fully controlled by Serbia, was increasing its numbers in Bosnia. One Croatian party leader told historian Viktor Meier that the state was occupied, and others informed him that the army would not permit Bosnia-Herzegovina to pursue an independent course (Meier, 1999: 207). As well, the Bosnian Serbs had already established a breakaway assembly and, in March 1992, proclaimed a separate Bosnian Serb Republic.

A referendum was held in March 1992, after which the Parliament of Bosnia-Herzegovina declared independence. The United States and the European Commission accepted it in April. Then the war began in earnest. The former federal army (referred to as the JNA and now representing Serbia) took control of weapons depots, so although the Bosnian army was created, consisting of former Yugoslavian, primarily non-Serb conscripts, it had no weapons. Paramilitary forces consisting of Serbs resident in Bosnia-Herzegovina were also organized together with volunteers from Montenegro. The UN Security Council, in May 1992, ordered the JNA and paramilitary units out of Bosnia, but the JNA was already bombing Sarajevo. The siege of Sarajevo involved months of bombing by the army, even though the Bosnians had few arms or munitions and had not had the time or the capacity to become organized before the assault. According to Bosnian general Jovan Divjak (2001: 160–1), the soldiers, most of whom were very young, had inadequate footwear or other clothing and were untrained for the trench warfare they faced during the first two years of the war. Divjak also claims that, by 1993, clergy became involved in the Bosnian territorial defence units, contradicting the secular, multicultural, multireligious, and democratic image that the volunteers were defending.

The strategy of Serb paramilitary forces was first to terrorize a Muslim village, so many inhabitants would voluntarily depart, then kill those who remained. Homes and property were taken. By the fall of 1992 there was also the systematic destruction of mosques, Muslim libraries, schools, and other cultural buildings. All these actions were accompanied by anti-Muslim propaganda put out over all available media.

In the early stages of the war, Serbs were pitted against Muslims, but before long there were also skirmishes between Serbs and Croats and then between Croats and Muslims. Unknown to the troops on the ground, Presidents Slobodan Milosevic and Franjo Tudjman had met in September 1991 and had agreed to divide Bosnia between their two territories (Rogel, 1998: 31). By mid-summer 1992 Bosnian Croats had declared the formation of an autonomous Croat state (Herceg-Bosna) in southwestern Bosnia. Tudjman supported it and later claimed credit. In 1995 Croats tried to take over Mostar. That city was destroyed, leaving in its ashes many dead civilians of both Croat and Muslim descent, and many more who became refugees.

Serb forces took Srebrenica in July 1995, even though Dutch UN forces were guarding it and had declared it a "safe zone." An estimated 6,000 Srebrenicans were killed, mainly men. Women and children were forced onto buses and sent outside the region, but those who attempted to flee were shot. Bodies were thrown into mass graves (Honig and Both, 1996). The previous month, Serbs had also taken 370 UN hostages.

The war ended in December 1995 when an agreement was reached, brokered by the United Nations, by which Bosnia-Herzegovina would continue as a legal entity, though it would have a Muslim-Croat federation in the middle and along the western border, and a Serbian republic in the northern and easterm regions. This agreement comes close to the secret one between the Croatian and Serbian presidents in 1991. The Dayton Accords satisfied no one, but they ended the fighting for the time being. While all parties continue to stew over the impossible division of powers, Radovan Karadzic, the civilian leader of the Bosnian Serbs, Ratko Mladic, the military leader, and Slobodan Milosevic, the president of Serbia, have all been indicted for war crimes by the Hague Tribunal.

The period from 1992 to 1995 involved bestiality, rape, torture, and murder – in short, genocide against Muslim civilians in Bosnia-Herzegovina by Bosnian and other Serb soldiers from the former federal army and also by Croatians resident in Bosnia. There were forced evictions of Muslims from territories bordering Serbia and wherever they were a minority. Rape was so prevalent that observers recognized it as a war strategy. One Bosnian argues that "organized rape of young girls and women" constituted a "systematic method of execution" (Kajan, 1993: 87). In April 1992 all but three leaders of the Party of Democratic Action (SDA), led by the elected president, were killed as they were coming out of a mosque. Many others were killed when their attackers bombed the mosque where they had sought refuge. The soldiers then urinated on the corpses (Kajan, 1993: 87–8). Numerous eyewitness accounts of this atrocity and many others have described their experiences for publication. They report repeated killings, looting of people's homes and stores, arson, and abductions. One frequent method of eradicating Muslims was to force all villagers into a house, seal it, and then douse the house with gasoline. Whole villages were burnt. A typical report from the village of Kosovo Poije reads: "The Chetniks [Serbs] came into the village on June 3, 1992 ... They went to my brother Sefket's house. They began kicking his wife Fatima. They demanded money and all her jewelry. My sister-in-law brought them what they wanted. They then locked her up in the house and raped her. After they had finished they set the house on fire with Fatima in it. The remains of her hair and bones were found" (Kajan, 1993: 91).

Women, especially in a strong patriarchal culture, are loath to talk about rape. It is a forbidden subject, and those who have suffered it consider it shameful, a degradation they do not want to admit to men or even to other women who have equally suffered. But one female foreign reporter, talking to women in a refugee camp near Zagreb, was able to elicit memories such as this one:

Yes, I knew that five of my school colleagues were raped and killed afterward. I saw them lying in a ditch. They were there for days and each time I passed by I didn't want to look, but I did. It was in June. Their clothes were torn off them and I could see that they had been tortured. I saw knife wounds on their breasts, on their stomachs. Then, one afternoon, when we were coming back from a concentration camp where my brother was imprisoned – there were about fifty women walking back to our village through the woods – we saw that armed Serb Chetniks were waiting for us. We knew what was going to happen, but it was impossible to escape. They stopped us and chose two women. Then about ten Chetniks raped them in front of us. We were forced to stand and watch." (Draculic, 1993: 118)

Bosnians fleeing ethnic cleansing (the phrase came into popular usage in the context of the Croatian war in Yugoslavia) numbered 1.5 million (a third of the population) by November 1992. The International Red Cross concluded that Serbs had perpetrated numerous human rights offences, and, in particular, an estimated 20,000 rapes (Rogel, 1998: 32). Serbian air bombardment of Sarajevo, concentration camps, rape, and ethnic cleansing continued to occur after the publication of the Red Cross and other reports. In 1995 thousands of Muslims were evicted, killed, or disappeared following Serbian attacks.

External reports on the events, especially a very detailed report by Helsinki Watch (1993), reiterated that Bosnian Serbian soldiers, their militias and volunteers, had perpetrated the majority of war crimes and human rights offences. The reports traced ethnic cleansing as a Serbian government policy in eastern Croatia to its rigorous application in Bosnia after Karadzic had proclaimed the Serbian Republic of Bosnia. Croatian soldiers had likewise become involved in attacks on Bosnian Muslims, despite an agreement of solidarity in the very early stages of the war.

Ethnic nationalism was the ideological rationale for the wars in both Croatia and Bosnia-Herzegovina. It afflicted both the Croatians and the Serbs in particularly heavy doses and took the form alternately of boasting about the superiority of whichever nationality the perpetrators assumed and complaining about the predations and history of all others. The strategy of raping women was pegged on the theory that, in this way, all people in the following generation would have Serb blood in their veins. As well, whether or not the women were impregnated, it was a means of humiliating both them and the men in their families and villages.

EXTERNAL INFLUENCES

The second incarnation of Yugoslavia emerged in the ashes of the Nazi occupation and the enmity of the Cold War. Britain enabled Tito to become the strongman of the region, and the United States provided him with military assistance and aid when it became clear that he was prepared to thumb his nose at Stalin. His independent socialism allowed the country to be treated as a buffer state against the USSR. But the problem with this arrangement was that it depended on the continuation of the Cold War. Once that ended, Yugoslavia was of no further interest to the Western powers.

Before the expiry of a federated Yugoslavia, European leaders, hitherto preoccupied with the fallout from the ending of the Cold

War, attempted to patch up the disintegrating union through prom-
ises of IMF funds. At that time, 1991, they were generally of the opinion that the federation should be saved, that the independent states
should not be recognized. When it became clear that the violence had
started and would not soon stop, both US and European Community
leaders negotiated a temporary cease-fire agreement (the Brioni Declaration), but failed to bring about a cessation of hostilities. European
Community forces were ineffective in peace enforcement, and NATO
treated the crisis as outside its sphere of activity. The United Nations
sent observers to examine the possibilities for an extended cease-fire
agreement, but UN troops did not arrive in Croatia until late March
1992. A UN-brokered cease-fire was promulgated at that time, and
the European Community recognized both Slovenian and Croatian
independent states after Germany broke ranks and did so unilaterally.
A brief respite followed for these states, while the war shifted its focus to Bosnia-Herzegovina.

The three major ethnic groups there were not able to reach an amica-
ble agreement on governance, partly because of mutual distrust following events in Croatia and Serbia. The European Community and the
United States nonetheless chose to recognize Bosnia-Herzegovina's independence, thereby inflaming, rather than resolving, the tensions. External groups again attempted to stop the conflict by devising a peace
plan: the Vance-Owen Plan of January 1993, which included a division
of Bosnia and Herzegovina into ten provinces. Though the parties
agreed under pressure to go along, fighting was renewed before the sig-
natures were on the paper. The UN forces proved to be ineffective in
protecting civilians even in "safe zones," and UN personnel were
themselves threatened with an inglorious death when they attempted to
broker peace agreements. The Dayton Accords that were finally established in 1995 are tenuous. They split Bosnia into two almost equal
parts: central and western regions to be called the Federation of Bosnia-Herzegovina, where Bosniaks (formerly calleds Muslims) and
Croats coexist; and northern and eastern portions called Republika
Srpska, dominated by Serbs. Of the three leaders of Serb forces since
indicted for war crimes, Karadzic and Mladic remain free. Republica
Srpska, or Serbia itself, continues to protect them.

Epilogue

Inequality is a normal feature of societies. But there are varying degrees and kinds of inequality, and varying degrees of permeability and flexibility in hierarchical systems. A system that combines class and ethnicity in rigid structures is more likely to break than to bend when confronted by unavoidable conditions that will oblige it to change. Change is no bad thing, especially when it has the power to dissolve cruel and oppressive systems: the problem is that the powerful and wealthy take out their fear of change on the weaker members of the society.

How satisfying it would be to say of the societies in our survey that they belong to the past, that such events would never happen today. Yet such events are happening today. Not surprisingly, they happen frequently in countries where there is a huge gulf between the powerful few and the powerless many. In such countries, whenever the powerless demand access to the political process in order to improve their economic conditions, they become a potential threat to the privileges of the few. Wherever they gain enough access to alter the system via political channels, the privileged are likely to stage a counter-thrust, even a counter-revolution, as in Chile.

The stage seems to be set now for a long-drawn-out civil war in Venezuela, one that could turn into a bloodbath if the army turns against a populist president seen by the poor as its champion. Hugo Chávez was, in fact, removed by force from the presidential palace during 2002 and kept incommunicado for several days while representatives of the privileged class tried to take control of the government. The counter-revolution was stopped and Chávez returned to office when thousands of working-class and poor Venezuelans demonstrated against the

usurpers and the army refused to go along with the coup. This pause is
not a conclusion to the Venezuelan crisis, nor is it the initial chapter:
rather, this civil-war-in-the-making has simmered for a long time, just
as it did in Argentina throughout the 1960s and 1970s. In Argentina,
however, the army was the government-in-waiting at every turn, and it
was the army that ousted the populist Juan Perón the first time, and his
unpopular third wife the second time. Much depends on the Venezuelan army in the current episode. It is a situation that those who recom-
mend international efforts to prevent crimes against humanity need to
monitor. Even more, they need to monitor the reactions in Washington:
Venezuela continues to be a source of oil for the United States, and US
leaders are not shy when it comes to protecting their energy sources.
With respect to Argentina, we continue to watch as a society, abused by
profligate governors together with IMF "market fundamentalists," as
George Soros calls them, makes desperate and brave attempts to reconstruct its tattered economy. The one hopeful ingredient in that scenario
is a weakened army, substantially downsized and obliged to obey civilian leaders in the aftermath of the 1976–83 state terror.

Africa is rife with examples of states in trouble. African states were
carved out arbitrarily by European powers of the nineteenth and early
twentieth centuries. Some of the descendents of the original people
speak French, some Portuguese, some English, a few, German, and, in
South Africa, Afrikaans, as a consequence of the rivalries and conquests of European peoples. Regardless of differences among the European powers that drew up their borders while plundering their
natural resources, all these states have continuing political and economic problems.

The Democratic Republic of the Congo (DRC) is a tragic example.
Occupying a territory in Central Africa a quarter the size of the United
States, and blessed – or cursed – with some of the world's most valuable
natural resources (oil, diamonds, emeralds, and many other industrial
and gem minerals), this region has been plundered, oppressed, and bedevilled from the time Europeans burdened it with their presence. Belgian King Leopold II's men came for its elephant tusks, then its minerals
and rubber, enslaving and killing its people along the way. When at last
the colonial ties were cut, the Central Intelligence Agency of the United
States, together with Belgian soldiers, arranged for the assassination of
its first elected president, Patrice Lumumba. He was just one of the
many victims of Cold War politics. From that time forward the country,
led by Mobuto Seki Seko, then Laurent Kabila, and now Kabila's son

Joseph, has been governed by coercion and corruption. Companies and soldiers from every sub-Saharan country are there now, competing viciously for a share of the valuable resources, in what they euphemistically call a civil war. Ugandan troops are in the northeast corner of the land, and Rwandans occupy the eastern areas. Zimbabweans take the side of the DRC against Ugandans and Rwandans, and profit in the same ways as they do. South African companies are engaged in the scramble. The Congolese army and police are unpaid, though this rich country, were it organized, could easily provide for its custodial staff. The problem here is not general poverty but, rather, such unconstrained greed that no funds are reserved for public sector employees: they have become bandits in order to survive. Canadians, like the others, "cultivate connections in high Congolese places to get away with deals giving them access to valuable state mining concessions on terms that conspicuously violate the needs of the public sector," says Jim Freedman, a Canadian member of a United Nations Panel of Experts charged with determining what was happening in the Congo. He circulated a description (2002) of a hair-raising trip in the south-central region still under Congo government control where the conflict is over diamonds. Violence in the northeastern DRC is similar to the Rwandan experience. Hema (Hutu) and Lendu (Tutsi) groups have formed militias. As in Rwanda, radio propaganda is accompanying an escalating conflict that may be the beginning of another genocide.* Angola, Nigeria, Chad, Sudan, Ethiopia, Zimbabwe, Mozambique, and other countries on the African continent have also experienced civil wars, or civil wars augmented by the armies supported by external powers, generally over valued resources or geopolitical position.

Where no one controls a territory and many would like to control it or its resources, the outcome is anarchy. Whoever controls the strongest force is likely to be the winner. There is no surprise here: the borders of the original states of Europe, and many of the states created under colonial control, were determined largely by force. When statesmen pontificate about the sacred rights of sovereignty as determined by the Treaty of Westphalia, they tend to ignore the arbitrariness of the world's political map. Both anarchy and strong-arm sovereignty can be terrible burdens to the hapless inhabitants of territories either contested by or under the control of ruthless dictators, military juntas, or militant

---

* Current information is available on website allafrica.com/stories/200305120003.html, hrw.org/press/2003/05/drc050803.htm, hrw.org/press/2002/10/easterncongo-bck.htm, and linked sites.

theocrats and other ideologues. Then concerned leaders of other countries ask whether they have the right to intervene, and what might be the appropriate forms of intervention.

A commission established by the Canadian government, but with international representation (the International Commission on Intervention and State Sovereignty, 2001), grappled with the question: When is it appropriate for states to take action, especially military action, against other states for the purpose of protecting people at risk? In 1994 the nations of the world ignored the terrible genocide in Rwanda even while the commander of UN forces, a Canadian, begged his superiors in the United Nations, Canada, the United States, and elsewhere for troops and military backing to stop it. Yet Canada joined the United States and many European nations in the NATO attack on Kosovo in 1999, where the stated reason for intervention was humanitarian. Other situations in the 1990s and early in the new century have elicited inconsistent responses from the United Nations and from individual states. In Bosnia in 1995 a UN force failed to prevent the massacre of civilians who, expecting the United Nations to protect them, sought shelter in UN "safe areas" in Srebrenica.

What might have been the appropriate form of intervention in Iraq while Saddam Hussein was in power? What about Iran, Afghanistan while it was under the Taliban rule, or the numerous African states under oppressive governments or experiencing anarchy? What would be needed to intervene in the affairs of a state that is under the military shield of the United States, such as Saudi Arabia between the late 1940s and 2003? When has a state contravened international morality to such a degree that outsiders deemed it appropriate or necessary to intervene? Is it essential for a state to threaten other states before they take action, or is it possible for a state to threaten only its own people to elicit a reprimand or a stronger response from the outside world?

The International Commission began with the argument that intervention had to meet four basic objectives: the rules, procedures, and criteria have to be clear; military intervention may be legitimate, but only if all other approaches have failed; military intervention may be undertaken only for the purposes proposed and must be undertaken so as to minimize human costs and institutional damage; and intervening states must attempt to eliminate the causes of conflict and seek ways of creating a durable and sustainable peace (2001: 11).

The commission chose to treat sovereignty not as an inviolable boundary between states, but as a responsibility. State authorities are responsible for the welfare of their citizens, and they are responsible, and therefore accountable, to the international community through the United Nations. Another change in perspective matches this stand: instead of talking about the right to intervene, the commission argues in favour of "the responsibility to protect." Protection begins with prevention and involves attempts to enable the offending state authorities to alter their behaviour. The commissioners referred to such potential causes of conflict as poverty and uneven distribution of resources and suggested that preventive strategies must work to "promote human rights, to protect minority rights, and to institute political arrangements in which all groups are represented." (23)

Key to the recommendations are requirements for international agreement and collective, not unilateral, action. These provisos would avoid the kind of intervention that occurred in Iraq when the divided voice of the United Nations and massive anti-war demonstrations throughout the world were shunted aside by the United States and Britain. But this response embodies an obvious caveat. The Security Council, established in the wake of the Second World War, has shown little capacity for united decision-making, let alone collective willingness to intervene in humanitarian crises. Rwanda and Burundi were ignored. They were of no strategic or economic interest to the major powers. Russia opposed the intervention in Kosovo because of its relationship to the Serbs, and NATO, rather than the United Nations, fought that war. The United States opposed UN leadership with respect to Iraq because it wanted to control the timing, the forces, and the outcome. Oil was the calling card; humanitarian concerns were not the original and never the primary reason for the war. Britain and France also had their own agendas, often linked to earlier colonial interests. The International Commission acknowledges the obstacles, but charges the Security Council with the duty to make tough decisions on humanitarian grounds. The alternative is to create a new global organization – and given the state of the world in the first decade of the twenty-first century, that is even less likely to succeed than remodelling the Security Council and the United Nations.

Another objection to the proposal is that intervention often means long-term occupation. The terrible war and genocide in Bosnia was finally stopped by UN intervention, but the peace there depends on the continuing presence of 12,000 NATO troops. The NATO war in Kosovo is likewise demanding of the presence of peacekeepers. Yet a further problem is the difficulty, in some situations, of separating, even identifying, the perpetrators and victims. Crimes against humanity were certainly perpetrated in Croatia, for example, but at the time it was not clear to outsiders whether both groups were equally at fault. Finally, if UN forces are to be used, they must be sufficient in strength to overcome the combatants, since a weak UN force, such as the one in place at Srebrenica in Bosnia, may be worse than none at all. It conveys false hope to the victims.

As the International Commission recognizes, the preferable route is preventive international action. Such organizations as the International Crisis Group, Amnesty International, Human Rights Watch, and the Fédération internationale des ligues des droits de l'homme are crucial humanitarian "canaries" that can warn the world of emerging conflicts that could easily turn into massive crimes against humanity. The question that remains is whether the United Nations as presently structured is capable of heeding such warnings and acting before it is too late.

The commission's report and recommendations were discussed in mid-July 2003 by fourteen "progressive" political leaders who voluntarily come together in an informal summit from time to time. They urged the United Nations General Assembly to give "urgent consideration" to establishing a legal code to guide international interventions. Canadian prime minister Jean Chrétien, who initiated the discussion based on the International Commission's report, admitted that it would take time to work out a legal framework for collective action by the United Nations, but pointed out that the convention against landmines, also spearheaded by Canada while Lloyd Axworthy was foreign minister, had a long route to follow before it was adopted.

For those who dismiss such efforts as "pie in the sky," the alternatives need sober reflection. Is it better to leave a poor and strategically unimportant country such as Rwanda or Burundi to drown in its own blood? Should Serbs and Croats be permitted to carve up Bosnia between them, killing or evicting the Bosniaks who stand in the way? Why is it that Radovan Karadzic and Ratko Mladic, both charged by the International War Crimes Tribunal with crimes against humanity during the war in Bosnia, are still at large? Should the world ignore the plight of Zimbabweans while their mad president, Robert Mugabe, tears apart their country? Should we merely watch and shake our heads in wonder as many of the world's soldiers and mining companies kill one another along with thousands of defenseless citizens of the Democratic Republic of the Congo? Why was world opinion ineffective in stopping the American colossus from invading Iraq? Why was it impossible, instead, to charge Saddam Hussein, his sons and allies, with crimes against humanity in the International Criminal Court (ICC)?

While good people advance an agenda in favour of "the responsibility to protect," the world continues to be organized on principles of aggression and intervention for reasons that have little to do with protection and much to do with control of vital resources or control of geo-political regions where markets might otherwise be interrupted.

The world in the first decade of the twenty-first century does not consist of equal and independent states, some governed by dictators, and others by the rule of law and democracy. Its states are extremely unequal in both power and wealth, and one state is becoming an empire. Empires have been dominant organizations throughout much of human history. They erupt whenever one group manages to gain control of more military force than any other or even combinations of others. That group uses its military and economic power to oblige neighbours and other more distant members of the human community to obey its dictates, accept its orders, adapt to its culture, share its religion or political ideology, and bow to its laws. The Holy Roman Empire, the Byzantine Empire, the Austro-Hungarian Empire, the Ottoman Empire, the Russian Empire, and the British Empire were all the most powerful military and economic geo-political units of their times: the American Empire follows suit. But always there are limits, and the limits are embedded in the same codes as the privileges. Empires disintegrate both at the centre and at the peripheries because they can no longer control all the conditions that introduce change and oblige the rulers to accept restrictions on their privileges.

The problems that face the American Empire are the same as those that finally brought down its predecessors. At the core of the United States there is extreme poverty; and there is racism that obstructs efforts to overcome that poverty. In its growth period, much of the United States was liberal and progressive, endowed with a vision of civil rights and the rule of law that marked it as one of the most advanced societies on earth. It had gross inequities between races and classes, but it struggled with these problems and attempted to overcome them. Unfortunately, before it succeeded in that feat, its major rival for world dominance caved in. With the collapse of the Soviet Union, the United States became a military power so great that no single state and no combination of other states can challenge it. Such supremacy gives rise to arrogance. Its leaders lose their sense of communal values, civil liberties, and shared inheritance of the planet. The refusal of its governments over the past decade to accept the ICC convention and other international agreements indicates that the political leaders do not see their country as an integral component of the human community; rather, they perceive it as superior and beyond the controls that bind other human societies. Not surprisingly, this arrogance is an affront to other states. Sour relations between former allies is the least of the problems. More serious is the proliferation of underground anti-American movements and organized groups of religious zealots who condemn the "evil empire." The world has entered into a period of turmoil between empire and peripheries, similar in many ways to the turmoil of earlier times with other empires and other hinterlands.

In this context, the International Commission's humane agenda has little chance of becoming international law. The strongest nation is unwilling to support the United Nations, and the United Nations has no military capacity of its own to intervene in humanitarian crises. It can do only what its stronger components are willing to do, relying on their military and economic capacities. Even so, the commission's report indicates a new route by which the developed and relatively wealthy states could take responsibility for improving the lot of many people in politically unsavory conditions. Simply by acknowledging the issues, the report opens up the discussion and obliges thinking people to consider how to bring about change.

I have argued throughout this book that state-sponsored crimes against humanity occur when those in control of state institutions are unable to sustain the existing system, with its embedded inequalities. The society in these cases generally lacks buttressing institutional sectors but has a substantial military force. The International Commission leans, instead, on the theory that poverty and maldistribution of wealth are primary causes of these crimes. The analysis matters because, if we wish to intervene, we need to know why the breakdown occurred: otherwise, our attempts to fix the system will misfire.

If the analysis in this book is valid, we must identify states at risk and consider how external groups and countries might enable such states to cope with the changing conditions that cause the impairment. That does not mean propping up dictators, however. Where alternative or successful political arrangements cannot be achieved without conflict, our strategy might focus on the political environment rather than the weak state. Publicity about human rights offences is often helpful. Warnings to tourists and cessation of trade in non-foodstuffs are possible ways of alerting leaders of such societies that the outside world has an interests in what occurs. Threats to take offenders to the ICC are credible now that the court is up and functioning. With international cooperation, the arms trade could be stopped. That cooperation would include investigation of financial transactions connected to the trade. The ICC lacks jurisdiction over financial crimes, but it can share information that is crucial to national court prosecutions. Luis Moreno-Ocampo, the first prosecutor of the ICC, has already initiated investigation into money laundering and other financial crimes connected with such atrocities as are occurring in the Democratic Republic of the Congo (*Globe and Mail*, 17 July 2003).

The international community can also provide positive incentives to enable weak states to accommodate change and to treat their populations humanely. International aid, for example, can be attached to demands for positive action that supports the population and reduces the size and power of armies. The world organizations that already exist – the World Bank and the International Monetary Fund – could recreate themselves as agents of support for people, rather than as supports for the lending banks. In the long-run, that reorientation would be in the interests of the lenders, since impoverished and oppressed people have nothing to invest. The developed world might eventually be persuaded to examine the contribution of its own trade barriers and other actions to the instability of other countries.

Genocide and politicide are viruses we can overcome. They provide no positive long-term results, and they divide populations for many generations after the outbreak. If stable nations are willing to act collectively, even without the support of the United States, they could identify states at risk, peoples in trouble, and could take preventive action long in advance of the predictable commission of crimes against humanity. With collective concern and action, the use of force against such states would be a rare event.

References

Adalian, Rouben P. 1997. "The Armenian Genocide." In Samuel Totten, William S. Parsons, and Israel W. Charny, eds., *Century of Genocide*, 41–64. New York: Garland.

Adelman, Howard, and Astri Suhrke, eds. 1999. *The Path of a Genocide: The Rwanda Crisis from Uganda to Zaire*. New Brunswick, NJ: Transaction Publishers.

African Rights [Organization]. 1994. *Death, Despair, and Defiance*. London: African Rights.

Aktan, Gündüz. 2002. Column in *Turkish Daily News*, 21 May.

Alexander, Robert J. 1978. *The Tragedy of Chile*. Westport, Conn.: Greenwood Press.

Alvarez, Alex. 2001. *Governments, Citizens, and Genocide: A Comparative and Interdisciplinary Approach*. Bloomington: Indiana University Press.

Aly, Götz. 1999. *"Final Solution": Nazi Population Policy and the Murder of the European Jews*. London: Oxford University Press.

Amnesty International. 1977. *Report of an Amnesty International Mission to Argentina, 6–15 November 1976*. London: Amnesty International Publications.

Andersen, Martin. 1993. *Dossier Secreto: El Mito de la Guerra Sucia*. Planeto: Espejo de la Argentina.

Andreopoulos, George J., ed. 1994. *Genocide: Conceptual and Historical Dimensions*. Philadelphia: University of Pennsylvania Press.

Archdiocese of Santiago, Chile. 1984. "Vicariate of Solidarity." Mimeo.

Arendt, Hannah. 1958. *The Origins of Totalitarianism*. London: Allen and Unwin.

Arendt, Hannah. 1964. *Eichmann in Jerusalem: A Report on the Banality of Evil*. Rev. Ed. New York: Viking Press.

Arendt, Hannah. 1969. *On Violence*. New York: Harcourt, Brace & World.

Argentina, Comisión nacional sobre la desaparición de personas. 1985. *Nunca Más: Informe de la Comisión nacional sobre le desaparición de personas.* Buenos Aires: Editorial Universitaria de Buenos Aires.

Arriagada, Genaro. 1988. *Pinochet: The Politics of Power.* Translated by Nancy Morris with others. Boston: Unwin Hyman.

Astourian, Stephan H. 1998. "Modern Turkish Identity and the Armenian Genocide: From Prejudice to Racist Nationalism." In Richard G. Hovannisian, ed., *Remembrance and Denial: The Case of the Armenian Genocide,* 23–50. Detroit: Wayne State University Press.

Avramov, Smilja. 1995. *Genocide in Yugoslavia.* Translated by Margot and Bosko Milosavljevic. Belgrade: BIGZ.

Barnett, Victoria J. 1999. *Bystanders: Conscience and Complicity during the Holocaust.* Westport, Conn.: Greenwood Press.

Bassiouni, M. Cherif, ed. 1994. *The Protection of Human Rights in the Administration of Criminal Justice: A Compendium of United Nations Norms and Standards.* Geneva: Centre for Human Rights, United Nations; New York: Transnational Publishers.

Bassiouni, M. Cherif, and Ziyad Motala, eds. 1995. *The Protection of Human Rights in African Criminal Proceedings.* Dordrecht: Martinus Nijhoff.

Bauman, Zygmunt. 1989. *Modernity and the Holocaust.* Cambridge: Polity Press.

Becker, Elizabeth. 1998. *When the War Was Over: Cambodia and the Khmer Rouge Revolution.* New York: Public Affairs.

Berkeley, Bill. 2001. *The Graves Are Not Yet Full: Race, Tribe and Power in the Heart of Africa.* New York: Basic Books.

Borys, Jurij. 1980. *The Sovietization of Ukraine, 1917–1923: The Communist Doctrine and Practice of National Self-Determination.* Edmonton: Canadian Institute of Ukrainian Studies.

Bracher, Karl Dietrich. 1970. *The German Dictatorship: The Origins, Structure, and Effects of National Socialism.* New York: Praeger.

Bracher, Karl Dietrich. 1982. *The Age of Ideologies: A History of Political Thought in the Twentieth Century.* London: Weidenfeld and Nicolson.

Bramsted, Ernest K. 1965. *Goebbels and National Socialist Propaganda, 1925–1945.* Ann Arbor: Michigan State University Press.

Brinka, Tone. 1995. *Being Muslim the Bosnian Way: Identity and Community in a Central Bosnian Village.* Princeton, NJ: Princeton University Press.

Browder, George C. 1996. *Hitler's Enforcers: The Gestapo and the SS Security Service in the Nazi Revolution.* New York: Oxford University Press.

Browning, Christopher R. 1992. *The Path to Genocide: Essays on Launching the Final Solution.* Cambridge: Cambridge University Press.

Browning, Christopher R. 1998. *Ordinary Men: Reserve Policy Battalion 101 and the Final Solution in Poland*. New York: Harper Collins.

Burg, Steven L. 1997."Genocide in Bosnia-Herzegovina?" In Samuel Totten, William S. Parsons, and Israel W. Charny, eds., *Century of Genocide: Eyewitness Accounts and Critical Views*, 424–33. New York: Garland.

Burgler, R.A. 1990. *The Eyes of the Pineapple: Revolutionary Intellectuals and Terror in Democratic Kampuchea*. Saarbrucken: Verlag Breitenbach.

Burrin, Philippe. 1989. *Hitler and the Jews: The Genesis of the Holocaust*. London: Edward Arnold.

Bushnell, P. Timothy, et al., eds. 1991. *State Organized Terror: The Case of Violent Internal Repression*. Boulder, Col.: Westview Press.

Carney, Timothy. 1989. "The Unexpected Victory." In Karl D. Jackson, ed., *Cambodia, 1975–1978: Rendezvous with Death*, 13–36. Princeton, NJ: Princeton University Press.

Carynnyk, Marco, Lubomyr Y. Luciuk, and Bohdan S. Kordan. 1988. *The Foreign Office and the Famine: British Documents on Ukraine and the Great Famine of 1932–1933*. Kingston, Ont.: Limestone Press.

Chalk, Isreal W., and Kurt Jonassohn. 1988. "The History and Sociology of Genocidal Killings." In Israel Charny, ed., *Genocide: A Critical Bibliographic Review*, 39–58. London: Mansell Publishing.

Chalk, Israel W., and Kurt Jonassohn. 1990. *The History and Sociology of Genocide: Analyses and Case Studies*. New Haven: Yale University Press.

Chandler, David. 1996. *Facing the Cambodian Past*. Chiang Mai, Thailand: Silkworm Books.

Charny, Israel W., in collaboration with Chanan Rapaport. 1982. *How Can We Commit the Unthinkable? Genocide, the Human Cancer*. Boulder, Col.: Westview Press.

Charny, Israel, ed. 1984. *Toward the Understanding and Prevention of Genocide*. Boulder, Col.: Westview Press.

Charny, Israel. 1992. "Early Warning, Intervention, and Prevention of Genocide." In Michael N. Dobkowski and Isido Wallimann, eds., *Genocide in Our Time: An Annotated Bibliography with Analytical Introductions*, 149–66. Ann Arbor, Mich: Pierian Press.

Chile. 1973. *Decreto Ley No. 81: Fija, por Razones de Seguridad del Estado, Sanciones para las Personas que Desobedezcan el Llamamiento Publico que Indica del Gobierno*.

Chile. 1975. *Decreto Ley No. 1.009: Sistematiza Normas Sobre Proteccion Juridica de los Derechos Procesales de los Detenidos por Delitos Contra la Seguirdad Nacional por los Organismos que Indica Modifica Disposiciones Legales que Señale*.

Chile. 1980. *De Los Tribunales Militares: Decreto Ley No. 3.425, de 14 junio de 1980.*

Chile. Corporación Nacional de Reparación y Reconciliación. 1996. *Informe Sobre Calificación de Víctimas de Violaciones de Derechos Humanos y de la Violencia Política.* Santiago: El Corporación.

Chile. Ministerio de Defensa (Sub. Guerra). 1978. *Decreto Supremo No. 400: Fija Texto Refundido, Coordinado y Sistematizado de la Ley No. 17.798, Sobre Control de Armas.*

Chile. Ministerio del Interior. 1975. *Decreto Supremo No. 890: Fija Texto Actualizado de la Ley 12.927, Sobre Seguridad del Estado.*

Church Report. See United States Senate Select Committee on Intelligence Activities, 1975a.

CODEPU. 1996. "International Seminar on Impunity and Democracy: Santiago Declaration." Santiago, Chile: CODEPU.

Cohen, Lenard J. 1992. *Regime Transition in a Disintegrating Yugoslavia: The Law of Rule vs. the Rule of Law.* Pittsburgh: University of Pittsburgh Center for Russia and East European Studies, No. 908.

Cohen, Lenard J. 1993. *Broken Bonds: The Disintegration of Yugoslavia.* Boulder, Col.: Westview Press.

Cohen, Philip J. 1996. "The Complicity of Serbian Intellectuals in Genocide in the 1990s." In Thomas Cushman and Stjepan G. Mestrovic, eds., *This Time We Knew: Western Responses to Genocide in Bosnia,* 39–64. New York: New York University Press.

Cohn, Norman. 1967. *Warrant for Genocide: The Myth of the Jewish World-Conspiracy and the Protocols of the Elders of Zion.* New York: Harper and Row.

Cohn, Norman. 1970. *The Pursuit of the Millennium: Revolutionary Millenarian and Mystical Anarchists of the Middle Ages.* New York: Oxford University Press.

Conquest, Robert. 1986. *The Harvest of Sorrow: Soviet Collectivization and the Terror-Famine.* New York: Oxford University Press.

Conquest, Robert. 1990. *The Great Terror: A Reassessment.* New York: Oxford University Press.

Conquest, Robert, et al. 1984. *The Man-Made Famine in Ukraine.* Washington, DC: American Enterprise Institute.

Cooley, John K. 1999. *Unholy Wars: Afghanistan, America and International Terrorism.* London: Pluto Press.

Corradi, Juan, Patricia Weiss Fagen, and Manuel Antonio Garretón, eds. 1992. *Fear at the Edge: State Terror and Resistance in Latin America.* Berkeley: University of California Press.

Crnobrnja, Mihailo. 1996. *The Yugoslav Drama*. 2nd ed. Montreal: McGilll-Queen's University Press.

Cushman, Thomas, and Stjepan G. Mestrovic, eds. 1996a *This Time We Knew: Western Responses to Genocide in Bosnia*. New York: New York University Press.

Cushman, Thomas, and Stjepan G. Mestrovic. 1996b. Introduction to *This Time We Knew*, 1–38. New York: New York University Press.

Dadrian, Vahakn N. 1995. *The History of the Armenian Genocide: Ethnic Conflict from the Balkans to Anatolia to the Caucasus*. Providence, RI: Berghahn Books.

Dadrian, Vahakn N. 1999. *Warrant for Genocide*. New Brunswick, NJ: Transaction Publishers.

Deac, Wilfred P. 1997. *Road to the Killing Fields: The Cambodian War of 1970–75*. College Station: Texas A&M University Press.

Dekmejian, R. Hrair. 1986. "Determinants of Genocide: Armenians and Jews as Case Studies." In R.G. Hovannisian, ed., *The Armenian Genocide in Perspective*. New Brunswick, NJ: Transaction Books.

Denitch, Bogdan. 1994. *Ethnic Nationalism: The Tragic Death of Yugoslavia*. Rev. ed. Minneapolis: University of Minnesota Press.

de Tocqueville, Alexis. [1856] 1955. *The Old Régime and the French Revolution*. Translated by Stuart Gilbert. Garden City, NY: Doubleday.

Deutsch, Sandra McGee. 1993. "The Right under Radicalism, 1916–1930." In Sandra McGee Deutsch and Ronald H. Dolkar, eds., *The Argentine Right*, 35–63. Wilmington, Del.: SR Books.

Dextexhe, Alain. 1995. *Rwanda and Genocide in the Twentieth Century*. Translated by Alison Marschner. New York: New York University Press.

Díaz Bessone, Ramón Genaro. 1988. *Guerra revolucionaria en la Argentina (1959–1979)*. Buenos Aires: Circulo Militar.

Divjak, Jovan. 2001. "The First Phase, 1992–1993: Struggle for Survival and Genesis of the Army of Bosnia-Herzegovina." In B. Magas and I. Zanic, eds., *The War in Croatia and Bosnia-Herzegovina, 1991–1995*. London: Frank Cass.

Dolot, Miron. 1985. *Execution by Hunger: The Hidden Holocaust*. Toronto: Penguin.

Draculic, Slavenka. 1993. "Women Hide behind a Wall of Silence." In R. Ali and L. Lifschultz, eds., *Why Bosnia? Writings on the Balkan War*, 116–21. Stony Creek, Conn: The Pamphleteer's Press.

Drake, Paul and Iván Jaksi, eds. 1991. *The Struggle for Democracy in Chile*. Rev. ed. Lincoln: University of Nebraska Press.

Drost, Peter N. 1959. *The Crimes of State*. 2 vols. Leyden: A.W. Synoff.

Dülffer, Jost. 1996. *Nazi Germany, 1933–1945*. London: Arnold.

Duvall, Raymond D., and Michael Stohl. 1988. "Governance by Terror." In M. Stohl, ed., *The Politics of Terrorism*, 231–71. Third edition. New York: Marcel Dekker.

Ensalaco, Mark. 2000. *Chile under Pinochet: Recovering the Truth*. Philadelphia: University of Pennsylvania Press.

Erikson, Kai. 1996. "On Pseudospeciation and Social Speciation." In C.B. Strozier and M. Flynn, eds., *Genocide, War, and Human Survival*, 51–8. Lanham, My.: Rowman & Littlefield.

Etchecolatz, Miguel O. 1983. *La otra campana del Nunca más: Por la reconciliación de los argentinos*. Buenos Aires: The Author.

Ezell, Walter K. 1989. "Investigating Genocide: A Catalog of Known and Suspected Cases and Some Categories for Comparing Them." In Y. Bauer et al., eds., *Remembering the Future*, vol. 3: *The Impact of the Holocaust on Jews and Christians*, 2880–92. Oxford: Pergamon Press.

Fein, Helen. 1990. "Genocide: A Sociological Perspective." International Sociological Association Journal, *Current Sociology* 38, 1. London: Sage Publications.

Fein, Helen, ed. 1992. *Genocide Watch*. New Haven, Conn.: Yale University Press.

Findley, Trevor. 1995. *Cambodia: The Legacy and Lessons of UNTAC*. SIPRI Research Report No. 9. Oxford: Oxford University Press.

Fischer, Klaus P. 1995. *Nazi Germany: A New History*. New York: Continuum.

Frank, André Gunder. 1979. *Dependent Accumulation and Underdevelopment*. New York: Monthly Review Press.

Freeman, Jim. 2002. "Canadian Business in the Congo." Manuscript.

Friedlander, Henry. 1995. *The Origins of Nazi Genocide: From Euthanasia to the Final Solution*. Chapel Hill: University of North Carolina Press.

Friedman, Benjamin M. 2002. "Globalization: Stiglitz's Case." In *New York Review of Books* 49, 13, 15 Aug.

Frontalini, Daniel, and Maria Cristina Caiati. 1984. *El mito de la guerra sucia*. Buenos Aires: Centro de Estudios Legales y Sociales.

Fruhling, Hugo. 1992. "Resistance to Fear in Chile: The Experience of the Vicaria de la Solidaridad." In Juan Corradi, Patricia Weiss Fagen, and Manuel Antonio Garretón, eds., *Fear at the Edge: State Terror and Resistance in Latin America*, 121–41. Berkeley: University of California Press.

Garreton, Manuel Antonio. 1994. "Human Rights in Processes of Democratisation." *Journal of Latin American Studies*. 26: 221–34.

George, Alexander, ed. 1991. *Western State Terrorism*. New York: Routledge.

Gerth, H.H., and C. Wright Mills, trans. and eds. 1958. *From Max Weber: Essays in Sociology*. New York: Oxford University Press.

Gilbert, Paul. 1994. *Terrorism, Security and Nationality*. London: Routledge.

Gillespie, Richard. 1982. *Soldiers of Perón: Argentina's Montoneros.* Oxford: Clarendon Press.

Goldhagen, Daniel Jonah. 1996. *Hitler's Willing Executioners: Ordinary Germans and the Holocaust.* New York: Alfred A. Knopf.

Gonzalez Pino, and Miguel y Arturo Fontaine Talavera, eds. 1997. *Los Mil Dias de Allende.* 2 tomos. Santiago, Chile: Centro de Estudios Publicos.

Gourevich, Philip. 1998. *We Wish to Inform You That Tomorrow We Will Be Killed with Our Families.* New York: Farrar, Straux, and Giroux.

Gow, James. 1992. *Legitimacy and the Military: The Yugoslav Crisis.* London: Pinter.

Gramsci, Antonio. 1971. *Selections from Prison Notebooks.* New York: Routledge.

Greenland, Jeremy. 1976. "Ethnic Discrimination in Rwanda and Burundi." In Willern A. Veenhoven, ed., *Case Studies on Human Rights and Fundamental Freedoms: A World Survey,* vol. 4: 95–134. The Hague: Martinus Nijhoff.

Guest, Iain. 1990. *Behind the Disappearances: Argentina's Dirty War against Human Rights and the United Nations.* Philadelphia: University of Pennsylvania Press.

Gurr, Ted Robert. 1985. "The Political Origins of State Violence and Terror: A Theoretical Analysis." In M. Stohl and G. Lopez, eds., *Government Violence and Terror: An Agenda for Research,* 45–71. New York: Greenwood Press.

Gutman, Roy. 1993. *A Witness to Genocide.* New York: Macmillan.

Haas, Michael. 1991. *Genocide by Proxy: Cambodian Pawn on a Superpower Chessboard.* New York: Praeger.

Harff, B. 1986. "Genocide as State Terrorism." In M. Stohl and G.A. Lopez, eds., *Government Violence and Repression: An Agenda for Research,* 165–87. Westport, Conn.: Greenwood Press.

Harff, B., and T.R. Gurr. 1988. "Towards Empirical Theory of Genocides and Politicides: Identification and Measurement of Cases since 1945." *International Studies Quarterly* 37, 3: 357–71.

Harff, Barbara. 1985. *Genocide and Human Rights: International Legal and Political Issues,* Monograph Series in World Affairs, vol. 20, book 3. Denver, Col.: University of Denver.

Helsinki Watch. 1992–9. *War Crimes in Bosnia-Hercegovina.* 2 vols. New York: Human Rights Watch.

Hersh, Seymour. 1983. *The Price of Power: Kissinger in the Nixon White House.* New York: Summit Books.

Herz, John H., comp. 1982. *From Dictatorship to Democracy: Coping with the Legacies of Authoritarianism and Totalitarianism.* Westport, Conn.: Greenwood Press.

Hilberg, Raul. 1985. *The Destruction of the European Jews*, 3 vols. New York: Holmes and Meier.

Hobbes, Thomas. [1651] 1957. *Leviathan*. London: J.M. Dent & Sons.

Hochschild, Adam. 1999. *King Leopold's Ghost: A Story of Greed, Terror, and Heroism in Colonial Africa*. New York: Mariner.

Hockenos, Paul. 1993. *Free to Hate: The Rise of the Right in Post-Communist Eastern Europe*. New York: Routledge.

Hodges, Donald C. 1991. *Argentina's Dirty War*. Austin: University of Texas Press.

Honig, Jan Willem, and Norbert Both. 1996. *Srebrenica: Record of a War Crime*. London: Penguin.

Horowitz, Irving Louis. 1980. *Taking Lives: Genocide and State Power*. New Brunswick, NJ: Transaction Books.

Hovannisian, Richard G., ed. 1986a. *The Armenian Genocide in Perspective*. New Brunswick, NJ: Transaction Books.

Hovannisian, Richard G. 1986b. "The Historical Dimensions of the Armenian Question, 1878–1923." In Richard G. Hovannisian, ed., *The Armenian Genocide in Perspective*, 19–41. New Brunswick, NJ: Transaction Books.

Hovannisian, Richard G. 1986c. "The Armenian Genocide and Patterns of Denial." In Richard G. Hovannisian, ed., *The Armenian Genocide in Perspective*, 111–33. New Brunswick, NJ: Transaction Books.

Hovannisian, Richard G., ed. 1998. *Remembrance and Denial: The Case of the Armenian Genocide*. Detroit: Wayne State University Press.

Howard, Rhoda, and Jack Donnelly. 1986. "Human Dignity, Human Rights and Political Regimes." *American Political Science Review* 80, 3: 801–17.

Hryshko, Wasyl. 1983. *The Ukrainian Holocaust of 1933*. Edited and translated by Marco Carynnyk. Toronto: Bhariany Foundation.

Human Rights Watch. 1998. *Proxy Targets: Civilians in the War in Burundi*. New York: Human Rights Watch.

Human Rights Watch Arms Project. 1994. *Arming Rwanda: The Arms Trade and Human Rights Abuses in the Rwandan War*. New York: Human Rights Watch.

International Commission on Intervention and State Sovereignty. 2001. *The Responsibility to Protect*. Ottawa: International Development Research Centre.

International Human Rights Law Institute, DePaul University. 2003. "Progress Report on the Ratification and National Implementating Legislation of the Statute for the Establishment of an International Criminal Court" Chicago: The Institute.

Jackson, Karl D., ed. 1989a. *Cambodia, 1975–1978: Rendezvous with Death*. Princeton, NJ: Princeton University Press.

Jackson, Karl D. 1989b. "The Ideology of Total Revolution." In Karl D. Jackson ed., *Cambodia, 1975–1978*, 37–78. Princeton, NJ: Princeton University Press.

Jackson, Karl D. 1989c. "Intellectual Origins of the Khmer Rouge." In Karl D. Jackson, ed., *Cambodia, 1975–1978*, 241–50. Princeton, NJ: Princeton University Press, Pp 241–250.

Johnson, Paul. 2002. *Napoleon*. New York: Viking.

Judt, Tony. 2002. "Its Own Worst Enemy." Review in *The New York Review of Books*. August 15.

Kajan, Ibrahim. 1993. "Is This Not Genocide?" In Rabia Ali and Lawrence Lifschultz, eds., *Why Bosnia? Writings on the Balkan War*, 86–97. Stony Creek, Conn.: Pamphleteer's Press.

Kiernan, Ben, ed. 1993. *Genocide and Democracy in Cambodia: The Khmer Rouge, the United Nations and the International Community*. New Haven, Conn.: Yale University Press.

Kiernan, Ben. 1996. *The Pol Pot Regime: Race, Power, and Genocide in Cambodia under the Khmer Rouge, 1975–79*. New Haven, Conn.: Yale University Press.

Kiljunen, Kimmo, ed. 1984. *Kampuchea: Decade of Genocide*. Report of a Finnish Inquiry Commission. London: Zed.

Kirakossian, John S. 1992. *The Armenian Genocide: The Young Turks before the Judgment of History*. Translated from Russian by Shushan Altunian; English edition prepared by Arman Kirakossian. Madison, Conn.: Sphinx Press.

Klinghoffer, Arthur Jay. 1998. *The International Dimension of Genocide in Rwanda*. London: Macmillan Press.

Koch, Fred C. 1977. *The Volga Germans*. University Park: Pennsylvania State University Press.

Krausnick, Helmut, et al. 1968. *Anatomy of the SS State*. Translated by R. Barry, M. Jackson, and D. Long. New York: Walker.

Kren, George M., and Leon Rappoport. 1980. *The Holocaust and the Crisis of Human Behaviour*. New York: Holmes and Meier.

Kuper, Leo. 1981. *Genocide: Its Political Use in the Twentieth Century*. New Haven, Conn.: Yale University Press.

Kuper, Leo, 1986. "The Turkish Genocide of the Armenians, 1915–1917." In Richard G. Hovannisian. 1986a. *The Armenian Genocide in Perspective*, 43–59. New Brunswick, NJ: Transaction Books.

Kuper, Leo. 1990. "The Genocidal State: An Overview." In Pierre L. Van den Berghe, ed., *State Violence and Ethnicity*, 19–52. Niwot: University of Colorado Press.

Lazar, Daniel. 2002. "False Testament and Archaeology Refutes the Bible's Claim to History." In *Harpers* 304, 1822 (March): 39–47.

Lefebvre, Georges. 1962, 1964. *The French Revolution*, 2 vols. Translated by John Hall Steward and James Friguglietti. New York: Columbia University Press.

Lemarchand, René. 1970. *Rwanda and Burundi*. London: Pall Mall Press.

Lemarchand, René. 1990. "Burundi: Ethnicity and the Genocidal State." In Pierre L. Van den Berghe, ed., *State Violence and Ethnicity*, 89–112. Niwot: University Press of Colorado.

Lemarchand, René. 1992. "Burundi: The Politics of Ethnic Amnesia." In Helen Fein, ed., *Genocide Watch*, 70–86. New Haven, Conn.: Yale University Press.

Lemarchand, René. 1994. *Burundi: Ethnocide as Discourse and Practice*. Washington, DC, and Oxford: Woodrow Wilson Center Press and Oxford University Press.

Lemarchand, René. 1997a. "The Burundi Genocide." In S. Totten, William S. Parsons, and Israel W. Charny, eds., *Century of Genocide*, 317–29. New York: Garland.

Lemarchand, René. 1997b. "The Rwanda Genocide." In S. Totten, William S. Parsons, and Israel W. Charny, eds., *Century of Genocide*, 408–17. New York: Garland.

Lemarchand, René. 2002. "The Logic of Mass Murder: The Cases of Rwanda and Burundi." Paper presented to State Terrorism Conference, Liu Centre for the Study of Global Issues, University of British Columbia, Vancouver.

Lemkin, Rafael. 1944. *Axis Rule in Occupied Europe*. Washington, DC: Carnegie Endowment for International Peace.

Lemkin, Rafael. 1947. "Genocide as a Crime under International Law." *American Journal of International Law* 41, 1: 145–51.

Levy, Daniel C. 1986. "Chilean Universities under the Junta: Regime and Policy." In *Latin American Research Review* 21, 3: 95–128.

Lewis, Paul H. 1992. *The Crisis of Argentine Capitalism*. Chapel Hill: University of North Carolina Press.

Liber, George O. 1992. *Soviet Nationality Policy, Urban Growth, and Identity Change in the Ukrainian SSR, 1923–1934*. Cambridge: Cambridge University Press.

Linden, Ian. 1977. *Church and Revolution in Rwanda*. Manchester: Manchester University Press.

Liotta, Ph. H. 2001. *Dismembering the State: The Death of Yugoslavia and Why It Matters*. Lanham, Md.: Lexington.

Longman, Timothy Paul. *Proxy Targets, 1998: Civilians in the War in Burundi/ Human Rights Watch*. New York: Human Rights Watch.

López, Ernesto, and David Pion-Berlin. 1996. *Democracia y Cuestion Militar*. Quilmes, Argentina: Universidad Nacional de Quilmes.

López, George. 1988. "National Security Ideology as an Impetus to State Violence and State Terror." In Michael Stohl and George Lopez, eds., *Govern-

ment Violence and Repression: Agenda for Research, 74–93. New York: Greenwood Press.

López, George A. 1988. "Terrorism in Latin America." In M. Stohl, ed., *The Politics of Terrorism*, 497–524. Third edition. New York: Marcel Dekker.

López, George A., and Michael Stohl. 1987. *Liberalization and Redemocratization in Latin America*. New York: Greenwood Press.

Lukacs, John. 1997. *The Hitler of History*. New York: Alfred A. Knopf.

Mace, James. 1983. *Communism and the Dilemmas of National Liberation: National Communism in Soviet Ukraine, 1918–1933*. Cambridge: Harvard University Press.

Mace, James. 1984. "The Man-Made Famine of 1933 in the Soviet Ukraine: What Happened and Why." In Charny, ed., *Toward the Understanding and Prevention of Genocide*, 67–83. Boulder, Col.: Westview Press.

Mace, James E. 1986. "The Famine in the Soviet Ukraine, 1932–33." In Widener Library, Harvard University, *Famine in the Soviet Ukraine, 1932–33: A Memorial Exhibition*. Cambridge: Harvard University Press.

Mace, James E. 1990. "Genocide by Famine: Ukraine in 1932–33." In Pierre L. Van den Berghe, ed., *State Violence and Ethnicity*, Niwot, 53–71. Col.: University Press of Colorado.

Mace, James E. 1997. "Soviet Man-Made Famine in Ukraine." In Samuel Totten, William S. Parsons, and Israel W. Charny, eds., *Century of Genocide: Eyewitness Accounts and Critical Views*, 78–90. New York: Garland.

MacKenzie, Richard. 1998. "The United States and the Taliban." In William Maley, ed., *Fundamentalism Reborn?* 135–44. London: Hurst & Company.

Magas, Branka, and Ivo Zanic, eds. 2001. *The War in Croatia and Bosnia-Herzegovina, 1991–1995*. London: Frank Cass.

Magocsi, Paul Robert. 1996. *A History of the Ukraine*. Toronto: University of Toronto Press.

Maksudov, M. 1986. "Ukraine's Demographic Losses, 1927–1938." In Roman Serbyn and Bohdan Krawchenko, eds., *Famine in Ukraine, 1932–1933*, 27–43. Edmonton: Canadian Institute of Ukrainian Studies, University of Alberta.

Maley, William, ed. 1998a. *Fundamentalism Reborn? Afghanistan and the Taliban*. London: Hurst & Company.

Malkki, Liisa H. 1995. *Purity and Exile: Violence, Memory, and National Cosmology among Hutu Refugees in Tanzania*. Chicago: University of Chicago Press.

Malloy, James M., and Mitchell A. Seligson. 1987. *Authoritarians and Democrats: Regime Transition in Latin America*. Pittsburgh: University of Pittsburgh Press.

Mamdani, Mahmood. 2001. *When Victims Become Killers: Colonialism, Nativism, and the Genocide in Rwanda*. Princeton, NJ: Princeton University Press.

Marchak, (M.) Patricia. 1991. *The Integrated Circus: The New Right and the Restructuring of Global Markets*. Montreal: McGill-Queen's University Press.

Marchak, Patricia, in collaboration with William Marchak. 1997–98. Unpublished interviews and fieldnotes, Chile.

Marchak, Patricia, in collaboration with William Marchak. 1999. *God's Assassins: State Terrorism in Argentina in the 1970s*. Montreal: McGill-Queen's University Press.

Martínez, Javier. 1992. "Fear of the State, Fear of Society: On the Opposition Protests in Chile." In Juan Corradi, Patricia Weiss Fagen, and Manuel Antonio Garretón, eds., *Fear at the Edge*, 142–60. Berkeley: University of California Press.

Martínez, Javier, and Alvaro Díaz. 1996. *Chile: The Great Transformation*. Washington, DC: The Brookings Institution.

Marx, Karl, and Frederick Engels. 1970. *The Communist Manifesto*. New York: Washington Square Press.

Meier, Viktor. 1999. *Yugoslavia: A History of its Demise*. Translated by Sabrina Ramet. London: Routledge.

Melson, Robert. 1986a. "Provocation or Nationalism: A Critical Inquiry into the Armenian Genocide of 1915." In R. Hovannisian, ed., *The Armenian Genocide in Perspective*, 61–84. New Brunswick, NJ: Transaction Books.

Melson, Robert. 1992a. *Revolution and Genocide*. Chicago: University of Chicago Press.

Melson, Robert. 1992b. "Revolution and Genocide: On the Causes of the Armenian Genocide and the Holocaust." In Richard G. Hovannisian, ed., *The Armenian Genocide: History, Politics, Ethics*. New York: Macmillan.

Melvern, L.R. 2000. *A People Betrayed: The Role of the West in Rwanda's Genocide*. London: Zed.

Milgram, Stanley. 1974. *Obedience to Authority: An Experimental View*. New York: Harper and Row.

Milton, Sybil. 1997. "Holocaust: The Gypsies." In Samuel Totten, William S. Parsons, and Israel W. Charney, eds., *Century of Genocide: Eyewitness Accounts and Critical Views*, 171–88. New York: Garland.

Moore Jr, Barrington. 1966. *Social Origins of Dictatorship and Democracy: Lord and Peasant in the Making of the Modern World*. Boston: Beacon Press.

Moore Jr, Barrington, 2000. *Moral Purity and Persecution in History*. Princeton, NJ: Princeton University Press.

Morris, Virginia, and Michael P. Scharf, eds. 1998. *The International Criminal Tribunal for Rwanda*. Vol. 1. New York: Transactional Publishers.

Moulian, Tomás. 1997. *Chile Actual: Anatomía de un mito*. Chile: Arcis Universidad.

Nalbandian, Louise. 1967. *The Armenian Revolutionary Movement*. Berkeley: University of California Press.

Nekrich, Aleksander. 1978. *The Punished Peoples: The Deportation and Tragic Fate of Soviet Minorities at the End of the Second World War*. New York: W.W. Norton.

New York Times. 2002. May 27 (on line).

Newbury, Catharine. 1988. *The Cohesion of Oppression: Clientship and Ethnicity in Rwanda, 1860–1960*. New York: Colombia University Press.

Niewyk, Donald L. 1997. "Holocaust: The Jews." In Samuel Totten, William S. Parsons, and Israel W. Charny, eds., *Century of Genocide*, 136–50. New York: Garland.

Nino, Carlos Santiago. 1996. *Radical Evil on Trial*. New Haven, Conn.: Yale University Press.

Nye Jr., Joseph S. 2002. *The Paradox of American Power: Why the World's Only Superpower Can't Go It Alone*. Oxford: Oxford University Press.

O'Brien, Philip J. 1982. *The New Leviathan: The Chicago School and the Chilean Regime, 1973–1980*. Occasional Papers of the University of Glasgow, no. 38. Glasgow: University of Glasgow.

O'Donnell, Guillermo. 1973. *Modernization and Bureaucratic Authoritarianism*. Berkeley: Institute of International Studies.

O'Donnell, Guillermo. 1978. "Reflections on Patterns of Change in Bureaucratic Authoritarianism." *Latin American Research Review* 13, 1: 3–38.

O'Donnell, Guillermo. 1979. "Tensions in the Bureaucratic-Authoritarian State and the Question of Democracy." In David Collier, ed., *The New Authoritarianism in Latin America*, 285–318. Princeton, NJ: Princeton University Press.

O'Donnell, Guillermo. 1988. *Bureaucratic Authoritarianism: Argentina, 1966–1973, in Comparative Perspective*. Berkeley: University of California Press.

O'Halloran, Patrick J. 1995. *Humanitarian Intervention and the Genocide in Rwanda*. London: UK Research Institute for the Study of Conflict and Terrorism.

O'Kane, Rosemary H.T. 1989. "Military Regimes: Power and Force." *European Journal of Political Research* 17: 333–50.

O'Kane, Rosemary H.T. 1991. *The Revolutionary Reign of Terror: The Role of Violence in Political Change*. Cheltenham, UK: Edward Elgar.

O'Kane, Rosemary H.T. 1996. *Terror, Force and States: The Path from Modernity*. Cheltenham, UK: Edward Elgar.

Öke, Mim Kemâl. 1988. *The Armenian Question, 1914–1923*. Nicosia: K. Rustem and Brothers.

Olcutt, Martha Brill. 1981. "The Collectivization Drive in Kazakhstan." *Russian Review* 40, April.

Oleskiw, Stephen. 1983. *The Agony of a Nation: The Great Man-Made Famine in Ukraine, 1992–1933*. London: The National Committee to Commemorate the 50th Anniversary of the Artificial Famine in Ukraine, 1932–1933.

Oppenheim, J. 1997. "The Rwanda Crisis. Historical Background," Part 1. In J. Oppenheim and W. van der Wolf. eds., *The Rwanda Tribunal*. The Netherlands: Wolf Global Legal Publishers.

Oppenheim, J., and W. van der Wolf, eds. 1997. *Global War Crimes Tribunal*. Vol. 1. *The Rwanda Tribunal*. The Netherlands: Wolf Global Legal Publishers. 1997.

Osiel, Mark J. 1997. *Mass Atrocity, Collective Memory, and the Law*. New Brunswick, NJ: Transaction Publishers.

O'Sullivan, Noel, ed. 1986. *Terrorism, Ideology, and Revolution*. Brighton, UK: Wheatsheaf Books.

Ould-Abdallah, Ahmedou. 2000. *Burundi on the Brink, 1993–95: A UN Special Envoy Reflects on Preventive Diplomacy*. Washington, DC: United States Institute of Peace Press.

Palast, Greg. 2000. "Argentinia's Economic Collapse Engineered by IMF, World Bank." In *The Canadian Centre for Policy Alternatives Bulletin*, May: 10–11.

Parsons, Talcott, ed. 1966. *Max Weber: The Theory of Social and Economic Organization*. Translated by A.M. Henderson and Talcott Parsons. New York: The Free Press.

Pavkovic, Aleksandar. 1997. *The Fragmentation of Yugoslavia*. New York: St. Martin's Press.

Peralta-Ramos, Monica. 1987. "The Structural Basis of Coercion." In Mónica Peralta-Ramos and Carl H. Waisman, eds., *From Military Rule to Liberal Democracy in Argentina*, 38–68. Boulder, Col.: Westview Press.

Peralta-Ramos, Monica, and Carlos H. Waisman, eds. 1987. *From Military Rule to Liberal Democracy in Latin America*. Boulder, Col.: Westview Press.

Physicians for Human Rights. 1994. *Rwanda 1994: A Report of the Genocide*. London: Physicians for Human Rights.

Pino, Miguel Gonzalez, and Arturo Fontaine Talavera. 1997. *Los Mil Dias de Allende*. 2 vols. Santiago: Centro de Estudios Publicos.

Pion-Berlin, David. 1983. "Political Repression and Economic Doctrines: The Case of Argentina." *Comparative Political Studies* 16, 1: 37–66.

Pion-Berlin, David. 1989. *The Ideology of State Terror: Economic Doctrine and Political Repression in Argentina and Peru*. Boulder, Col.: Lynne Rienner.

Pion-Berlin, David, and George Lopez. 1991 "Of Victims and Executioners: Argentine State Terror, 1975–1979." *International Studies Quarterly* 35, 1: 63–87.

Pipes, Richard. 1964. *The Formation of the Soviet Union: Communism and Nationalism, 1917–1923.* 2nd rev. ed. Cambridge, Mass.: Harvard University Press.

Polanyi, Karl. 1994. *The Great Transformation.* Boston: Beacon Press.

Ponchaud, Francois, 1989. "Social Change in the Vortex of Revolution." In Karl D. Jackson, ed., *Cambodia, 1975–1978,* 151–79. Princeton, NJ: Princeton University Press.

Prevent Genocide International. 2002. "Info on the Genocide Convention." on-line.

Prunier, Gérard. 1995. *The Rwanda Crisis, 1959–1994: History of a Genocide.* New York: Columbia University Press.

Quinn, Kenneth M. 1989a. "The Pattern and Scope of Violence." In Karl D. Jackson, ed., *Cambodia, 1975–1978,* 179–208. Princeton, NJ: Princeton University Press.

Quinn, Kenneth M. 1989b. "Explaining the Terror." In Karl D. Jackson, ed., *Cambodia, 1975–1978,* 215–40. Princeton, NJ: Princeton University Press.

Ransdell, Eric. 1994. "The Wounds of War." *US News and World Report,* 117, 21 (November 28): 74–5.

Rapoport, David C., and Yonah Alexander, eds. 1982. *The Morality of Terrorism: Religious and Secular Justifications.* New York: Pergamon.

Reiff, David. 1995. *Slaughterhouse: Bosnia and the Failure of the West.* New York: Simon and Schuster.

Report of the Independent Inquiry into the Actions of the United Nations during the 1994 Genocide in Rwanda. 1999 (December 15). On line at un.org/News/ossg/rwanda_report.htm.

Robertson, Geoffrey. 1999. *Crimes against Humanity: The Struggle for Global Justice.* London: Penguin.

Rogel, Carole. 1998. *The Breakup of Yugoslavia and the War in Bosnia.* Westport, Conn.: Greenwood Press.

Ronayne, Peter. 2001. *Never Again? The United States and the Prevention and Punishment of Genocide since the Holocaust.* Lanham, Md: Rowman & Littlefield.

Rummel, R.J. 1990. *Lethal Politics: Soviet Genocide and Mass Murder since 1917.* New Brunswick, NJ: Transaction Publishers.

Rummel, R.J. 1992. *Democide.* New Brunswick, NJ: Transaction Publishers.

Rummel, R.J. 1992. *Nazi Genocide and Mass Murder.* New Brunswick, NJ: Transaction Publishers.

Rummel, R.J. 1994. *Death by Government*. New Brunswick, NJ: Transaction Publishers.

Schabas, William. 1999. "The Genocide Convention at Fifty." Washington, DC: United States Institute of Peace.

Scheltema, C., and Willem-Jan van der Wolf, eds. 1999. *The International Tribunal for Rwanda: Facts, Cases, Documents*. Nijmegen, The Netherlands: Global Law Association.

Schmitter, Philippe, Guillermo O'Donnell, and Laurence Whitehead, eds. 1986. *Transitions from Authoritarian Rule*. Baltimore, My: Johns Hopkins University Press.

Seale, Patrick, and Maureen McConville. 1968. *French Revolution, 1968*. London: Penguin.

Sederberg, Peter C. 1989. *Terrorist Myths: Illusion, Rhetoric, and Reality*. Englewood Cliffs, NJ: Prentice Hall.

Serbyn, Roman, and Bohdan Krawchenko, eds. 1986. *Famine in Ukraine, 1932–33*. Edmonton: Canadian Institute of Ukrainian Studies, University of Alberta.

Shawcross, William. 1984. *The Quality of Mercy: Cambodia, Holocaust and Modern Conscience*. New York: Simon and Schuster.

Shirer, William L. 1941. *Berlin Diary: The Journal of a Foreign Correspondent*. New York: Alfred A. Knopf.

Shirer, William L. 1961. *The Rise and Fall of the Third Reich: A History of Nazi Germany*. London: Secker and Warburg.

Shirwin, Martin J. 1996. "Hiroshima and the Politics of History." In Charles B. Strozier and Michael Flynn, eds., *Genocide, War, and Human Survival*, 41–50. Lanham, Md: Rowman & Littlefield.

Sigmund, Paul. 1977. *The Overthrow of Allende and the Politics of Chile, 1964–1976*. Pittsburgh, Penn.: University of Pittsburgh Press.

Smith, William. 1985. "Reflections on the Political Economy of Authoritarian Rule and Capitalist Reorganization in Contemporary Argentina." In Phillip O'Brien and Paul Cammack, eds., *Generals in Retreat: The Crisis of Military Rule in Latin America*, 37–88. Manchester: Manchester University Press.

Smith, William. 1989. *Authoritarianism and the Crisis of the Argentine Political Economy*. Stanford, Cal.: Stanford University Press.

Soros, George. 2002a. *George Soros on Globalization*. New York: Public Affairs.

Soros, George. 2002b, *Open Society: Reforming Global Capitalism*. New York: Public Affairs.

Speer, Albert. 1970. *Inside the Third Reich*. Translated by Richard and Clara Winston. New York: Avon.

Spooner, Mary Helen. 1994. *Soldiers in a Narrow Land: The Pinochet Regime in Chile*. Berkeley: University of California Press.

Staub, Ervin. 1989. *The Roots of Evil: The Origins of Genocide and Other Group Violence*. New York: Cambridge University Press.

Stiglitz, Joseph E. 2002a. "A Fair Deal for the World." Review of George Soros, *On Globalization*, in *The New York Review of Books*, May 23.

Stiglitz, Joseph E. 2002b. *Globalization and Its Discontents*. New York: W.W. Norton.

Stohl, Michael. 1987. "Outside of a Small Circle of Friends: States, Genocide, Mass Killing and the Role of Bystanders." *Journal of Peace Research* 24, 2: 151–66.

Stohl, Michael, ed. 1988a. *The Politics of Terrorism*. Third edition. New York: Marcel Dekker.

Stohl, Michael. 1988b. "Demystifying Terrorism: The Myths and Realities of Contemporary Political Terrorism." In M. Stohl, ed., *The Politics of Terrorism*, 1–28. Third edition. New York: Marcel Dekker.

Stohl, Michael. 1988c. "National Interests and State Terrorism in International Affairs." In M. Stohl, ed., *The Politics of Terrorism*, 273–92. Third edition. New York: Marcel Dekker.

Stohl, Michael and George A. Lopez, eds. 1985. *Government Violence and Repression: An Agenda for Research*. New York: Greenwood Press.

Strozier, Charles B., and Michael Flynn, eds. 1996. *Genocide, War, and Human Survival*. Lanham, Md: Rowman & Littlefield.

Talavera, Arturo Fontaine. Nd. "Revolution from the Top and Horizontal Mediation: The Case of Chile's Transition to Democracy." Mimeo distributed by Centro Estudios Publico, Santiago.

Thurston, Robert W. 1996. *Life and Terror in Stalin's Russia, 1934–1941*. New Haven, Conn.: Yale University Press.

Tottle, Douglas. 1987. *Fraud, Famine and Fascism: The Ukrainian Genocide Myth from Hitler to Harvard*. Toronto: Progress Books.

Totten, Samuel, William S. Parsons, Israel W. Charny, eds. 1997. *Century of Genocide: Eyewitness Accounts and Critical Views*. New York: Garland.

Townsend, Charles. 1987. "The Necessity of Political Violence." *Comparative Studies in Society and History* 29, 2.

Toynbee, Arnold. 1915. *Armenian Atrocities: The Murder of a Nation*. London: Hodder & Stoughton.

Toynbee, Arnold. 1916. *The Treatment of Armenians in the Ottoman Empire, 1915–1916*. London: His Majesty's Stationery Office.

Turkish Daily News. 2002. Editions of May 21 and 22.

United Nations. 1951. *Convention on the Prevention and Punishment of the Crime of Genocide.*

United Nations. 1984. *Convention against Torture and Other Cruel, Inhuman, or Degrading Treatment or Punishment.*

United Nations. 1994a. *Report on Yugoslavia.*

United Nations. 1999. *Report of the Independent Inquiry into the Actions of the United Nations during the 1994 Genocide in Rwanda.* 15 December on line: un.org/news/ossg/rwanda_report.htm.

United Nations. Commission of Experts Established Pursuant to Security Council Resolution 935 (1994), on Rwanda. 1994. *Final Report.*

United States. Commission on the Ukraine Famine. 1988. *Report to Congress, Commission on the Ukraine Famine, 1932–33.* Washington: United States Government Printing Office.

United States Congress Commission on Security and Cooperation in Europe. 1993.

United States Official Documents on the Armenian Genocide. 1994, 1995. Compiled and introduced by Ara Sarafian. 5 vols. Vol. 2: *The Peripheries*; vol. 3: *The Central Lands.* Watertown, Mass.: Armenian Review.

United States Senate Select Committee on Intelligence Activities. 1975a. *Alleged Assassination Plots Involving Foreign Leaders.* Washington: U.S. Government Printing Co.

United States Senate Select Committee on Intelligence Activities [Church Report]. 1975b. *State Report. Covert Action in Chile, 1963–1973.* Washington: U.S. Government Printing Co.

Universal Declaration of Human Rights, 1948.

Valaskakis, Kimon. 2002. "Might makes right? Wrong. Toronto: *Globe and Mail.* 17 September.

Valenzuela, Arturo. 1978. *The Breakdown of Chilean Democracy.* Baltimore, My.: Johns Hopkins University Press.

Van den Berghe, Pierre L., ed. 1990a. *State Violence and Ethnicity.* Niwot, Col.: University Press of Colorado.

Van den Berghe, Pierre L. 1990b "Introduction." In Van den Berghe, ed., *State Violence and Ethnicity,* 1–18. Niwot: Col.: University Press of Colorado.

Verstappen, Bert, comp. 1987. *Human Rights Reports: An Annotated Bibliography of Fact-Finding Missions.* London, H. Zell.

Vickery, Michael. 1984. *Cambodia, 1975–1982.* Boston, Mass.: South End.

Waller, David. 1996. *Rwanda: Which Way Now?* Oxford: Oxfam.

Waller, James. 2002. *Becoming Evil: How Ordinary People Commit Genocide and Mass Killing.* Oxford: Oxford University Press.

Wallerstein, Immanuel M. 1979. *The Capitalist World Economy: Essays.* Cambridge: Cambridge University Press.

Wanandi, Jusuf. 1989. *The Cambodian Conflict.* Jakarta: Centre for Strategic and International Studies.

Widener Library, Harvard University. 1986. *Famine in the Soviet Ukraine, 1932–1933.* Cambridge, Mass.: Harvard University Press.

Wolpin, Miles. 1986. "State Terrorism and Repression in the Third World: Parameters and Prospects." In M. Stohl and G.A. Lopez, eds., *Government Violence and Repression: An Agenda for Research.* New York: Greenwood.

Wright, Martin, ed. 1989. *Cambodia: A Matter of Survival.* London: St. James Press.

Zimbardo, Philip, in Craig Haney, Curtis Banks, and Philip Zimbardo, "Interpersonal Dynamics in a Simulated Prison," *International Journal of Psychiatry* (1968): 279–80, as reported here by Bauman.

Index

Entries for case studies begin with two overviews: *analysis*, the major section(s) in Part One containing analytical material; and *case study*, the empirical study in Part Two. References to the country follow, with identical references in each case for the major theoretical categories: class/inequality, bureaucracy (where applicable), ethnicity/religion (where applicable), economy, genocide/politicide, history, ideology, institutions, legitimacy, material interests, political paralysis, and social change. Other entries (names, events) specific to the country are also provided.

Individuals famous for events singular to a country are named only in the country entry.

The "theories of crimes against humanity" entry provides locations of discussion on the range of theoretical insights in the field of study, including, but not restricted to, those put forward by the author.